# The Rising of a King

## KING DAVID
## A MAN AFTER GOD'S OWN HEART

## Cynthia Crumbaugh

TRILOGY CHRISTIAN PUBLISHERS

*Tustin, CA*

Trilogy Christian Publishers
A Wholly Owned Subsidiary of Trinity Broadcasting Network
2442 Michelle Drive
Tustin, CA 92780

*The Rising of a King*

Trilogy Christian Publishers A Wholly Owned Subsidiary of Trinity Broadcasting Network

2442 Michelle Drive Tustin, CA 92780

Cover design by Jeff Summers

For information about special discounts for bulk purchases, please contact Trilogy Christian Publishing.

Trilogy Disclaimer: The views and content expressed in this book are those of the author and may not necessarily reflect the views and doctrine of Trilogy Christian Publishing or the Trinity Broadcasting Network.

Manufactured in the United States of America

10 9 8 7 6 5 4 3 2 1

Library of Congress Cataloging-in-Publication Data is available.

ISBN: 978-1-63769-962-1

E-ISBN: 978-1-63769-963-8

# Dedication

To my beloved husband, I dedicate this book to you because you have been an inspiration the entire time we have been together. You have been a great example of how to stay strong in faith and take a stand.

I dedicate this book to my children and grandchildren. I found God early in my life and have always tried to teach you of His goodness and His love for us. I especially want my grandchildren to learn how fun the Word of God can be and how rewarding it is to study it. I want to name each of you, Scheeli, Bronwynn, Piper, Wesley, Levi, Aria, Cora, Elliot, and Ezra. I have to include any grandchildren yet to come. I also want to dedicate this to my other two grandchildren, Dalton and Elyssa. I love each and every one of you!

I dedicate this book to *all* my nieces and nephews; I dedicate this work to you because I want you to know how great God is. He loves you and wants a relationship with each of you.

I dedicate this book to Erica, Tiffany, Myron (Randy) and Jennifer, and your families. God loves you, and so do I. God is a loving God and wants to guide you daily.

I would like to dedicate it to every foster child who ever came through our house and to every child who has ever been in my children's church. That is quite a handful! I have always worked to instill how precious God's Word is and how great it is to commit your life to Him. Jesus came that we might have life and live more abundantly. I hope you have found that as you've gone on with your lives.

I love each of you!

Love, Cindy

(Aunt Cindy, Pastor Cindy, mom, grandma, and wife)

# Acknowledgements

When writing a novel, many people influence and have a part in inspiring your thoughts and ideas. There are so many people that have had a small part in my writing of this manuscript. I will attempt to thank them and not miss anyone.

My very first acknowledgment goes to my Father God. I asked Him to make studying the Word of God fun for me. I knew all the steps to studying, but it felt more like homework except when finding that rhema word. Of course, nothing compares to a rhema word from God. But I desired to have fun when studying. Matthew 7:7-8 says, "Ask, and it shall be given unto you. Seek, and ye shall find... Knock, and it shall be opened to you."

I asked, and one day, God said, "Write a book on the life of King David."

I had no idea where this would go or how it would come together, but it has been one of the most amazing adventures in my life! Fun doesn't begin to explain the experience it has been. Writing and studying the Scripture has been fulfilling, rewarding, and, dare I say, blessed. I have been blessed over and over while writing. I found many truths just by adding history, foreshadowing through prophetic scriptures, adding in details from archeological digs, studying the geography and agriculture, and interpreting scripture with scripture. Thank You, Father, for this experience. May we have many more to come!

My precious husband, Dave, has been by far my greatest supporter. You have listened to me read and reread each chapter, sometimes multiple times, as I changed the initial and added new ideas and details around each chapter. After working all day, you'd come home and enjoy listening to what God gave me to write that day. I cannot thank you enough for all the encouragement you have given me. You have boasted about how you see God's hand on this work. Thank you, sweetheart! There are not enough words to tell you how much your support has meant to me and will always mean to me.

The second person who has inspired me so very much is my aunt Lesia. I could write a book about the countless ways you have encouraged me. We have enjoyed a massive number of hours on the phone talking about our writing endeavors. You are excellent at so many graphic designing skills. Thank you for designing my book two cover, for taking my personal picture, and so much more. We talked about such issues as copyrighting my work and the endless hours of discussing publication. Your warm smile and encouraging words will always be a part of this book.

My own daughter and son and their families have been a large influence as well. Whether it was watching my daughter prepare for Shabbat or discussing foods from that time, I was greatly inspired when watching the interaction of my grandchildren in their younger years. Many little ideas and thoughts have been inspired around my family, my son-in-law's military career, my son's determination, and my husband's dedication. Each one has been an inspiration from time to time.

I would like to thank Kimberly Bueby, my hairstylist and colorist. She owns Salon Blu Ave in Boyne City, MI. Thank you, Kimberly, as we've talked through different colors and the adventure of growing my hair out again. She has listened to me talk about my book as I've worked with Trilogy to prepare everything for publication.

I cannot begin to thank the ministers and ministries that I have listened to over the course of writing King David. I'd find an inspiring thought that would cause me to dig deeper into God's Word. Perhaps someone would mention something about an animal or a plant that grows in that area, and I'd find myself looking and searching for every minute detail. Many ideas were never used, but they always inspired more studying and more research. I can say that because I focused on God as my guide.

I would like to give a special thank you to our pastors, Mark and Rhonda Garver, with Cornerstone Word of Life Church. They are located in Madison, Alabama. We first came to your church after pastoring for a number of years. I needed the love and support I found from both of them. I grew strong and stronger while sitting under their ministry. This refreshed my spirit and caused me to rise up and take the victory. The Word of God took root in me in a deeper way than ever before. Thank you very much! I love you both and those who touched our lives during our stay in Madison.

If I missed naming anyone, then please know that I am deeply grateful for all you've done to assist me along the way.

# Contents

# Foreword

*The Rise of a King* is a book I'll never tire of reading. Since the inception of this book many years ago, I've had the pleasure of reading each chapter as well as having it read to me. My wife and I bounce things off of each other, including books that we write. This book is no exception other than I looked forward to each time she would want to bounce another chapter off me.

This book is not only awesome but also a book that every Christian should have in their library. Cynthia has spent hundreds of hours researching every scripture related to David (King David) and brought each scripture to life.

Most people know about David and Goliath, but few know much about David's life apart from that story. When you start reading this book, you will have a very hard time putting it down. I have read it many times and never tire of it and learn something new every time, much like we do when reading the Bible. This book not only brings the scriptures to life but is written as a story that will captivate you.

I am convinced that every Bible school/college should have this book as required reading. I have a hard time deciding what part is my favorite because I enjoy every bit of it. It is not a boring read but just the opposite. As a pastor, I would highly recommend this book to anyone who would like to know more about King David. As Cynthia's husband, I find it an honor to be able to write this foreword and encourage everyone to get a copy to read and keep in your home library.

—Pastor/Husband David Crumbaugh

# Preface

Dear Reader:

It is my greatest prayer that this book will bless you. God put it in my heart to write about King David. He is truly one of my favorite people in the Bible. He was a strong man and yet a humble man. He knew God personally and chose to follow Him. As we all know, this didn't make him a perfect man but a "real" man.

I have the pleasure of knowing a few men that I had fun fashioning David's strong character after. The key man would be my own wonderful husband, my own David. He has always stood strong on his faith and has always been proud to serve God. Another man would be my son, Joshua David. Joshua is very determined and has taught me much over the years as I've watched his determination to succeed and enjoy life. I remember one time when he and his sister were traveling back from college together. The car was overpacked, and a tire blew. By all-natural circumstances, he should have rolled the car. Later, I asked him how he kept from rolling the car. He answered very nonchalantly, "It wasn't an option." I spent a lot of time processing that statement. How many times do we surrender to a bad situation instead of taking charge of it? I see David as doing the same thing; when he saw Goliath challenging the Israelites, he had that same nonchalant attitude, "It wasn't an option." Then there's my wonderful son-in-law, Nathan. During most of my writing, Nathan has been working on a military career. When I tried to envision a soldier's point of view, I'd think of Nathan and his leadership skills and look for insight into the man that David was.

I fashioned my timeline for the events of David's life around two key sources, the *One Year Chronological Bible* and the *Thompson Chain Bible*. When they didn't line up together, I went to research to best determine the correct path to take.

Several hundred hours of research have gone into understanding the Bible times in which David lived and the way the land looked at that time. Although you will have your own interpretation of some of the passages, the goal was to add insights into what it would have been like to walk or to ride along with David. What would it be like as he sought his time writing his psalms? Did he notice the land next to him? What were the human emotions that he dealt with through these biblical passages? Then there is understanding the things that don't line up with how we interpret the Bible today, as in, "... more than one wife..." or the whole scenario with Uriah. It is my prayer that reading through this book will allow you to see how many of these events may have unfolded.

Much geography research went into understanding the land in which David lived and walked. Great effort was incorporated to give insight to where these areas would be today. When possible, I added updated geological notes to bring out details on these areas. Though many factors are missed when reading only one passage, much more is added when you include the whole Bible. The Old Testament is quoted repeatedly throughout the New Testament and provides additional insights. Then there are added teachings that provide extra understandings throughout the Bible. Since David lived in what was titled the "Promised Land," there is much history and insight provided from those who lived prior to David. Then there are comments throughout the rest of the Bible that teach us. One such example is Isaiah 2:6 (NIV) where it talks of the Philistines, "You, Lord, have abandoned your people, the descendants of Jacob. They are full of superstitions from the East; they practice divination like the Philistines and embrace pagan customs." Add verses like this together with other verses on the Philistines, and before you know it, you have insight into what the Philistines were like, and pictures of that time begin to form in your mind. Although much insight comes from geological research, it is still best to interpret scripture with scripture. When we do this, we come to understand God more thoroughly than ever. As you study out the word "divination" in this context, it starts to build a picture of the lifestyle of the Philistine nation. Then if you add it to research, you quickly learn that they were not always part of that region but appear to be originally called the "Sea People," indicating they came from across the sea and are thought to have invaded Egypt around 1190 BC. This would be around the time the Israelites arrived to the Promised Land. They were a violent people, as the scriptures indicate, and on goes the study...

I prayed every time I sat down to write, and quite often, I felt the leading of the Holy Spirit in the words that I wrote. It has been an incredible journey. I'd encourage everyone to take time to tear apart a favorite passage and write about it. Search it out and learn all the geographical information you can find. Then paint in the pictures around it. An example could be Matthew 17:27, "But so that we may not cause offense, go to the lake and throw out your line. Take the first fish you catch, open its mouth, and you will find a four-drachma coin. Take it and give it to them for my tax and yours." If you have ever gone fishing, you can see the land, the trees, a gentle breeze blowing, and finally, the lake. Determine the type of fish by the fish that swim in that region today. Make it a large one, at least large enough to hold this particular coin in its mouth. Then, was there sea weed, cattails, or flowers by the shore? Was there drift wood? What trees are in the region today? How was Jesus dressed? Was the ground barren as desert or plush with tall grasses flowing from the nourishment of the water? Did Peter let the fish live, or did he take it back and cook it for dinner? Did he share the story with the tax collectors? Did Jesus have a twinkle in his eye as He saw Peter's excitement? Did other disciples go with him? "The word of God is alive and powerful. It is sharper than any two-edged sword cutting between soul and spirit, between joint and marrow. It exposes our innermost thoughts and desires" (Hebrews 4:12, NLT). As you take time to search it out, God will come to you with understanding and insights. Studying His Word was meant to be enjoyed. That is exactly what writing about the life of David has been for me.

I have a few favorite chapters that I pray bless you as much as they blessed me. The first one is the very first chapter. It was fulfilling and yet a challenge to pray about how to begin writing the story. I felt God's leading in many areas of this book and believe God paved the way in the very first chapter. My second favorite chapter was when David killed Goliath. It was challenging to bring new insights that would set this apart from all the other stories of Goliath. One of the scenes that blessed me most was when Goliath died. I believe we should care about a soul lost to eternity, and that is what I tried to bring out with his death. It was also amusing to imagine David and his brothers fighting together in the war against the Philistines. Then, my next favorite chapter is when David marries Michal. It was exciting foreshadowing events that would later explain many of Michal's decisions and choices. It was also a time to bring in much of the influences that the Israelites dealt with from the Egyptians. I hope these chapters and all the others will bless you like they have blessed me.

I found a natural love for God's Word early in my life as I grabbed hold of the simple truths I knew as a child. With that love came a deep love for God's Word. My prayer is that this book will allow you to see how exciting it can be to read and study God's Word for yourself.

Have fun as you journey through the life and the land of David...and may God bless you!

—*Cynthia Crumbaugh*

# Section I

## *David's Journey from Shepherd Boy to Warrior*

# Chapter 1

*"Praise be to the Lord my Rock, who trains my hands for war, my fingers for battle" (Psalm 144:1, NIV).*

Swoosh, swoosh. "Watch out, bear, here it comes! I told you to leave my sheep alone. Now, you must d—i—e!"

"Father Jehovah, thank You for guiding my hands. Together we have hit many targets, but this is the biggest target yet."

Swoooooosh! Thump!

"That will teach you; down you go, you big black bear!"

A few minutes earlier, a big black bear came after David's herd of sheep. The bear had wandered out of the woods in search of an appetizing meal. He tried to chase it away, but the thought of fresh meat had a great appeal to the hungry bear. This very moment the bear was heading straight for one of the little lambs. Reaching down into his waist belt, David pulled out his sling along with a near perfectly rounded stone.

Jesse, David's father, had spent hours teaching him and all his brothers how to fashion a sling. Their father knew it would be useful in multiple ways but would serve his sons most in hunting and protection. He also knew that their practice time would serve as an excellent sport.

During the cold winter evenings, their family would gather around the fire in the living room. They started with a solid but rather thin piece of deer hide, approximately an eight to ten-centimeter square. Next, they tied strings on the corners of the solid piece. The string was also cut from the deer hide. Then, they would rub it and work the hide until it was soft and flexible. At these times, Jesse would proceed to teach his sons about the many famous slingers that had lived throughout their history. They always enjoyed listening to their father teach them about their heritage. Their father was a particularly good storyteller. His voice was always rich and filled with excitement. He knew how to make his voice fall at the lowest points and rise with each climax peak of the story. He was excellent at capturing a moment from the past. David and his brothers would sit by the hours listening and rubbing their leather. All of Jesse's sons soaked in the truth of the stories in a way that resembled their bread as they dipped it into their broth. No matter what the story, they always found themselves involved and sitting on the edge of their seats with expectation. Sometimes they wanted to cry with the people in the story, and other times they found themselves repenting with those that Jehovah was trying to reach. Often, their mother, Nitzevet[1] bat Adel, would sit there listening along with her sons. Sometimes she would get a twinkle in her eye as she would question him, "Now...Jesse, are you sure that is how it went?" He never embellished the stories to where they were not true, but he would often fill in the details lost with time. She would keep the fire going, and she would be preparing for tomorrow's meals, but Nitzevet always had one ear tuned to the conversations that flowed from her family.

*****

David could already feel the victory! He would have so much fun telling his family about killing the bear. Reaching down, he grabbed his sling. He always carried three to five perfectly rounded, smooth small rocks in his bag. They were there for his protection. Sometimes he would, however, use them as a sport to pass the hours as he tended the sheep. Even when using his sling as a sport, David was careful to never leave himself without ammunition. He had learned to never leave himself unprotected, for most assuredly, that is when the enemy will hit the hardest.

The bear reached down to grab a small white lamb. The rest of the herd was bleating very loudly as they cried for help. The sheep scrambled frantically to get as far from the bear as they could. It was certain that David would have to do something quickly, or this little lamb would become the bear's next meal. David picked the rock out of his leather bag. Next, he took the necessary time to gain his stance. As he stood preparing to sling the rock at the bear, David estimated his strength and the force that he would need to drive this rock right into the bear's forehead. Carefully and yet quickly, David placed the rock in the middle of the sling. Then he braced the two strings on the left, one under his little finger and the other under his third finger. The other two strings on the right side of the sling were held tightly between his thumb and first finger. These two strings would be released at just the right time to allow the rock to fly at the target. Each time David swung the sling around, he would shift his weight back and forth from one foot to the other. He focused on the bear's forehead with all his might. Then, he arched his right hand at the elbow and swung his hand around one time, then two times, now three times, and then he released the sling with all his might at the bear, swoosh.

"Right in the forehead!" David exclaimed. "A perfect shot!" The bear shook its head from side to side. The rock had startled the bear enough to cause it to release the lamb but not enough to kill it. David reached out and pushed the lamb out of the way. He made sure that it was out of reach of the bear. The bear was very angry now and stretched out its big claws to attack David. Acting quickly, David grabbed the bear by its beard. He hit the bear again and took the knife and slit its throat. There was a loud thump as the bear fell to the ground. In fact, the ground immediately surrounding him shook at the bear's weight. Meanwhile, the little lamb had run very quickly to the thick of the fold, searching desperately for safety. Its eyes were full of terror. After killing the bear, David went over and picked up the little lamb. He checked it out all over and then comforted it. There were a few scratches on the lamb where the bear had grabbed it, but otherwise, the lamb was fine except for the fright. Within just seconds, the little lamb's heart started to slow back to the normal rate. The lamb found safety as it nestled its nose into the crook of David's arm. The other sheep were still bleating and panicking. David knew that this was due to the smell of the bear's blood in the air. The odor that permeates from a bear is strong and potent. The smell alone kept the sheep alert and fearful for their safety. Later, David found himself reflecting on how we are so much like these sheep were today. *Yes, they are a perfect example of us...we run in fright even when Jehovah has protected us, and the danger has passed. Our fear blinds us from seeing that we are no longer in danger.*

*What an awesome kill, David thought, but I needed more force. I should have put the bear on the ground the first time. If I tweak my elbow just a little more and use the force of my forearm...that should be all it takes...maybe a little more snap of the wrist...*

After critiquing himself, his thoughts turned back to his own appetite and skinning the hide of the bear. David suddenly felt very hungry. He was sure that his appetite had been aroused due to all the excitement.

A few hours later, David sat relaxing as he leaned against the tree. He'd skinned the bear, and tomorrow he'd work on tanning the hide. It would bring a good profit from the foreigners who travel the area. He would need to build a frame on which to stretch the hide. That could be done in the morning. He gave thanks to Jehovah for the small stream that was close by. The fresh water assisted him with cleaning the blood off himself. It had been necessary to move downstream away from the bear scent. Dead animals draw other wild animals. He'd heard that heathens actually eat bear, but according to their law, the bear was considered unkosher meat, meat not blessed by God.

The hide would be the most valuable part as far as his brothers were concerned. His brothers wouldn't believe he killed the bear without the hide to prove it. David marveled at his success. However, he was quick to give Jehovah all the credit. His mother always appreciated his adventures. He could picture her now, bent over the garden working on the leafy vegetables or separating the milk for butter and cheese. She was a very hard worker. Her hair was starting to gray and showing signs of thinning. Abigail, his sister, helped their mother with all these tasks, but his mother seemed to work circles around Abigail. Her name, Nitzevet, means "to stand." Just as her name, she was someone David could rely on...someone he could count on. Yes, she would believe him, and she would be proud of him.

He was sure that his oldest brother, Eliab, would think that he had gotten the bear hide from travelers. Eliab would probably accuse him of trading one of the family sheep. David liked Eliab, but Eliab often thought he knew everything about any subject. David wondered if this was an "Eliab thing" or the "oldest brother thing." He supposed that his brother's "take charge" attitude came from being the oldest.

"Baah, baah," the sheep bleated.

# Chapter 2

*"...Man looks at the outward appearance, but the Lord looks at the heart" (1 Samuel 16:7, NKJV).*

A few weeks had passed since David killed the bear. He was enjoying resting under a tree. He did not consider himself prideful, but David did delight in remembering the thrill of that moment. He did not know very many people who had killed a bear, let alone kids his age. Each time he relived his victory over the bear, he found himself taking the time to analyze each step to slinging the rock. He needed more force behind the rock. *Maybe some more daily pushups would do it...* David would scrutinize every detail and determine what he would do differently the next time...next time... He wasn't going looking for another bear, but he was sure that in time another enemy would raise its ugly head. David enjoyed relaxing and watching the sheep and lambs wandering about as they grazed on the grass.

Another winter season had passed, and spring would soon be here. Soon there would be fresh new grass for the sheep to eat. David found such comfort in hearing the sound of the sheep bleating. His father had often told how this herd of sheep descended from wild moufflon, a breed of sheep that had been purchased and brought over from Assyria. David had always thought that the male sheep, called rams, looked funny with their large curling horns. These sheep had been a part of his family for several years. His grandfather Boaz had taken the time to breed them and to enhance the herd. He had been one of the wealthiest men of the land.

The day had warmed to a nice temperature. The sun was shining brightly, and there was a gentle breeze blowing about. The wind was warmer than David had felt it in the past few weeks. This wind was bringing in warmer temperatures from the south. These were the times that David found life the most exciting. During these times, he relaxed and took time to talk to Jehovah. As long as the sheep were taken care of, he could take the time to relax. He found himself creating songs about his Jehovah, the God of Abraham. The words and music just seemed to flow out of him.

David was the youngest boy in his family. His parents had been richly blessed by having eight boys and only two girls. It was important that you had many boys in the family. After all, sons are a father's heritage. David, being the youngest, had been given the job of tending the sheep. His brothers had "more important" tasks now. It appeared as though David's oldest three brothers would soon be going off to war for their king, King Saul. Therefore, they were currently working hard to get the spring fields planted. The fourth oldest brother was engaged and planned to be married in the fall. He was busy building a home for himself and his betrothed. His oldest sister was married and had three sons. They had built their home close by, so his nephews were over at his house often. Occasionally, their parents would let them accompany David while taking care of the sheep. Two of his brothers had wood-carving skills that kept them busy buying and selling in the marketplace. They would bring home some very interesting stories from town. Their skills assisted greatly with their family's food and supplies. The next youngest brother was given the task of working with their father around the house. He assisted both of their parents in many ways. This left David alone with the sheep out in the fields most of the time. They had some servants, but there was much to be done with their other livestock and the fields. His father would send the servants out from time to time to give David a break when his brothers could not. David loved being outside with the sheep. He had become protective over them while studying and observing how vulnerable sheep really are. His thoughts would turn to how we are so much like sheep and Jehovah is our great shepherd. David rarely found himself lonely; instead, he was comforted by the songs he would create. He found companionship by talking to Jehovah and the sheep. Sometimes he'd strike up a conversation with those passing by. He loved to talk to the travelers. David enjoyed hearing the news of different places and the many exotic lands. Maybe he would travel someday, but not this day.

David's brothers loved to tease him about "someday growing up." Of course, you were only "grown up" when you graduated from taking care of the sheep. Then there were the "sheep" jokes that each of them had heard when it had been their time to tend the sheep. None of this bothered David, though, because he loved his time out in the fields.

David was leaning back against the tree trunk and taking in the moment with great pleasure. Soon the leaves would be in full bloom, and he would enjoy the shade of the Eucalyptus tree. This tree was big enough that the sheep could also be shaded. But for now, the sun was before him and warming him. This tree was a special tree because it was a natural enemy to the bees and wasps. They would also be out in full scale soon. David's chest rose and fell as he breathed in a deep cleansing breath while savoring the moment. It was so easy to think of the Lord Jehovah during times like this. Reaching over to pick up his harp, he meditated on what he should play. Should he create a new song for the Lord, or should he sing one of his old favorites? David loved his harp, and it seemed as though the sheep loved it too. Sometimes it appeared as if the sheep were singing along while he played. Their bleating seemed to take on the sounds of praise. It was as though their baaaaaahh sound became "praise the Lord." He could even imagine their bleating sounds being transformed into a whole choir. At this point, David would often imagine the Lord laughing with him at his own silliness. However, all humor aside, David truly believed that the sheep did bleat out praises to Jehovah, their Creator.

As he ran his fingers over the canvas bag, he took just a few minutes to dream about the full-size harp that he planned to have someday. That harp would be the full size of a man's body. He had heard that the Egyptians made theirs that way. On the front at the base, it was said that they carved images of their gods, although David would not have a graven image of a false god on his. His harp would be an instrument of praise dedicated to bringing glory and honor to Jehovah. The Egyptians' harps were made with the finest strings that would last for many years. The craftsmen that David talked with said that the Egyptians used braided horsehair to make their strings.

When making these harps, the craftsmen used the most excellent pieces of wood. It would be fun when he could make his own; perhaps one of his brothers could help with the carving at the base. For now, he was too busy with the sheep to make one, but someday, he would have the time...someday. David reached inside the canvas bag and pulled out his little harp. His harp was a handheld one that he played with his fingers. The distance from David's elbow to his fingertips matched the size of his harp. There were ten strings on the harp, and all the strings were of different thicknesses to produce different tunes. The wood was not as grand as the large harps made by the Egyptians, but it was still of a good quality. He knew that by the sound that came from his harp. There were keys at the top of it made from soft bamboo. These keys allowed David to tighten or loosen the strings and to tune them as needed.

David did not really remember being taught how to play the harp. He had worked for one of the craftsmen in town when he was seven years old. It was all small jobs and cleaning, but he received his pay in merchandise. When asked what he would most like to earn, David told the man, "A harp." He had always loved music, and his eyes lit up every time he heard it played. His soul seemed to start dancing on its own with the very first note. Music made him feel alive; he felt as though it opened a direct line of communication with Jehovah. Playing the harp was a great way to pass the hours. When David started to strum the strings, something magical happened to his fingers. They seemed to know just which strings to play to make the sounds he wanted. When a mistake occurred, it took on the effect of new sounds and a creative touch.

Lost in worship and music, David looked up to see one of his brothers coming toward him. It was Nethaneel, the fourth-eldest brother. Nethaneel appeared excited about something and was hurrying toward him. When he thought of how hard Nethaneel was working to impress his betroth's father, David could not help but snicker. It reminded him slightly of the story of Jacob and Rachael. He determined that he would never be caught in that kind of situation. Girls are mostly pretty but clearly not worth the bother. Someday he may want to marry, but certainly not any time in the near future. But if he were to marry, he would hope for someone as refined as, well, as "a king's daughter." Now those girls were worth taking notice of, or so he had heard. However, marriage was not something he planned to consider for a very long time.

His thoughts drifted off to his great-grandmother Ruth. Their father had shared the love story about his grandparents. The love and devotion that Ruth showed for her mother-in-law, Naomi, and for Jehovah God had been a testimony to all who heard. Jehovah blessed Ruth by giving her favor with Boaz.

David carefully placed his harp back into his canvas bag. As he climbed to his feet, he placed the bag on his shoulders. He walked toward Nethaneel to meet him. His brother was panting as he approached and tried to catch his breath. David and Nethaneel always enjoyed each other and could talk rather easily. Nethaneel was clearly excited about something, probably something to do with his betroth's dowry. The cattle that his father was setting apart for them seemed to be multiplying daily.

Panting from the run, Nethaneel tried to talk to David between the gasps for air. He inhaled deeply and bent over with the palm of his hands on his knees, "David...you...will never believe...what has happened!" Straightening and walking out the short distance that remained between him and David, he continued, "Do you remember Father...telling us...about the Prophet Samuel...and how he...was coming...to town?"

By this time, they had closed the distance between them and were now face to face. David smiled at his brother's excitement as he recalled their father telling them about the Prophet Samuel and how he had anointed King Saul to be Israel's first king. But what was this news that had his brother so excited? Nethaneel's breath had almost returned to normal. Excitement seemed to exuberate from him. Bending down to place his hands on his knees again, he inhaled, taking a deep breath. Straightening himself, Nethaneel began excitedly to tell David what events had occurred.

"Yes, of course, I remember Father telling us about him. But you look as though you ran all the way from town; what is it that has caused you to hurry so?" asked David.

"Do you remember Father talking about being invited to offer sacrifices with Samuel?"

"Yes, we were all wondering why Father was *really* invited."

Standing tall, Nethaneel continued, "Well...Father was also asked to bring his sons, so we went with him. We assumed we were going to offer sacrifices among the elders. In fact, the only thing that we were sure of is that it was to be a 'peaceful' visit." David recalled his father telling that a council of elders had gone to Samuel when he first came to their town. These men feared that "their sins had found them out." Those were the words that their father had used.

"So what happened? Was his visit just to offer sacrifices?" David was anxious for his brother to get to the point. David had been known to be of a curious nature. Although he still considered himself a patient person, he loved to get to the matters at hand. When a task needed to be done, he would do what needed to be done as quickly and efficiently as he could.

With a grin starting to raise the corners of his mouth, Nethaneel continued, "All of us went with Father but you because you were busy tending to the sheep. The elders of the town continued to take the time to prepare a sacrifice and to set themselves apart for worship. Once our family arrived, the prophet led us to a house. Sharing glances, we were most curious about this. He then proceeded to talk privately to Father. It was odd because when Father and the prophet finished talking, Father looked rather excited and yet apprehensive. Samuel then asked Father to have us pass by him, one at a time. First, Father told Eliab to stand and walk in front of the prophet. The prophet seemed very pleased with Eliab. It was easy to see that Samuel looked favorably upon him. Samuel seemed to be pondering something over as he studied Eliab's built. He walked slowly around Eliab, bringing the palm of his left hand up under his bearded chin and folding his right arm across his chest. He then rested his left elbow on his right wrist. There was a slight drumming action going on in Samuel's left fingers upon the side of his cheek. Clearly, he was thinking or meditating about something.

"Suddenly, Samuel turned to Father and said, 'Surely the Lord's anointing is before him.' As you can imagine, our father's face was beaming with a big broad smile. His beard might be thick, but you could see it nonetheless. As quickly as the prophet spoke, he stopped and closed his eyes.

"While Samuel was praying, the Lord spoke to him and said, 'Look not on his countenance, nor on the height of his stature because I have refused him, for the Lord sees not as man sees, for man looks on the outward appearance, but the Lord looks on the heart.'

"Samuel addressed Jessie, 'The Lord has not chosen this one...' then he continued on sharing Jehovah's words.

"Of course, we all thought this a bit odd, but we just watched to see what would happen next. At the prophet's leading, Father asked Abinadab to pass before Samuel. After a few seconds of looking him over and studying Abinadab, the prophet turned to Father and said, 'The Lord has not chosen this one either.'

"Chosen him...chosen him for what?" Nethaneel continued. "We all found ourselves looking at each other, wondering the same thing: *what was one of us being chosen for?*

"Father then nodded at Shammah to pass before the prophet. Samuel was much quicker this time in looking at father and saying, 'Neither has the Lord chosen this one.'"

Nethaneel continued to speak. His breathing had relaxed some, but he still seemed very excited. He had straightened to a standing position. His hands were moving very quickly as he spoke, helping to paint the picture. "Each one of us passed one by one before the Prophet Samuel, Eliab, Abinadab, Shammah, me, Raddai, Aram, and Ozem. I found my chest pounding as I walked past him." Instinctively, Nethaneel's right hand started to thump up and down upon his chest. "I found it to be an honor and a scary thing to be that close to a prophet. I wondered if he could read my thoughts or if he could hear how loud my heart was beating.

"Finally, Samuel turned to Father and said, 'The Lord has not chosen any of these. Jesse, are these all of your children?'

"Father answered him, saying, 'Only the youngest remains, and he is out tending to the sheep.'

"Samuel told Father to send and to fetch you and that no one would be allowed to sit down to dine until you come.

"Isn't it exciting, David? Samuel has requested you personally. You must be the one that the Lord has chosen." Nethaneel's hands relaxed and rested upon both of his hips as he took a proud stance. A smile spread over Nethaneel's face as excitement shone from his eyes.

Now, it was David who had questions, "Chosen...chosen for what? This could be exciting, but for what might I be chosen? Maybe Jehovah is looking for someone for a task bigger than I am ready for. Perhaps the prophet has seen into the darkest corners of my heart and has seen some evil that I do not know is there..." Slowly, methodically David spoke, "I guess that I better hurry into town..." Suddenly, the realization of all that was happening began to show on David's face as the rest of his sentence burst forth, "...because I won't know what this is all about until I go to see the prophet." Were these words coming from his lips or just bursting forth within his heart? He did not know for sure until Nethaneel smiled at him and said, "I don't know what this is all about, David, but I know that we need to hurry. I will be right behind you. I can see the servant coming now. As soon as he gets here, I will run to catch up with you. Then we can find out if you are the one that the Lord has chosen and for what!"

At this statement, David caught sight of their servant hurrying across the field to where they were standing. David quickly grabbed his leather bag that carried his harp and took off in a hastened sprint. Nethaneel was chuckling to himself as he watched David rush off with great anticipation and excitement. Just a few minutes later, Nethaneel caught up with David, and together, they went to the house where Samuel and his brothers were waiting. Nethaneel made David walk the last few feet so that his breathing could start returning to normal. David hated to slow down for even a moment but thought it wise to not walk in breathless. Just before entering the door, they looked at each other and took a deep breath as if to bring their excitement in control. As David entered, his father came to him and led him over to the prophet. David stood in front of the prophet for what seemed like hours. It was exciting to meet the prophet personally. But David was curious and had many questions running through his head.

As Samuel looked at David, he prayed and waited on the Lord. Samuel thought to himself, *This boy is just a lad. Could he possibly be the one that the Lord has chosen to take King Saul's place?*

For just a few minutes, Samuel's thoughts drifted back to another time and another place when he anointed another young man to become king. Israel had come before him and asked to have their own king. Samuel tried to tell the people that God had a better way for them, but they refused to listen.

Instead, the people insisted that they needed a king to lead them, just as other nations. As Samuel went to God in prayer about their request, God led him to Saul. It was a rather curious journey. God gave many signs to Saul as a testimony to establish His will. Finally, the journey ended in a special anointing in front of the townspeople. During the last few years, King Saul had turned his back on God. Now, God was turning His back on Saul. God was going to replace Saul with a new king; that was why he was here. Soon Samuel would know who the new king would be. This time, there would be no big public anointing. This anointing would be done in private, for Samuel feared for his life. He knew that to go and anoint a new king openly would be considered treason. He'd be signing his own death warrant with King Saul. So God gave him the plan to find and to anoint the new king under the guise of offering a sacrifice.

Samuel's thoughts continued within him. The first thing Samuel noticed was the lad's rosy cheeks. They were bright with color, perhaps from rushing to get here? This lad had beautiful light red hair. There was a touch of brown to his hair, probably from the sun. It was currently messed up and could use a good combing. But being a shepherd did not allow much time for grooming, nor the need. Although his cheeks were rosy, his complexion was clear, and he had fair skin. There was clearly something rare about this lad. He had appealing brown eyes that seemed to shine. Samuel could not get over the sincerity that radiated from the lad's eyes. He could sense God's blessing upon this boy. He paused for a few minutes just to study David's eyes. He looked into the soul of the young boy. His eyelashes were full and thick, matching the color of his hair. It was true that he was going to be a fine man someday. His shoulders were broad for his small frame, a sign that he would have a muscular full built one day. Samuel found it easy to look upon this lad. Although he was a young boy, he was a handsome lad for sure. But would he be the next king?

As he prayed, God spoke to Samuel and told him, "Arise and anoint him. For he is the one."

Samuel turned around and went over to the table where he had placed his woven cloth sack. Reaching down, he opened his sack and began to take out some supplies. First, he took out a ram's horn. Next, he removed a container of oil. Opening the oil container, Samuel began to fill the ram's horn. Turning around to Jesse and his sons, Samuel took a few minutes to explain that God had sent him to anoint the next king of Israel.

Samuel looked at Jesse and said, "This is the one that the Lord has chosen."

Samuel's thoughts reflected on how true it is that God's ways are not our ways. To begin with, God selected the smallest tribe of Israel, the Benjaminite tribe, for the first king; and now God was choosing the smallest boy in a family of eight fine young men.

He turned to David and said, "You are chosen of God to lead Israel. You are to be the next king."

Jesse's face was shining. Without audibly speaking the words, his eyes spoke for his lips, saying, "My son is to be the next king...*my* son...*my* David."

All of David's brothers gasped with excitement. They began to shout and to dance, swinging each other in excitement. As quickly as the excitement began, it ended. All of David's brothers continued to watch the prophet.

Nethaneel just knew that whatever it was he was chosen for would be something really good. So this was the big news! This is what one of them had been chosen for...the next king! "Wow, this is very exciting!" Nethaneel knew in his heart that this was what they had learned to call "a God thing." Nethaneel knew that this was right, just as sure as if God had told him personally. He could not help but smile from ear to ear. This was turning out to be a very special day indeed. "Wait 'till Mother hears the news. There will be a party at home tonight!"

Samuel walked over and stood in front of David. He looked down at the young lad and reached his hand out until it was over the top of David's head. He tipped the ram's horn and let the oil flow over David. It ran down into his hair and over his face. It flowed down the back of his hair and onto his clothes. God had spoken to Samuel and said that when he anointed David, He would be putting His own character and nature in the oil.

David knew that he was saturated in the anointing oil, but all he could feel was the presence of God. David felt as if God was personally there with him. An abundance of joy flooded over his soul. David felt totally encircled in the presence of God. He could hear his father and his brothers laughing and shouting for joy, but it was all so distant. David hoped that this feeling would never leave him. So many times, he had longed to be in God's presence. Although he had felt close to God many times, this was different. This time it was God who was drawing close to him. It was as though he was consumed in God's glory, much the way he imagined Moses when the bush was on fire but not burning. Should he take off his shoes as Moses did? Was this holy ground? The oil had a beautiful fragrance to it. It was a fragrance that he would remember throughout his whole life.

Then he heard Samuel's words of prophecy over him. Samuel prayed over the kingdom that David would have someday. The prophet prayed that he would be a king worthy of our Lord. He also prayed that David would never forget that God was anointing him for this position.

"Yes, Lord, may I never forget that You are establishing me as the next king and that *You* can just as easily remove me from this position."

Samuel went on to pray that God's Spirit would remain with David always and that God's Spirit would give him the wisdom and knowledge to lead the people. Then, Samuel finished the prayer by praying that he would live an obedient life unto the Lord.

It was a glorious moment. David found himself praising God in a way that he never had before. David felt set free. He had never felt chained before, but this was a freedom that he had never experienced.

# Chapter 3

*"In the Lord I take refuge. How then can you say to me: Flee like a bird to your mountain..." (Psalm 11:1, NIV)*

After Samuel left Bethlehem, David found it hard to return to the sheep. He loved the sheep just as he always had, but he had so many questions. At first, his brothers were all very happy for him. They shared thoughts of marrying a king's daughter. They talked about assisting him when he ruled the kingdom. They talked of the riches that they would most certainly have. It was fun imagining the servants David would have and how they would order them around. One night when they were gathered around the fireplace in their living room, they had fun imagining how David would come to be king. Although this was fun, David knew that the king had a son and wondered what his part would be in all this.

Often, one of his brothers would stop working a few hours early to join him out in the fields. Together they would sit and talk for a while. Sometimes they just wanted to dream ahead, to try to fill in the pieces of how things would end for King Saul. His brothers would come out for a few hours to share a new idea about his kingship. They were all sure they would have a place of position at the palace. The palace...oh, did they have fun building a palace in their thoughts, especially David's two brothers who worked in wood trade. They had the biggest and grandest palace ever built in their minds. They had an entire wing built on for David's parents. They imagined parties and learning to dance. The fun went on and on. Everyone except Nethaneel had David bringing in kings' daughters from all over the region. At this point, their mother would always remind them not to marry from a heathen tribe. Every heathen tribe has idols. David's mother loved hearing every detail over and over. She never tired hearing about the favor that God had given her Jesse. She was a praying mother, and she thanked God for His anointing upon her family and, more importantly, her son.

Always Jesse would caution each one of his sons to keep their excitement in check. He reminded them of why there was no public anointing. He would say, "King Saul will most likely kill anyone who would take his kingdom. These words that the prophet has spoken were meant just for our family." Or he'd say, "If word were to get out prematurely, the king might try to imprison or to assassinate David or all of us. No, we want God to work all things out in His own way and in His own time."

Over the last few weeks, Eliab had started to express some anger toward David. Eliab seemed to get increasingly more short-tempered with him. It was obvious that Eliab was disappointed that God had not chosen him to be the next king. With each conversation Eliab would have with David, he added insulting comments like, "...and you think you will be a king." David did not find fault with Eliab because David knew that it was the Israelites tradition that the oldest son receives the blessings. Therefore, David knew that this was why Eliab felt like he should have received the blessing. It was their custom that the eldest son receives the father's blessings prior to his death. However, this blessing was different. This was a blessing from God that David was quite sure that he was not worthy to receive. In fact, David had to wonder, *Was it a blessing... or a commission? Being a king and leading the people...* Indeed, it was a blessing bestowed upon him. Although he felt as if he understood Moses' apprehensions when God spoke to him and said that he would lead all of Israel out of Egypt, his father had found humor in Moses when he said that he was not eloquent in speech. Moses was raised and taught by the best scholars. The Egyptians considered themselves the most advanced society of their era, and what did God do? He used an uneducated Israel slave to be the spokesman before Pharaoh.

Jesse was a very wise man of God. Jessie could see David's anxiety over the prophet's words, so he took David aside and told him that patience is a virtue. "When God starts something, He always finishes it. Don't be anxious; just trust God and wait."

His father's words were definitely from God. Immediately, he was able to relax and worship God. David was no longer anxious. The songs that he enjoyed writing to God took on new meaning. They seemed to be psalms of praise more than songs of attribute. The psalms became words from David to God and words from God to David. The music started to flow from his heart more than ever.

# Chapter 4

*"David said to the Philistine, 'You come against me with
sword and spear and javelin, but I come against you in the
name of the Lord Almighty, the God of the armies of Israel,
whom you have defied'"* (1 Samuel 17:45, NIV).

*How much further could it be?* David thought. It had been early
this morning when David left Judah. He couldn't help but smile
as he thought of his father. The men in the area called him
"Jesse the Bethlehemite." They always said it with such pride.
David loved his father very deeply. His father was truly a man
of God. He raised David and his brothers to love the Lord. It
wasn't hard either! Father made it so easy, as he told all the
stories of old, the stories of God talking to Adam and Eve and
Moses. *Oh, that had to have been so awesome when God spoke to
Moses through the burning bush.* Why, when Father told the story,
you were sure that you were right there seeing the events as
they were unfolding. You would feel your confidence building
as you listened to the words spoken by the prophets.

*Prophets...* After pausing in his thoughts, David smiled,
remembering meeting the Prophet Samuel. Months had
passed since he had met with Samuel, and there had been many

changes. But the words that Samuel had spoken would forever stay close to David's heart.

*Not long now*, David thought as he continued his journey. It would be good to see his friend Jonathan again. They'd only known each other for a few months, but David had grown closer to Jonathan than any of his seven brothers, including Nethaneel. As David came up over the hill, he could see the men who had gathered to fight to protect Israel. He could hear the cries of the Philistines. David rushed to the largest tent. Finding the supply tent was not hard. For it had many cows, sheep, and goats, all of which were there either to provide milk and butter for the soldiers or for food.

Jesse, David's father, had been anxious for a word on his sons. Many days had passed since his three oldest sons left to join King Saul in battle. His father had asked David to take a bushel of roasted grain and ten loaves of bread to his brothers. Jesse had also asked him to take ten loaves of cheese to the commander of his brother's unit. Jesse had urged David to hurry. Upon getting word that his brothers were fine, David was to bring back a token, some spoil of war for their father. This would give Jesse proof that they were winning the battle. Early that morning, David left his father's sheep with a keeper. He felt confident that the sheep would be fine in his absence because keepers were trained to protect. A keeper had such a strong understanding of protection that they compared their protection to placing a hedge around the animals. He loaded up the food items that his mother had prepared, and then he set out for Shochoh in Judah. When David arrived at the supply tent, there was a young boy helping the cooks and those in charge of the supplies. David could feel the anticipation and the exhilaration of war. Although he was not quick to fight, he loved the victory. David quickly asked the young boy to take care of his cart and his supplies. He then headed out to find his brothers. The men were in a line on one side of the Valley of Elah with the tents and supplies behind them. The Philistines were on the next hill in a line facing the Israelites. Between both armies was a deep valley with a small creek running through the middle. The creek was not big this time of the year. One could easily step over it. As David looked at the Israelites, he saw many men that he had either met or knew well. He noticed that although most of the men were older, there were some teens his age. His eyes searched the numerous men. Some of the men turned around to see who was coming up behind them. David smiled, sending a greeting their way. Some of the men just turned back to face the Philistines, and some of them nodded a slight smile back. One detail, more than anything else, caught David's attention. The men's eyes...some of the men looked defeated already, and others looked very tired. But surprisingly, none of the men looked eager to fight the Philistines.

"There they are...my brothers." David hurried over to where they were. He was very anxious to hear about every detail from his three oldest brothers, Eliab, Abinadab, and Shammah. David was so full of anticipation waiting to hear the stories that he could hardly wait to get past the formalities. The Philistines just did not understand that they would never win against Israel. God would always fight their battles. At least, as long as the people continued to worship God and serve Him first. David was confident of one thing. As long as God was in control, God would win the battle, and the Philistines were wasting their time.

As David was greeting his brothers, one of the Philistines stepped out of line and walked toward the Israelites. David knew without anyone saying a word that this warrior had to be the one they called Goliath. Philistines boasted about how Goliath was their champion. The tales went far and wide around the countryside. Much was also said about Goliath's brothers and the rest of these giants. They talked about how huge Goliath was, as though that alone would bring about their victory. The stories told how Goliath was over eleven feet tall. They said that his armor was of the finest quality and made of the strongest materials to protect him. His helmet was made of brass plates laid over each other. Often, people would refer to the scales on a fish to describe these brass plates. His legs were so long that they came to the chest of the average man. They told how he wore brass boots so that the soldiers he fought could not use his legs as a target. The stories said that his coat weighed about five thousand shekels or 125 pounds. As impressive as Goliath's size and armor were, David did not find himself impressed at all, for he knew God's power. Nothing could ever be as impressive as the God of Abraham.

Eliab was the first to see David and to greet him. He was David's oldest brother. Eliab was the tallest of his brothers and had wide, firm shoulders. He had the eyes of a leader. All his brothers looked up to him for answers, and of course, Eliab loved that. Eliab reached out to shake David's hand as he inquired what brought him out to the battlefield. Before David could answer, Abinadab came up and hugged him; Shammah smiled and stepped in to hug him next. Abinadab also had a tall and sturdy build. However, he was a few inches shorter than Eliab, and he was more of a follower than a leader. Shammah was shorter than Abinadab, and he had a soft heart, just like David. He had most wanted to be like him when he was a young lad. Now he was older, and he just wanted to fashion himself after God. David had always loved to see Shammah smile. His teeth had not come in as straight as he and his brothers. This gave him what the family had named "the crooked smile." Sometimes Shammah was self-conscious of his smile, but David had always thought it gave him a unique character. It was good to see them again. They were having a great time talking about their father, their mother, and the other brothers. They laughed as David caught them up on all of Nethaneel's steps to impress his new bride and her father. David was just telling them how anxious their father had been to hear about them when Goliath, the Philistine champion, stepped forward and shouted a challenge to the Israelites.

His deep voice resounded loud and arrogant across the valley, *"Why do you come out and line up for battle? I am a Philistine, and you are the servants of Saul. Choose a man and have him come down to me. If he is able to fight and kill me, then we will become your slaves, but if I overcome him and kill him, you will become our slaves and serve us! This day I defy the armies of Israel! Give me a man and let us fight each other!"*

David found himself repulsed to see this arrogant enemy defying *his* God. His brothers were quick to explain that Goliath had been doing this for the past forty days. It was quite a surprise to see all the Israelite men running away in fear from

Goliath. A handful of men, excited to share the details with someone new, started talking at once to tell David about how this giant kept coming out and challenging them. Not only had he been doing this for the past forty days, but Goliath also came out twice a day, every morning and every evening. Twice a day for the last forty days, they had heard this challenge. As they all fought to talk over each other, one of the men started talking about how he would like the king's reward for killing Goliath, "If only there were a way to outsmart this giant and to kill him without being killed...then I could receive the king's rewards... his daughter's hand in marriage...great wealth...and my father's land would be tax-exempt from taxes forever!"

Suddenly, time was standing still around David at the words he thought he had just heard. Over the past few months, prior to the war, the king had sent messengers to request of David's father that he be allowed to come and play his harp for the king. It was said that evil spirits were tormenting King Saul. David loved to play the harp and worshipped God by the hours. Often, shepherds with their sheep or merchants would pass by when David was out in the fields. Frequently, they would stop and sit with David as he played. Therefore, David had become known for his beautiful talent. As the king's attendants were looking for a way to soothe the evil spirits, one of the king's servants told them of Jesse's son, David. It was said that he played an instrument with great skill. The servant said, "I have seen a son of Jesse of Bethlehem, who knows how to play the harp. He is a good lad and a great protector of his sheep. He speaks well and is a fine-looking man...and the Lord is with him."

Immediately, King Saul sent out messengers to Jesse and said, "Send me your son David, who is with the sheep."

Therefore, Jesse took a donkey loaded with bread, a skin of wine, and a young goat and told David to take them to Saul. Upon arriving, David entered the king's service. King Saul liked David very much. In a short time, he became one of the king's armor-bearers. After a while, King Saul sent word to Jesse and said, "I am pleased with David. So allow him to remain in my service."

Having felt the huge responsibility of this title of armor-bearer, David knew a lot of the king's burdens would fall to him. He was expected to continuously bear up the king. Normally, he might question his ability to perform such a task, but with God, he was learning that he could perform whatever it was that God had set before him. David determined to be the best armor-bearer possible. He would lift the king up and support him to the best of his abilities. Whenever the evil spirits came upon King Saul, he would take his harp out and start to play. Relief would come over the king, and he would feel better as the evil spirits would leave him. The king did not know why, but David did. From the very first time he could remember, he had been taught about "God's power." He also knew that where God was, evil could not stay. God's presence was why the evil spirits had to leave King Saul. David was inviting God into the room. He believed himself to be pretty good on the harp, but it wasn't just his playing ability; it was God's presence and David's prayers. Most of the time, David prayed silently, but if the king was really bad off, in a violent raging way, David would work prayers into his songs.

After some time, Saul sent word to Jesse, saying, "Allow David to remain in my service, for I am pleased with him."

David remembered his father chuckling about it. "Should I argue with a king? No, if the king wants my son in his service, then, of course, David can return to him. May the Lord bless you and my son."

When King Saul went off to war against the Philistines, he sent David home to his father's house.

In private, his father gave him a word of caution before he left. "David, do not covet the king's position. God has already spoken. You will be the next king. Be patient. Let God bring it to pass in His timing."

David appreciated his father. He had such comforting ways about him. He smiled and nodded his head in agreement with his father. He had no intention of doing anything else. God had filled him with peace and confidence. There were no longer any doubts or questions haunting his peace.

During the time David had been with King Saul, he had much opportunity to see the great wealth that King Saul had acquired. He had also become best friends with Jonathan, and David had definitely noticed Michal and her older sister, Merab. The first thing that he noticed about Michal was her long, shiny, black hair. It bounced in a multitude of curls as it flowed down her back and almost to her waist. He knew that she was a king's daughter by the way she walked, with such grace. Watching her almost left him speechless. It was such a contrast to the girls that David had been raised around. Those girls worked hard in the fields and in the house. He admired this fact about the girls but found it most intriguing to see the contrast between them. Michal had been raised with everyone doing everything for her; that was obvious. Merab was pretty too, but she was too old for David and more like the "big sister" type. She also had long black hair, but hers was straight and kept braided on the top of her head most of the time. She was a little taller than Michal, almost as tall as Jonathan, her brother. She was pleasant, but it was Michal that had caught his attention. She had such dainty features about her, such long thin fingers. He had even found himself wondering if he might ever be able to hold them...David realized that there were so many opportunities in the king's words. Although he was not planning to marry anytime soon, it still was a pleasant thought to think of the king's daughters. Maybe he would not have to wait to be a king to marry someone as refined as a king's daughter. As he meditated on the possibilities, his thought turned to his father and his aging health. His father's house would be free in Israel, free from all tolls, tributes, customs, and services to the crown. What an opportunity.

David suddenly heard himself talking as though coming out of a trance. He spoke to the men near him, "What will be done for the man who kills this Philistine and removes this disgrace from Israel? Who is this uncircumcised Philistine that he would defy the armies of the living God?"

As the seconds that seemed like minutes passed by, the reality of the king's words hit him again. Eliab, listening to David speaking to the men, became incessantly angry with him. David had seen his brother angry many times. The flame in his cheeks was rising, covering his whole face as he raised his voice at David. David always compared it to the fire in the fireplace once it gets going really well.

"Why have you come down here? And with whom did you leave the family sheep in the desert? I know how conceited you are and how wicked your heart is! You came down only to watch the battle!"

David had felt Eliab's stab of jealousy ever since Samuel had come to his father's town and anointed him to be the next king. When Samuel said that the next king of Israel would come from his father's house, Eliab was sure that it should and would be him. After all, he was the first-born son and the strongest built of all his brothers. David was not afraid of his oldest brother, but for just a split second, he had that all too familiar "little brother" feeling, and for a split second, there was the old thought to cower away.

Looking at Eliab, David asked, "Now what have I done? Can't I even speak?"

Before Eliab could respond, David turned away and started talking to another man from Israel. He asked this man the same question, and again the man quoted the king's words of reward for the conqueror of this Philistine. Again, David's thoughts were swimming with possibilities as he heard the man repeat the words, "The man who kills Goliath will receive great wealth from the king. King Saul will also give the man his daughter in marriage, and he will exempt his father's family from taxes in Israel."

Some of the men standing nearby overheard David's inquiries to the king's words. One of them quickly went to King Saul and told him all that he had just heard. King Saul delighted in this inquiry and sent his servant out to bring back this either very brave or very foolish soul.

As David was approaching King Saul, David looked confidently at the king and said, "Let no one lose heart on account of this Philistine; your servant will go and fight him."

King Saul smiled and said, "You are not able to go out against this Philistine and fight him; you are only a boy, and he has been fighting men from his youth."

David's reply came so naturally, as he remembered back to his shepherding days. He knew without a doubt that God had been grooming him for this day.

"Your servant has been keeping his father's sheep. Once a lion came and grabbed one of our sheep to carry it off. I grabbed it by its beard and slit its neck. Then a bear came and carried off a sheep from the flock. I went after it, struck it, and rescued the sheep from its mouth. When it turned on me, I struck it and killed it. Your servant has killed both the lion and the bear; this uncircumcised Philistine will be like one of them because he has defied the armies of the living God. The Lord who delivered me from the paw of the lion and the paw of the bear will deliver me from the hand of this Philistine."

What could King Saul say to this? He gave David a look, mixed with hope and uncertainty, and said, "Go, and the Lord be with you."

King Saul then called his armor-bearer over to him. He was the young man who had accompanied him to the front lines of battle and told him to help him with his tunic. The king took it off and started to dress David in it. First, he put his coat of armor on him and then his bronzed helmet. David fastened the king's sword over the tunic and tried to walk around. The tunic did not fit him at all, and he was unsure of his abilities in the outfit. He felt clumsy and fought to even keep a good balance.

As well-meaning as the king's actions were, King Saul stood a good two feet higher than David, and the armor made him feel cumbersome.

David turned to King Saul and said, "I cannot go in these because I am not used to them."

The armor-bearer took the tunic, armor, and the king's bronzed helmet, returning them to the king. David took his staff and walked down to the stream. He reached down and carefully chose five smooth rocks from the stream. He took extra time to select them. They had to be smooth and well-rounded. However, they were almost flat on each side. Then he placed the five stones in his shepherd's bag, and he picked up his sling. He loved his sling, and it felt right in his hands. David could feel the exhilaration of the moment rising. He knew his brothers doubted his abilities. He also remembered when he came home and told them about the lion and the bear. Neither time had they really acted like they believed him. If it weren't for the pelts he brought home for his father to sell, he was sure they would not have believed him at all. David was not happy about their attitude, but he took comfort in the fact that he knew the truth. He remembered the strength that he had felt rise within him each time that God had assisted him in killing the animals. He knew for a fact that it was not his strength alone that had killed these animals but rather God's strength in him. Strength was what he was feeling this very moment; a supernatural strength was growing. As David was walking up to Goliath, the people saw just one young shepherd boy, but David knew the God of Israel was with him, or rather, his presence surrounded him. Some people called it overconfidence, but David called it authority. Although his brothers loved God, this was where he was different. David didn't want to just believe in God and worship Him; he wanted to know everything there was to know about the God of Israel. David knew where he stood with God and, consequently, the enemies of God. It had also angered him that anyone would challenge the God of Israel. This Goliath was a stranger. He was not circumcised, and he had no covenant with God!

David could hear many conversations from the Israelites behind him. He knew what they must be thinking. They didn't hold out much hope for a shepherd boy coming against a warrior like Goliath. He could see them now as they sized up the situation: Goliath having on all that armor while David had only his shepherd's coat. Goliath had a spear while David had a staff. Goliath had a bow while David had a sling. Goliath had five or more arrows while David had five smooth stones. David almost found humor in their thoughts. He also knew that Eliab would be criticizing him and certain that he would die. He found humor in the thought that Eliab was most certainly trying to formulate a plan to tell their father. He was running different excuses around in his head as to why he let him go out there in the first place. Poor Eliab, would he ever learn to trust God? He didn't know for sure, but he would keep praying for him. A smile crept over David's face as he imagined what their faces must look like. David was not alone at all. In fact, he was ready for this victory that he knew unquestionably was his. He knew that God had been preparing him for today most of his life.

David approached Goliath; his shield-bearer was walking in front of him. They came closer to David. Goliath told his shield-bearer to stop and wait behind him. He would not need his assistance since his enemy would be crushed so easily. Goliath looked the boy over and saw that he was only a lad about fourteen years of age. He had dark brown hair with a cast of red marbled in, and his skin was fair in color. Goliath almost felt sorry for the lad in a rather sarcastic way, "...pity this boy has to die." Goliath had a job to do. Someone was going to die, and if that someone was a boy...then, so be it. Immediately, Goliath's feelings turned to bitter hatred, and he despised the boy who had come out to meet him.

He started yelling at the boy, "Am I a d-o-g that y-o-u-u-u come to me with s-t-i-c-k-s?"

Goliath started cursing the boy by his gods. Then he yelled at him, "I'-l-l-l give your f-l-e-s-h to the b-i-r-d-s of the a-i-r and the b-e-a-s-t-s of the f-i-e-l-d!"

David very boldly shouted back to the Philistine, "You come against me with sword and spear and javelin, but I come against you in the name of the Lord of hosts, the God of the armies of Israel, whom you have defied. This day the Lord will hand you over to me, and I'll strike you down and cut off your head. Today, I will give the carcasses of the Philistine army to the birds of the air and the beasts of the earth, and the whole world will know that there is a God in Israel. All those who are gathered here will know that it is not by the sword or spear that the Lord saves, for the battle is the Lord's, and He will give all of you into our hands."

Goliath threw back his head so hastily that his helmet fell off and left his broad forehead a fair mark for David. Goliath was full of scorn for David as he moved closer to attack him. As he did, David ran quickly toward the battle lines to meet him. There was not an ounce of fear in David, only the victory and excitement of what God was about to do. His eyes were only seeing one thing, the victory God would have this day! Maybe this time, the Philistines would actually see that there is only one God, the God of Israel. All the gods that the Philistines believe in are false gods. This uncircumcised Philistine will meet his fatal end.

David found himself elated. *This Philistine has no idea who comes with me. No, I am not alone. If only this Philistine knew what the Lord of hosts really means...the God of angel armies...* David found total delight to be standing with the God of angel armies against this soon fallen enemy.

David felt the rock between his thumb and index finger, just as he had many times before. He took the necessary time to gain his stance. As each second passed, the giant laughed at him and tried to antagonize him. David stood there preparing to sling the rock at Goliath; again, he estimated his strength and the force that he would need to drive this rock right into his forehead. He prayed a silent prayer. This prayer was not for help, as many of the men might have assumed, but it was of thanks. He already knew how this battle was going to end. He was thanking God that together they were a great team.

As many times before, he braced the two strings on the left side of the sling under his little finger and his third finger. The other two strings on the right side of the sling were held tightly between his thumb and first finger. He would release these at just the right time, allowing the rock to fly at this uncircumcised target. He then shifted his weight back and forth from one foot to the other each time he swung the sling around. David arched his right hand at the elbow and swung his hand around one time, then two times, now three times, and then he released the sling with all his might at Goliath's forehead. Swoosh! The rock sank deep into the middle of Goliath's forehead just above his eyebrows. "Bull's eye! Another perfect shot!" The earth shook much more when Goliath fell than he remembered from the bear.

David ran over and stood on top of Goliath's chest. He had a victory stance as he stood on top of him. As much as David wanted to lift his arms up in the air or pump his fists in victory, he had another gory yet victorious task to do. He reached for the Philistine's sword and drew it from its sheath. *Crazy giant, he didn't even pull out his sword or lift up his shield. He didn't even try to defend himself! He was so certain that I would not succeed.*

After David knocked him out, he cut Goliath's head off with the giant's own sword. The sword was a one-handed weapon for Goliath. However, for David, it took both hands to hold it. But it was amazing. David thought to himself, Even though the Philistine's sword would normally feel heavy to someone my size, it feels light and easy to lift. The triumph of the moment filled David completely. Although he was full of pride, it was not pride about him. It was pride that the God of Israel was the conqueror. David heard his father quoting scriptures to his brothers before they left, "Let not the strong man glory in his strength, not the armed man in his armor. Rather, glory in the God of Israel."

\*\*\*\*\*

Goliath felt his body falling to the ground. There seemed to be nothing that he could do to stop from falling. *What is happening?* His mind was dazed. *Oh yes...the rock...the lad. I curse you, boy...I curse the king of Israel...and I curse your God!* Hatred filled his heart more than at any other time. Goliath tried to open his eyes, but nothing seemed to happen. He heard voices. What was going on? *Oh no...the boy...he is pulling my sword from its sheath. Why didn't I kill him before he could do anything? Why didn't I use my shield? Where is my shield-bearer? Why aren't my own men helping me? Where are my brothers? If I die...we will become their slaves. Why aren't my eyes opening?* As Goliath lay there, his heart filled with a hatred that was blacker than the darkest night or deepest cave. This darkness came from evil. His thoughts were being overtaken with...with sounds...sounds and confusion...confusion that was thick and filled with the cries of an angry mob...it was a sound that seemed to grow...and grow...and grow...until it was taking over his entire being. There were faces, ugly faces, and hideous, grotesque faces jumping out at him. It was frightful, and nothing had ever scared him. These faces were coming straight at him; they were laughing and mocking him...he tried to gasp for air...evil loathed from everywhere around him. It grew and grew...he could no longer lie to himself...he knew where this evil came from...he knew...he knew... An intense pain filled Goliath's being as the cold, sharp edge of the sword cut into his neck. Then, suddenly and silently, his heart stopped beating...and his soul was lost for eternity.

*****

The Israelites stood watching in total amazement at what this shepherd boy had just accomplished. Some of the men were shouting victory chants. Some of the men were silent while they stood there marveling at what they had just witnessed.

King Saul stood there relieved that this "thorn in his flesh" was gone. David's brother Eliab stood there, getting angrier and angrier by the moment. His jealousy was growing as he felt insulted by his little brother's behavior. Not only did David get the anointing from Samuel to be the next king, but now he was going to win favor with all the men of Israel. This brother of his seemed unstoppable. Abinadab and Shammah were jumping around shouting and clapping their hands as they watched their youngest brother. It was going to be a wonderful time when they arrived back home and told the rest of the family what had just happened.

Shammah could not help but smile as he thought of all the famous slingers he remembered hearing about in Israel. He had no doubt that his little brother just went to the top of the list. He recalled quickly the story of when Israel attacked the Benjamites. An Israelite and his concubine had been traveling, and they stopped to spend the night. During the night, they were attacked by these Benjamite men. They raped and killed his concubine. This was a dangerous move on their part because he called for all the Israelite brethren. They decided to retaliate by attacking them and killing them. This would be a justice that would stop these men from doing such atrocities again. They had seven hundred chosen men who were left-handed. Each of them could sling a stone at a hair and not miss. Though there was so much more to the battle and this story, it was the words "seven hundred chosen men who could sling a stone at a hair and not miss" that caught Shammah's attention. *What will they say about my brother? "A giant killer...perfect shot... The giant had a sword, spear, and shield... David had only his sling...and, of course, his faith in God."* What more did David need? His imagination ran on with the possibilities.

Abinadab couldn't help but remember how he used to teach his younger brothers how to use a slingshot. However, he knew that he was not the one responsible for today's defeats. Just as their father had raised them, he knew that God was the real hero here. They used to practice when they were done with their chores, but none of his brothers had taken a liking to the sling as much as David did, nor did they all realize the degree that David had perfected this skill.

*****

When the Philistines saw that their champion was dead, they turned around and started running. No one stopped to pick up his tent. No one grabbed any of his things. They didn't take time to formulate a plan. No, they were running fast and hard. They knew that they were in danger for their lives. They ran with panic in their eyes.

Had David the time to sit and just watch all that was going on, he might have had fun watching the cooks as they came running out of their tents to see what was happening. The cooks

45

had been in the tents preparing the noon meal. Everyone knew the routine. Goliath challenged the Israelites and taunted them with all his criticisms, but now there were shouts and hollering coming from the battlefield. These were not the victory shouts that the cooks had been waiting for; no, this was different.

It was exciting to watch as God filled the Israelites with faith and victory. The victory that David felt from God seemed to flow over to all the Israelite and the Judean army. David had slew Goliath, and he was ready to take down the rest of these uncircumcised Philistines. David stood with one foot on Goliath's chest; he raised the giant's head high in the sky with his left hand, and he pointed the sword toward the heavens with his other hand. Then he let out a victory cry that seemed to fill the air for miles. The Israelites joined in, and the atmosphere became electrifying as all the men joined him, shouting and charging ahead. There was no doubt that everyone could feel God's presence, just as David did. David grabbed the first man that ran down the hill. "You, come here and stand guard over Goliath. I will be back as soon as we kill those Philistines. Do not let anyone touch Goliath...or his head!"

The man smiled with a firm salute, "Yes, sir! I will guard him and his head with my life." The man barely had time to respond as David threw the giant's head at him. Blood was running down the front of the man's clothes. The trail of blood was still seeping from the head. The man didn't have time to ask if he would like him to watch over the sword too. Before he could get the words out, David was running at full speed with the sword raised high in the sky; Goliath's blood was still covering the blade. The man felt proud to be watching over such a trophy for someone so young. Young or not, this lad had just saved them, and he felt honored to serve him.

David led the men into battle. They started charging after the Philistines that were on the run. They chased after them until they came to the valley and the gates of Ekron. As David led the way into battle, his brothers were right behind him. The rest of the Israelites followed hard on their heels. They were killing the Philistines as they went. As they chased them into the Hebrew valley, the Philistines were stopped by the gates of Ekron. They had run to their own city, but the keepers of the gates had not figured out what was happening quickly enough to open the gates. The Philistines were trapped just as God had planned, with no place to run. David could see the men inside the city trying to get them to move back so that they could open the gates. But the panic the men were feeling kept them from succeeding. David laughed out loud, delighted at God's plan to destroy the enemy. Raising their swords together, they would have victory.

As they were using their swords, David found laughter coming upon him as he heard his brothers counting the men they were killing. Abinadab and Shammah, it seemed, were having a contest. First, he heard Abinadab saying, "I have now killed fourteen of these worthless Philistines."

Shammah responded with, "I have two to the good of you, Brother."

David could have rolled with laughter when he heard Eliab making his claim to fame. "Remember that I taught both of you how to fight with a sword. I shall defeat more of these uncircumcised Philistines than either of you."

Even though David and his brothers had never fought before in war, there was a unity that reminded him of days gone by. It was as though every bit of fight had left the Philistines, and they were just waiting to die. David could only be thankful that he had never put his faith in men as the Philistines had. No, David knew that they must be conquered. To stop now would mean that more Israelites would die at the hands of these men. This was war, and the enemies of God had to die. As he raised his sword to kill another Philistine, he heard words to a psalm forming in his mind, *Praise be to the LORD my rock, who trains my hands for war, my fingers for battle. He is my loving God and my fortress, my stronghold and my deliverer, my shield, in whom I take refuge, who subdues peoples under me.* David would have so much fun later finishing this psalm. For now, there was a battle to finish winning.

As the men were returning from battle, they seized all the items of value left behind by the Philistines. They destroyed their tents and enriched themselves with the spoils. They left Philistines dead all along the Shaaraim road that led to Gath and Ekron. The conversation that David had with Goliath just a few hours ago rang through his mind as he looked at all the dead carcasses.

> This day will the Lord deliver thee into mine hands;
> and I will smite thee and take thy head from thee; and
> I will give the carcasses of the host of the Philistines
> this day unto the fowl of the air, and to the wild beasts
> of the earth; that all the earth may know that there is
> a God in Israel.[2]

Goliath should have listened and repented. But David knew that would never have happened. So just as he had said, the fowls of the air and the wild beasts of the earth would have their feast, and everyone would know that there was a God in Israel!

David would enjoy taking spoils of war back to his father just as he had requested. It would be a real delight to share the details of this victory with his father. He knew his father would appreciate all that God had done in him and through him.

*****

King Saul stood there almost in shock that this small shepherd boy had been able to kill such a strong enemy as Goliath. He knew that this boy had been determined, and King Saul had wished the best for him, but he did not believe that he would actually be able to kill the giant. The king had even hesitated to send a youth to his most certain death. He knew that the people would frown upon such an action. David had made killing the giant look so easy that he could not help but wonder why no other warriors had stood up to Goliath. For just a split second, the king remembered back to days that he had felt the power of God. Saul realized that this victorious feat had nothing to do with the boy's size or age, but it had everything to do with the God of Israel living in his life. As quickly as the king remembered what it felt like to walk in the presence of God, he drifted back into his dazed state that no longer was accompanied by God's presence. The king's thoughts were suddenly back on David. David had not just killed the giant, but he had made it look so easy. Then, as a valiant statement of victory, David cut off the enemy's head! The king was proud of this new warrior. David would no longer be seen as a small shepherd boy but as a warrior for the king, and not just any king but himself. The king was suddenly filled with pride of what the people would say. "King Saul has done it again! He has conquered the enemy! Goliath is killed, and King Saul is our hero!" His thoughts escalated with all that lay ahead for him as they entered the city. There would be a parade and marching. The townspeople would be there to greet their king with song and dance. His people would once again see him as their fierce leader, and they would know that God had been with him again. Feeling a jab of anger, King Saul swelled with hatred for the Prophet Samuel. Personally, he believed that Samuel should be killed. But even Samuel would not be able to deny what God had done here today. This was the victory that King Saul had been waiting for. The people would bow to him once again.

As David led the men into battle against the Philistines, King Saul asked Abner, commander of the army, "Abner, whose son is that young man?"

"As surely as you live, O king, I don't know," Abner replied.

King Saul gave a command, "Find out whose son this young man is."

After the battle, David returned to Goliath's body and released the man he had guarding Goliath's head and body. Reaching down, he grabbed the giant head, clutching a hand full of hair, which was both greasy and bloody by this time; greasy, of course, from the lack of baths. David pondered about what he would do with the head; he wasn't sure, but he knew that it had to make a statement for the one true God of Israel.

Abner came out to greet David and to take him back to King Saul. David was still carrying the head with the blood, veins, and neck bones showing when he approached King Saul.

As David came closer, the king looked at David and said, "That is quite a trophy that you have there, son. Tell me, whose son are you?"

David answered him, smiling ear to ear, "I am the son of your servant Jesse, from Bethlehem." David knew it had been a while since he had played his harp for the king, and he knew that the king was not in good mental health. Therefore, David was not surprised to realize that the king had not recognized him. As if a lightning bolt of understanding had flashed across the king's mind, a startled look spread across his face. He realized that this "son of Jesse from Bethlehem" was the David who had played the harp for him on many occasions. King Saul was quite taken back. Uncertain of how this was all coming together, the king determined at that very moment that David, this shepherd boy, would no longer go home but would come to live with him forever. David was proving to be very useful to the king's purposes.

David finished cleaning up from war. He took the head of Goliath into Jerusalem. Climbing the hill named Golgotha³, David mounted the head as a warning to all those who would come against the God of Israel. David then picked up Goliath's weapons and armor and headed to his supply cart.

The young boy that David left to watch over his cart and supplies felt honored to assist him. He didn't wait to be asked to set up a tent for him but had it done before David returned from war. A smile spread across David's face at the boy's enthusiasm. Realizing that he was not much older than the young boy, he inspired the lad to seek God. Taking his spoils from war into the tent, he sat down and invited the boy in.

"Weren't you *afraid* of Goliath, the *giant?*" the boy asked David, overemphasizing the words "afraid" and "giant." Awe and excitement exuberated from the boy's face. He appeared to David as if he were ready to bounce right off the stool from excitement. David told the boy how God fills us with His power to do the things that we need to do. He also told the boy how victory was stronger and more powerful than fear and how, with God, we could win battles and defeat those who would oppose the God of Abraham, Isaac, and Jacob. The lad could have talked to David all night. David was very tired by this point, but he also realized that teaching...yes, teaching and sharing the truths of God, was what life was all about. Appealing to the boyish ways within them both, David relished sharing a few gory details of the battle with the lad, although David was careful to never stray too far from the victory he had achieved and to keep himself humble through God. The boy had too many questions for one evening. David promised to take more time with the lad tomorrow. Before the boy left, David prayed that God would be the one to have the greatest impression on the young lad instead of himself.

It was David's decision to give the sword of Goliath to the priest to be stored in the tabernacle. Upon requesting this, the king and the priest both agreed. The priest said that he would consecrate the sword to God. He would also make a memorial for the victory the sword represented to God.

\*\*\*\*\*\*

The day had been long for David. He was tired, but he did not want such a victorious day to end without finding time to finish the psalm that he felt growing in his heart. He had brought his harp and left it with his supplies. As David looked around his tent at the spoils from war, his heart felt joyously light, although his body was growing tired. He had the armor from Goliath, which was made of the finest quality and from the strongest materials. This included his brass plate, his coat of mail, his helmet, his greaves of brass that Goliath wore to cover his legs, and his incredibly heavy coat. His eyes sparkled as he examined the other fine brass and gold objects that he had taken from other Philistines. It had been a very good day. Now the only thing that would allow this day to come to an end correctly was to take time with the God of Israel, who made all of this possible.

# Chapter 5

*"As they danced, they sang: 'Saul has slain his thousands,
and David his tens of thousands'"* (1 Samuel 18:7, NIV).

King Saul ordered Abner to arrange for David to be taken
to his palace. Abner sent servants out immediately to make all
the necessary arrangements. David was to be one of the king's
top warriors. He was to live in the palace now and never return
to his father's home to live again. Abner was very loyal to King
Saul, and the king valued him greatly as one of his top advisors.
King Saul took the time to assure Abner that David would only
be first in command "under" him. However, the king puffed up
with pride and knew beyond a doubt that he couldn't let go of
such a fine asset as this new young warrior. Abner had been
there as a faithful assistant since the beginning of Saul's reign
as king. Saul was grateful for the support and faithfulness that
Abner devoted to him, although there were times when Saul
questioned Abner's loyalty. Did he believe in him as the king
or because he was his cousin? Their fathers were brothers, and
maybe he just wanted to get nearer to the throne. Every once in
a while, he wondered how safe his children were; would Abner
ever try to get closer to the throne by hurting them, or worse,

killing them? These conspiracy thoughts were becoming more frequent. However, they always passed, and Saul's thoughts would return to days gone by when they grew up together, sharing boyhood secrets.

Saul's thoughts drifted back to the people...his kingdom. A big boastful smile spilled across his face as he thought about how they would adore their king once again. This was such a mighty feat of valor to have killed this particular Philistine! Not for one moment did the king question the praise that he would be receiving. Saul was so excited that he could hardly contain himself. Slowly, the glimmer in his eyes began to fade as he thought of the Prophet Samuel. Disgusted with himself, he found it hard to admit that he still secretly longed for the prophet's blessings and approval. Years earlier, Samuel had been the prophet who anointed him to be Israel's first king. His eyes darkened, and his thick eyebrows arched down toward the creases that burrowed deep between his eyes. His memory drifted back to when Samuel betrayed him. Within just a few minutes, the king relived the entire event as though it was only yesterday.

\*\*\*\*\*

After just two years of building a kingdom and fighting many wars, Saul chose three thousand men of Israel. There were many more well-trained soldiers. However, he sent the remaining soldiers home. King Saul personally led two thousand of the men into battle. His son Jonathan led the remaining one thousand men, taking them over to Gibeah in

Benjamin. King Saul ordered Jonathan to take the Philistine military post by surprise and destroy it. The garrison consisted of a memorial built by the Philistines and located in an area they had conquered. The Philistines recorded their conquests on the memorial. Jonathan had been ordered by the king to kill the Philistine officer and soldiers that were protecting it, therefore making a statement to the Philistine people. It had been a great battle plan. The corners of Saul's mouth turned up as he recalled the look of pride on Jonathan's face when he returned from a successful mission.

His thoughts continued as he recalled next how Jonathan took a trumpet and sounded it throughout the land to announce his victory. He shouted, "Let the Hebrews hear we have just conquered the Philistine's garrison." All of Israel *did* hear what Jonathan had done, and they felt the full blow of these words. This action was not acceptable. The people knew that the Philistines would see this action as a true sign of defiance and a just cause for war.

As quickly as the smile came to Saul's face, it dissolved in disgust. He could not help but sneer as he recalled how the Philistines called Israel "a stench." Both armies viewed it as Israel not keeping their word, but he had seen it as a good strategic plan and nothing more. Yes, it had been very treacherous indeed, but wasn't that what war was all about? Being very angered by this bold act, the Philistines assembled a massive army to fight and destroy Israel. Their regiment included three thousand chariots, six thousand charioteers, and a vast number of soldiers. The stories later told that the Philistines were as numerous as the sand on the seashore. Even Saul felt fearful when he saw the magnitude in which the Philistines came out against them. However, Saul stood in his favor with God and believed he'd protected them as always. He forgot that God had always gone before him, leading him, not the other way around. Saul grew angry when he remembered how cowardly the Israelites had acted. When they saw the multitude of the Philistine army, the Israelite's began to abandon their king. Being terrified, many of the men ran and hid in caves and in thickets. Some hid among the rocks and in pits, while others jumped into the cisterns. Many others swam across the Jordan to escape the Philistines by running to Gad and Gilead. The number of deserters grew daily.

Prior to Saul's decision to attack the Philistines, the Prophet Samuel had anointed him and prayed over him. Samuel then instructed Saul to go to Gilgal and to wait there for him for seven days. As midday approached on the seventh day, Samuel still had not arrived. With each passing hour, more men were losing hope. Fear was filling them, and they were beginning to scatter. Abner went to the king with continual updates of the men's status. This only added to the pressure the king was already feeling. Many of the men commented, "If the prophet, the man of God, will not come to our aid when there's an army this size, then God's blessing will most certainly not be upon us."

Many of the men uttered in desperation, "We will surely die."

The men became more and more discouraged with each passing hour. Seeing that they were losing hope, King Saul acted in haste. He decided to offer up the burnt offering and the peace offering. Recalling the days of his anointing as king, he once again heard the men saying, "Is Saul also among the prophets?" Feeling entitled, he asked God's blessing upon himself and his men. Saul was certain that to wait for the prophet would prove to be a fatal mistake. The fact that only a priest or a prophet was allowed to offer up this offering seemed a minor detail to King Saul. The requirement to be pure before coming to God was so strong that the custom called for the priest to wear bells on the hem of his garment and to have a rope around his waists. The rope was to be long enough to reach outside the holy place. If a priest came before God's presence, having even the slightest amount of sin in his heart, he would die immediately. If the bells stopped ringing as the priest was moving around, it was presumed that the priest had died. The people would immediately pull on the rope until they pulled the priest's body out of the holy of holies. No one dared to make a joke about what just happened or to find error with the priest. They all knew and respected the incredible responsibility that a priest had, seeking the Lord for forgiveness for each one of their sins.

When Jonathan heard his father order the men to prepare the burnt offering and the peace offering, he begged his father to wait just a little longer. Saul answered Jonathan with a firm and final "No!" Jonathan tried further to talk to his father, but he knew his father's look all too well. He had seen his father's countenance change with that same unyielding look too many times over the years. His father had made up his mind and tried as he would to convince his father he was about to make an unforgivable error; Jonathan would not be able to persuade him to change his mind. Jonathan was almost appalled as he heard his father exclaim, "After all, I am a worshipper of God. Many times, I have witnessed exactly what the prophet does to prepare the offering and to handle the prayer. Yes, I can offer the sacrifices and ask God to bless us. Something has to be done right this moment so that the men will be encouraged."

Foreseeing the danger, Jonathan pleaded with Saul a few more times, trying to explain the depth of the holiness upon this position. Jonathan could not reach his father because of his stubborn pride. Saul had already sinned by not consulting God for the battle plan, and now he was compounding that sin.

When Samuel arrived at the end of the seventh day, Saul accused him of not keeping his word and arriving on time. After all, didn't Samuel remember that he was the king, the more important one here? "A prophet should realize that he should be the one waiting on the king, not the other way around."

Upon his arrival, Samuel saw the smoke still rising from the altar. He saw the look of shame and regret on many of the men's faces. He knew instantly what had happened, and the pious look on the king's face told him who had made the offering. The very first words out of Samuel's mouth were, "What have you done?"

No one questioned the intensity with which the prophet disapproved. Jonathan felt embarrassed for his father. King Saul's actions of rebellion were causing his heart to be hardened. Puffing up his chest, he used his deep, authoritative voice to answer the prophet, "When I saw that the men were scattering and that you had not come at the appointed time and the Philistines were assembling at Micmash, I thought, *I have not sought the Lord's favor.* So I decided to offer the burnt offering and the peace offering myself!"

Samuel stomped toward the king, closing the distance between them. Expressing full disapproval, he firmly spoke, "You acted foolishly...you have not kept the command the Lord your God gave you; if you had, He would have established your kingdom over Israel for all time."

Samuel spoke with an emphasis on the word "all," using his voice and expressions to accentuate how serious of an offense this was. "But now, your kingdom will not endure; the Lord has sought out a man after his own heart and appointed him leader of his people because you have not kept the Lord's command."

King Saul was never exactly sure what happened next, but he assumed that it had been God accepting his offering and answering his prayer that had confused the enemy. Just as he had spoken, God had protected them. Saul did not realize that their victory came from his son. Jonathan went to God in prayer and asked Him to give them favor over the enemy. God intervened on their behalf. Jonathan and his armor-bearer defeated many Philistines the next morning. God used their attack to strike panic in the heart of the whole Philistine army. Their panic was a fear created by circumstances; only God Almighty could create such a scene.

The noise of a guard packing the king's tent to go home brought the king's thoughts back to the present moment. The memory of how Samuel acted caused Saul to determine that he was better off without a prophet. As Saul savored the anger that he had toward the prophet, the evil spirit started to rise up inside of him. He crushed the anger with pride as he redirected his thoughts back to the victory of how his people would receive him.

# Chapter 6

*"How good and pleasant it is when God's people live together in unity!" (Psalm 133:1, NIV)*

Jonathan adored David from the very first moment they met. As soon as the king finished talking to David, he headed back to his tent. Jonathan walked quickly to catch up with him.

Jonathan first met David when he came to play the harp for his father. The transformation his music made was amazing. When David played the harp for his father, the effect was like the taming of a wild animal. However, in this case, the wild animal was an evil spirit living in his father. The music calmed or soothed the evil spirit. This allowed his father to relax and the anger to leave momentarily.

Jonathan could remember his father teaching him about God's ways when he was a young boy. They used to pray together as a family. His father would teach him of the times men walked and talked with God. He remembered back to when he first noticed his father changing.

The changes started to occur a few years after his father began ruling as the king. His pride seemed to get in the way of his devotion to God. He always remembered his father as a strong, proud man, although his father had always been devoted to following God. Over the past few years, he watched his father drift further and further away from God. Jonathan felt like the change really started at the battle against the Philistines' garrison. It was the time that he and a thousand men defeated them and conquered the garrison. As he recalled the turning point in his father's life, he recalled how he had not known about the agreement with the Philistines and followed the king's orders. Then to make matters worse, his father had not waited for the prophet, Samuel. Jonathan always found himself coming back to the same question, "Why? Why did he do that?" He was certain that he would never find a satisfying answer. It was common knowledge that only the priest or a prophet could make the offerings. He relived how he pleaded with his father to wait for Samuel many times since the event. *What was Father thinking?* His father had raised him to know the holiness that went into the office of a priest or a prophet. It was as though his father could change all the rules now that he was king. God's rules were not exempt from this line of thinking. Someday... when he became king, he would always keep God first. Since he was the first-born son, it was certain that he would take over the throne for his father someday. Once again, he gave thanks to God for rescuing them. If he hadn't, they would have all died for sure.

As Jonathan closed the distance between David and himself, he was filled with pleasure as he thought of his father's plans to bring David to the palace. He was delighted at his father's decision. Jonathan was old enough to be a father to David, but their relationship was more of a friendship than the mentoring relationship of a "father and son."

It saddened Jonathan to think about his father's state of mind. He thought back to when he first met David. David was brought to the palace to play the harp for his father. There would be times when his father would fall into horrid fits of rage. His mouth filled with cruel, hateful accusations... accusations that were totally insane. Sometimes his father would accuse the cooks of poisoning him. He would accuse Jonathan of plotting against him to take over *his* kingdom and to steal all *his* wealth. The king would be so full of hate during these times that peace was nowhere in sight. The physicians examined Saul and determined that evil spirits had taken over and were tormenting his mind. The priests were called in on countless occasions to perform ceremonies that would cleanse him and chase away the evil spirit. These ceremonies, however, only seemed to bring temporary relief...if that. Then there were days that the king seemed fine, and everything had the appearance of returning to normal. Everyone around the palace had become aware of the king's state of mind, from his family to the servants, including the guards. There were many days when the talk was kept to a minimum around the palace. The staff hated to go to the king for even the simplest issues. At these times, they would come to Jonathan as much as was possible. Of course, this only seemed to add to the king's conspiracy theories.

David's arrival had been like a breath of fresh air. He was a young boy, around thirteen, when they met. Instantly they both liked each other. David quickly became Jonathan's closest friend. Though David was small for his age, the exuberance he experienced soon captured those around him. At first glance, you saw a small boy with a few pimples, freckles, and fair skin. But within just minutes, all you saw was how intelligent he was and that there was something very special about him. Smiling did not just come easy for David but was a part of him. His eyes were a dark brown. His hair was a mix of red and brown colors. The red colors showed up most often in the sunshine. Because David was always out with the sheep, he kept his skin covered, preventing a tan. Therefore, his skin was quite fair, nothing that a little sunshine wouldn't cure.

When David was not playing the harp for the king, he would often assist Jonathan in his daily activities. It was here that their friendship grew. They talked about everything, from battles and girls to views on life. Jonathan was surprised at how much he was learning from someone so young. David talked about God as though he had walked personally with Him, just as Adam and Eve did in the garden of Eden. The depth of David's knowledge surprised Jonathan greatly. David had knowledge that only came from studying under the great teachers of their time. What intrigued Jonathan the most was the way David viewed life. He loved life and lived it to the fullest. Jonathan had met people before that seemed to find pleasure in every aspect of life. But never before had he seen anyone who lived life with such fullness and high expectations as David. He always had a positive outlook, no matter the situation. Some would say he saw the sun shining behind every cloud. Confidence radiated through every fiber of David's being. Upon spending time with him, you found yourself inspired to do the same.

You found yourself enjoying life just because you were around him. During this time, Jonathan and David's hearts were knit together. Jonathan loved David almost from the moment they met. Now, after this mighty feat of valor, his admiration was so great he knew he had to make a covenant with David.

"That was unbelievable!" Jonathan smiled a big wide smile that seemed to reach from one ear to the other. "I knew that you had a special connection with God, but that was incredible! People will be talking about this for years to come. Perhaps you will be one of the great heroes of our time. Then the fathers will teach their children about you."

Although Jonathan very much meant what he was saying, he was poking fun at David with a tease in his voice.

David smiled and walked toward Jonathan. "Thanks, but I don't understand why you weren't the one out there."

Jonathan loved the humor that flowed between them. "Wow! Nothing like punching a guy in the gut to make a point." David smiled slightly and continued talking, "You could have killed that big, ugly, uncircumcised Philistine. They called him a giant, but the only thing giant about him was his size...oh, and his mouth. If his brain had been a little larger, he might have put his helmet back on or used his shield. Instead, he just stood there waiting for me to kill him, then he collapsed to his death. I warned him what would happen. You would have thought the big idiot would have listened."

Chuckling at David's comments, they approached each other and reached their arms out to embrace one another with the customary greeting hug.

Jonathan took the bait and responded to David's comments, "I didn't go after him because I was waiting for the real champ to get here. So what took you so long to get here anyway? Out with the sheep again?"

"Yeah, what did you expect? My older brothers were here lining up with you and the other men, listening to Goliath's idle threats. I was surprised to see how he was terrorizing the Israelite men. They were running away in fear when he hollered out to them. I would have expected you to go out and take Goliath down."

"I guess it took someone your age to show us 'men' how to do it. I think it would have been hard for you to make it look any easier than you did. I guess that is what comes from hours out in the fields with nothing but a sling, a harp, and lots of sheep." Jonathan laughed.

David decided to turn the attention off himself and asked Jonathan, "Did you go out to battle with us and kill the rest of the Philistine soldiers? Or did you stay here with your father and go after the spoils in the Philistine tents?"

Jonathan tried to act slightly offended when he responded, "Of course, I went out with you, and you'd have seen me too if you weren't so busy showing us 'men' how to kill the enemy."

"And did you count the Philistines you killed as my brothers did?" David asked with a twinkle in his eyes.

Jonathan smiled and replied as if he had an image to keep up with, "Every one of them. I always count those I kill when I go into battle. It was amazing how easy it was to kill them when you took away their hero. I'd have to say that their foundation was built upon one man. How sad it is to think that they could not accept the one true God."

David still had his youthful height and had to look up at Jonathan. He stood almost a head and a half taller than he.

Although David might never be as tall as him, he was hopeful that he would not be this short for long. He was on a growth spurt and knew that his robe would soon be showing more of his legs than he hoped to have showing. Jonathan looked a lot like a younger version of his father. David imagined that King Saul looked just like Jonathan when he was his age. Jonathan was tall; in fact, he was taller than most of the men who worked under him. His shoulders were very broad. The women admired the muscular frame that he had from staying fit for battle. You couldn't see his neck unless he turned sideways because of a well-groomed short beard that was as black as the darkest night. His hair was black, with small tight curls circling around his head. His eyes were a dark brown and were filled with deep sincerity and admiration for all those around, especially those who shared his faith in Jehovah.

Jonathan's thoughts turned toward the palace, *It will be fun to have David living there with my family.*

When his father was first anointed king, they began immediately to build a palace. Until it was completed, they moved into the largest house in the area. From there, the king continued to have laborers, masons, and architects working on the palace. When they first finished building the palace, it had felt like home. It was a very nice place to live indeed. But what he had valued the most was that they had been a family. They laughed together and enjoyed life. Sadness started to surface in Jonathan's heart as he realized how much his family had changed since that time. Then, as quickly as the sad thought came, a happy and refreshing thought came to him, *Yes, it will be fun having David living there permanently.*

Jonathan asked David, "Has Abner or one of the king's men informed you yet that you will be returning to the palace with us?"

"Yes, actually, your father told me. I have to say that it will be fun to live in the palace, especially around you. I will miss my parents but not my noisy brothers. I do hope the king will allow me to visit them now and then."

Jonathan was quick to say, "I am sure that he will, but if he doesn't, just let me know. As any intuitive son, I know how to handle Father. Perhaps you should approach him after you have played the harp for him. Father is always agreeable after your music, though it is clear to see that he is *not* so before."

David smiled, finding humor in Jonathan's words. *Timing is everything*, David thought. Perhaps Jonathan wasn't just making a joke but speaking from wisdom. Changing the topic, he asked,     "So Jonathan, do you think that the king will still give me his daughter in marriage now that he knows who I am?" David tried not to crack a smile while using his deepest adolescent voice.

With a very mischievous grin on his face, Jonathan gave David a slap on the back and continued, "I was wondering how long it would take you to bring up the rewards. So which one of my sisters shall it be? You do remember that it is customary for the oldest daughter to be married first. I say that because I am aware that you and Michal have noticed each other..."

Shocked at Jonathan's words and slightly embarrassed, he interrupted him, "What are you talking about? We have done no such thing. We are just friends."

David's embarrassment showed as his adolescent voice cracked. This caused him further embarrassment as his face turned bright red.

"Oh, the 'just friends' bit, I know about that one." Jonathan's eyes were twinkling now with a grin on his face that could not be hidden, not that he wanted to hide it. He was having way too much fun teasing his friend. "That is how I came to know my wife. We, too, were...'just friends.' Since it is customary for the oldest sister to be given in marriage first, I'd say stay friends for a while longer."

David breathed slowly as if to consider what words he would speak next. He also knew his face had turned red and hoped to gain control of his emotions. "God knows how things will turn out. I am not admitting any special interest in Michal, but you do know that your sister, Merab has eyes for someone already, don't you? I overheard her and Michal talking one day, quite by accident, I assure you. She was talking about Adriel of Abel-Meholah, and how 'fine' he looks in uniform. The way she accented the word 'fine' spoke volumes of her interest for him."

"Yes," Jonathan responded, "...I have become somewhat aware of her interest. So are you going to wait to collect on your rewards until she has been betrothed to Adriel?" Pausing, Jonathan added, "Don't answer that, or you will be admitting that you do have a special interest in Michal."

A playful laugh spilled from his lips as Jonathan teased his dearest friend. He knew there was an interest that flowed between them, and he found pleasure in the thought of having David as his brother-in-law. Although Michal was a little spoiled, she would take good care of a husband. His only concern was that she might tire easily of him. She seemed rather selfish at times. Then one more thought occurred to him that he just had to share with David.

CYNTHIA CRUMBAUGH

"David, can't you just imagine you and Michal standing before the priest in wedding apparel? What a fine wedding yours would be. We would have all the trimmings of royalty. We can use some of the fine-spun material they have brought in from the East for Michal's robe..." Before Jonathan could continue, David gave him a look of rebuke. His stance said that he meant business. David had his hands on his hips, and his jaw was set firm with determination, or was that a smile he was trying to hide? Jonathan wasn't sure which one, but either one caused Jonathan to burst out laughing.

"Jonathan, you are really enjoying this, aren't you? Now stop with all this foolishness before my brothers or any of the other men hear you. I am sorry I brought the subject up at all."

Secretly, David loved the thought of Michal in that soft-spun robe that Jonathan referred to. It was quite an intriguing thought, indeed. He was quite certain that God would work things out. Either he would never have to marry Merab, or he would fall in love with Merab. Maybe he would just have two wives early in life, like Joseph, who married Leah and Rachel. Now that was too exhausting of a thought for David.

Jonathan paused to watch David for a moment seeing that his thoughts were somewhere else. "David, you know how important you are to me."

Turning his attention back to Jonathan, David said, "Yes, and you to me."

"It is in my heart to put my mantel upon you. I am giving you my robe, my sword, my bow, and my belt. I am anointing you with the blessing that I have been given."

David bowed in humbleness before Jonathan. It was a very tender moment between them. For just a second, David hesitated to accept them. Then he felt as though God was speaking to him and telling him to accept them, that this was part of His divine plan.

Reaching down to take David's hands, Jonathan exalted him. It was a moment they would never forget. They bowed their heads together and prayed over each other, dedicating their friendship to God. Then, as if to add a light-heartedness to the conversation, Jonathan teased David, saying, "Besides, we cannot have you running around looking like a shepherd boy anymore, can we? Especially not if you are to marry one of the king's daughters." Jonathan knew when people saw David wearing his garments that they would know that he considered David to be equal to himself.

They could have talked all night, but they both had much to do. They agreed to find each other and spend time together once they were back at the palace. David still had much to do before this very big and exciting day could end.

# Chapter 7

*"I will sing to you a new song, O God; on the harp of ten-strings I will make music to you..." (Psalm 144:9, BSB)*

After washing himself in the stream and cleaning all the blood of battle off himself, David changed clothes and picked up his harp. He headed out of the camp to be alone. It was hard to avoid the men. They all wanted to give him praise. David kept telling them that it was the God of Israel who had killed Goliath. He was only the vessel God chose to use. Many of the men didn't understand this statement. Most of them thought David was the one who deserved the praise for all that happened today. David did not grow impatient with any of them. He knew it would take time to teach them. However, they would eventually learn this fact and grow close to God for themselves.

The sun was starting to set by this time. David gathered enough wood to build a small fire. Some of the men had tried to follow him, but he refused to allow them to do so. He needed time with God to praise Him and to finish the psalm that was burning in his heart.

As David sat silently, he reflected over the events of the day as they unfolded. He recalled the first lines that came to him during battle, *Praise be to the Lord my rock, who trains my hands for war, my fingers for battle. He is my loving God and my fortress, my stronghold and my deliverer, my shield, in whom I take refuge, who subdues people under me.* These first few lines had flowed from him so easily. Now he just needed to take the time to seek God and see what would follow.

After only a few minutes, the words continued to flow again. "O Lord, what is man that you care for him, the son of man that you think of him? Man is like a breath; his days are like a fleeting shadow. Part your heavens, O Lord, and come down; touch the mountains so that they smoke. Send forth lightning and scatter the enemies, shoot your arrows and rout them. Reach down your hand from on high, deliver me and rescue me from the mighty waters, from the hands of foreigners whose mouths are full of lies, whose right hands are deceitful. I will sing a new song to you, O God, on the ten-stringed lyre, I will make music to you, to the One who gives victory to kings, who delivers his servant David from the deadly sword. Deliver me and rescue me from the hands of foreigners whose mouths are full of lies, whose right hands are deceitful. Then, our sons in their youth will be like well-nurtured plants, and our daughters will be like pillars carved to adorn a palace. Our barns will be filled with every kind of provision. Our sheep will increase by thousands, by tens of thousands in our fields; our oxen will draw heavy loads. There will be no breaching of walls, no going into captivity, no cry of distress in our streets. Blessed are the people of whom this is true, blessed are the people whose God is the *Lord*."

Wow! David knew that God was giving him a big vision, but only now was he beginning to realize how big. It would be awesome to see how he would become king. It would be a lot of responsibility, but he was beginning to look forward to the privilege. Although he had never dreamed of being a great leader, he was beginning to have the heart of one.

The stars shined brightly down on David. His heart felt very warm as he basked in God's presence. He was very tired. It had been an incredibly long day, but he still had much to process in his mind. He still needed to think about each reward that the king had promised to the man who killed Goliath. Would he really marry the king's daughter, and which one would it be, Michal or her older sister? He had not thought much about it before. But as his head started to fill with thoughts of the future, he realized that things could get a whole lot more exciting.

# Section II

## *David's Journey from Warrior to Fugitive*

# Chapter 8

*"In peace I will lie down and sleep, for you alone, Lord, make me to dwell in safety" (Psalm 4:8, NIV).*

Upon defeating Goliath, David's life had changed in almost every way. The king made plans for their newest conquering soldier to enter the city with him. David and his brothers packed their spoils of war in the cart that he had brought from his father's house. His brothers planned to follow the army back into the city, and then they would return to their home until the next time there was a war or until they were once again needed for the king's service. David's thoughts turned to the future. Although he was unsure of where he would be staying in the palace, he chose to keep some of his treasures with him. This line of thinking provoked many questions. He tried not to give in to aimless wondering, but it was a rather difficult task. Some of the questions that began to plague him were, how would things end for King Saul, and how would they begin for him? He was confident that God was in charge but quite curious about it all. Sometimes he wondered about Jonathan. Would Jonathan despise him later when God put him on the throne? Would Jonathan be able to handle submitting to him as the next king?

The love between the two of them went very deep. He didn't know how everything would unfold, but he was confident of their loyalty to one another. Every time these questions came to mind, David would turn his thoughts to God the Father. He would once again turn it all over to God. He allowed his father's words to come back to him and to gently guide him. David's father told him to not be anxious but to trust in God and wait. Live life in total surrender to God's plans, and it will all come to pass as God has ordained.

Generally, after having many questions and thoughts, David would purposely relax his brow followed by a soft smile that would cover his face. Once again, he would realize that he had given into aimless questions and surmising. Of course, these thoughts were more "worrisome," but there were the "more fun" thoughts that plagued him as well. These thoughts surrounded the promises made by the king to the man who killed Goliath. They included thoughts of the king's daughters and a royal wedding. He still found the very thought of being with a girl in that *special* way to be rather embarrassing. As he imagined being a husband and a wedding night, he could feel his face turning beet-red. Perhaps he could wait a while to collect that gift. Then there was establishing his father's house to be free from taxes and the other such privileges that would be bestowed upon his family. Should he wait for the king to bring this up to him? Would it be all right to ask Jonathan about the rewards, or would it be more proper to approach the subject with Abner?

A few days had passed before they were finally ready to head back to town. King Saul instructed Abner to place David directly under him in the army. Most of the fighting men and officers were very excited about this new command. During this time, the king gave David many tasks and assignments. Everything David did was a success; this encouraged the men even further. David's youth and size were being lost to his achievements and his success. His victory seemed to boost their morale. The men flocked to David. As far as they were concerned, he was a giant killer or a great man of faith. Some said, "He has a direct line to God." They no longer saw him as a teenager with a few freckles but as a natural-born leader.

Suddenly, David was in a position of status over his brothers. He was surprised at how the events of the past few days had changed so many things. For him to be the next king, he knew that this change would occur. He determined that he would not take advantage of things when it came to his brothers. However, it would be fun to order Eliab around...just a little... After all...he deserved it. Why? Eliab used his position as the oldest of the family to order David and his brothers around. But David also knew that Eliab was having a hard time with this promotion. He chose to excuse his brother's actions. He knew Eliab had a good heart, but he also had a lot of pride to go with it.

*I will give him time and let him accept things as they are,* he thought. He knew that Eliab still felt that much of what was happening belonged to him as part of the eldest son's inheritance. Being the oldest, he should have been anointed as the next king. Being the oldest, he should have killed Goliath or at least received the rewards that David was receiving. David was quite certain that Eliab felt like he should be promoted in the king's army instead of his "youngest" brother. He determined to keep praying for Eliab that he would see the hand of God in all that was happening. He needed to see that it was God who was promoting him and not the king. Eliab wasn't a bad person; he just thought more highly of himself than he ought.

Abinadab had no problems submitting to David's leadership. In fact, once David caught a glimpse of him elbowing Eliab when he was grumbling. It was as if David and Abinadab were reading each other's thoughts as their eyes made contact. They shared a slight smile between them; it was a silent moment of joy. He knew that Abinadab would help Eliab to realize that David was not out to advance himself. In fact, killing Goliath had nothing at all to do with David's future. His intentions had been only to take down the enemies of God. He saw himself as a humble vessel that God chose to use. But if he was able to defeat the enemies and receive rewards for it along the way, well, that was even better. Abinadab was a good big brother. David enjoyed the times that they were alone. With a small house and seven boys and two girls, time alone rarely happened. He was confident that Abinadab would help Eliab to understand the motives of David's heart. No...Abinadab was not going to have any problems supporting David's decisions...or his promotions.

*Time is what Eliab needs. Our father raised us to believe in each other and to believe in God. In the meantime, I will not take advantage of my position and use it to order him around...although it would be a whole lot of fun,* David contemplated.

Next, David's thoughts turned to the sheep, and he wondered who was taking care of them. Most likely, their new shepherd would be Ozem, his brother closest to him in age, or maybe Joab, his nephew, his sister Zeruiah's son. He would miss the quiet times out on the hillsides with the sheep, but life does bring changes, and these were good and exciting changes. He smiled to himself when he realized that he had finally outgrown the sheep jokes. He hadn't minded them, but it was a sign of maturity...leastwise as far as his brothers were concerned. Shammah, of course, was the most supportive of his three oldest brothers. Shammah was having the most fun with his new position. His smile went from ear to ear when his little brother was promoted.

Shammah would say things like, "Did you see what David did? Did you see how he took that giant down? Wow! He will be one of the famous slingers of our time. That was my youngest brother! Did you see how God's anointing was upon him?"

The soldiers would agree with him, and their conversations would turn to all the events that had occurred. They talked about the victory over Goliath, and they talked about the battle that followed that victory. Each had his own take on how the events unfolded, and each had another story to add as to details surrounding Goliath's death, the next gorier and more gruesome than the last.

Shammah would stand to attention with extra pride. He marched with extra enthusiasm to each step. He was very proud of his little brother. David was quite certain that Shammah would be one of the key people to promote and to have working right next to him. It blessed David's heart to see his brother's pride in him.

\* \* \* \* \*

The journey from Shochoh to Gilgal was about sixteen miles away. Shochoh was where David had defeated Goliath for King

Saul's kingdom. Gilgal was seven miles north of Bethel and was where the united tribes of Israel formally received King Saul as their king. Some of the men had an ox or an ass to carry their packs. However, the men completed their journey by foot. It had taken the men a full two days to cover the distance.

King Saul was leading the march into the city by riding his most prized stallion. Jonathan and David followed behind King Saul on their horses. Next in line was Abner. Abner was rather annoyed that he was behind David. He was beginning to resent the young shepherd boy rather quickly. He murmured under his breath so that only he would hear his complaining,

"I am 'the' captain, not this insignificant shepherd boy. He should be behind me. What... It's not enough that he killed the Philistine giant; now he wants my job too." Abner pasted on a smile and nodded toward the crowd while pretending to enjoy the ceremonies.

David would have been fine with being at the end of the march instead of riding next to Jonathan. However, Jonathan insisted that he ride into the city next to him. He also insisted that he wear the apparel that he had given him. This way, the people would understand and see that they were to treat David with the same level of respect as Jonathan. David had argued against this, but in the end, he surrendered to his friend's bidding. He could tell the whole idea hadn't settled well with Abner, but he chose to let Abner deal with his own attitude. After all, no sense in apologizing for something that was not of his doing.

David had been given his very own horse, and she was a beauty! She was one of the king's most valued stallions. King

Saul had a few of the finest Egyptian bred horses brought in from Egypt. The horse had been named Bedouin. Her name meant that she came from desert dwellers. She was from a pure bloodline, a tall and beautiful dark brown champion. She had a long beautiful neck, and her mane and tail were braided with jewels and fine ribbons that set her apart as one of the king's horses. David couldn't help but enjoy the moment. Things were beginning to come together. It was going to be awesome to live in the palace, and this was only the beginning.

They were almost to town now. All the men could hear the cheers and shouts of joy from the crowds of people. Riders had been sent ahead to update the people and to tell them about the victory over Goliath and the Philistine army. They had been living in fear of being taken into bondage by the Philistines should Goliath defeat King Saul. Now, the fear was replaced with shouts of celebration. All the women came out of the cities of Israel singing and dancing. It was the custom of the women to line up and to greet the men as they entered the city. They were playing tambourines and lutes, making beautiful music for King Saul and the men. The women had on their best gowns of bright colors and fine fabrics. Their gowns flowed freely around their ankles as they danced. They sang almost in unison. Their welcome was a beautiful sight that David treasured. He noticed the young lady's hair bouncing gently on their shoulders and flowing down over their backs as they danced.

Suddenly, without warning, King Saul felt an overwhelming chill flow through his entire body. The chill was so intense that it compared to an unexpected lightning bolt coming down from the skies. The words his people were singing echoed through his head. At first, he thought he must have heard them incorrectly. But as he listened again, there was no mistaking what they were singing, "Saul has slain his thousands, and David his tens of thousands."

The words to their song filled him instantly with anger and rage.

The king had such high expectations for this moment. This was to be "his" moment of fame, the moment that would elevate him! He was to be exalted back into the kingly position that he had been struggling to keep since his illness. King Saul had been waving and smiling at the people. Had anyone in the crowd been watching the king, they would have noticed the change in his demeanor as the cold chill crept over the king. He turned white, and then slowly, the anger began to rise in his cheeks, turning them a fiery red. For a few seconds, his smile totally disappeared. At first, his smile was replaced with an expression of shock and then instantly replaced with anger. Regaining control, he planted a smile on his face, determined to cover his feelings. He made an effort to raise his hand back up and to continue to wave at everyone, just as he had only seconds ago.

The king murmured under his breath, "They have ascribed unto David ten thousand, and to me, they have ascribed but thousands and what can he have more but the kingdom...'my' kingdom!"

From that very moment, King Saul was filled with overwhelming jealousy. He determined to watch David very carefully. Immediately, he regretted bringing this young "shepherd boy" back with him. Thoughts of anger filled the king as he thought, *What are these crazy women doing? Don't they know that if it weren't for me, that giant would still be roaming our land? I found the shepherd boy. I let him go out to face the giant... I loaned him my armor... I authorized it all... I oversaw it all... I told them to go out and finish off the Philistine army... This is my moment, the moment that they pay homage to me, their king. They want to exalt this boy; then, they'll pay for it.* Practically screaming inside, he shouted, "*I am your king!* Is this the thanks that I get for winning the battle against the Philistines? Maybe I should send him back to his sheep."

His thoughts were going crazy with jealousy...so much to sort out...so much to think through...but one thing was for certain...this boy was not to be trusted! As he chewed on his lip, determination filled the king. The king's thoughts turned back to the words the Prophet Samuel had said, *Could David be the one...the one that Samuel referred to as a "neighbor" of mine...the one that Samuel said was better than me...the one God intends to give my kingdom to? We'll see about that!*

David felt humbled as he listened to the words of the people's song. No flowery show from receiving their praise did he make. His fair-skinned cheeks flushed almost with embarrassment at their praise. As David smiled at everyone, he could not help but pray that God would help everyone to see that it was not he that won the victory, but rather, it was God in him. David knew that his strength alone did not allow him to stand up to Goliath and the other Philistines. He found it very exciting to be a part of this celebration. He was among the king and his army riding on a beautiful horse into Gilgal. The moment was truly one to be treasured. There were beautiful maidens lining the streets of all ages. They had tambourines and triangles in their hands as they were playing, singing, and making music. It would have been exciting enough to have just been in the crowd watching King Saul's army returning from war. However, to have everyone cheering and singing songs about him...like he was a hero...it was very humbling. Suddenly, a tingling sensation surged through David as he thrilled over what his brothers must be thinking this very moment. Aware of the goosebumps that were on his arms, he didn't allow pride in his heart, but it was exhilarating knowing his brothers were witnessing all of this. If he had any trouble with pride upon this celebration, it was not with the people, their praises, or the king but with his brothers. As the youngest brother, he had been through a lot, and it was quite fun indeed to know that they were seeing and hearing all the praise he was receiving.

*****

Getting settled in the palace was a busy time. First, David went to the stable with Jonathan and bedded down Bedouin. David thanked God for her by saying a silent prayer over his new horse. He had been in the stables enough with Jonathan while staying at the palace earlier on that he knew how to properly care for horses. Seeing the brush hanging by the stall, he reached for it and began to brush her down. Jonathan told him to let the servants do the brushing, but David did not mind delaying his entry into the palace by spending time with his horse.

David was given a room of his own, not directly in the palace but adjacent to the palace. It was small, like most of the bedrooms in the palace. There was only one window, but it faced the morning sun, and that pleased David very much. The room occupied a small bed with a feathered mattress and a small table in the middle of the room. There was a chair that looked rather hard for sitting on, but it would serve its intended purpose. Maybe he would order some furniture from his brothers; their wood carving skills had developed quite nicely. He looked around with a smile of pleasure upon his lips while thinking about his new home. Jonathan had shown David where he would be staying. His brothers had brought his spoils of war over for him, and Shammah had loaned him a change of clothing. David had only intended to be gone for one, maybe two days at the most. It had been a few weeks by now, and even with rinsing out his garments, he needed something to change into. His brothers intended to have his clothes and few belongings sent over to him once they returned home. His brothers ribbed David about his new adventures and teased him fiercely about the king's daughters and his "royal" life. However, with all of their teasing, each one of David's brothers was careful not to express what they really wanted to say. Each one of them wondered where this would work into God's plans to make David the new king. Being cautioned by both Samuel and their father, they knew that the king's violent rages might cause him to turn on David once he knew what God had planned. Their whole family would be in danger once King Saul knew of God's plans. Though not much for hugging, David felt a new closeness with his brothers and hugged each one of them before they left. This new emotion caused David to sit on the bed for a few minutes, thinking about all the changes over the last few weeks. He believed that his brothers respected him more now, and that was something to give thanks for. It didn't take David very long to arrange his room. His spoils of war enhanced the room nicely. Before joining everyone for supper, he took time to wander around the grounds. David always found it easier to pray and to worship God out in the fresh air. Although he stayed at the palace in the past, he had never actually been any further than the stable, so he found pleasure in checking out the area. Without intending to, he came upon the house where Abner lived and the gathering hall for the soldiers. Most of the soldiers returned to their homes once they were back from war, but there were a few soldiers who chose to stay on the palace grounds, often because their home was too far away. Of course, there were some soldiers that lived there permanently due to working in the service of the king. Their job was to guard the grounds and protect the king. Jonathan instructed David to regularly join them for meals and informed the cook of this new change. After dinner, David decided to retire to his room. The day had been long, and he needed time to pray. He also wanted to pray for King Saul, who had been unusually quiet at supper. David wondered if it was because of him. Had he done something wrong? Maybe tomorrow, if the king were still acting strange, he might ask him if there was anything wrong. For now, it was time to call it a day and spend time in prayer.

David had his window opened and enjoyed the sound of birds singing close to his window. The window offered a small view of the stars and the moon. Sitting on his bed with no lights on, he played his harp and sang some songs to the Lord. After he had been playing for a while, he rose and went to the window. The breeze was so gentle and soothing.

Caught by surprise, David saw the form of someone standing near a window looking down at him. "But what have we here?" David asked softly, speaking only to himself. Upon spotting him, they backed quickly into the shadows.

"I do believe that it is a fair maiden that has made her way to the window. Is it... Who is it? Is it Michal? I think that it is..." A smile spread across his face as he mused to himself, "It will be grand to live here...yes, it will be."

# Chapter 9

*"Reach down your hand from on high; deliver me and*
*rescue me from the mighty waters,*
*from the hands of foreigners..." (Psalm 144:7, NIV)*

The next day brought some surprising events for David. He had just finished preparing for the day and had not been praying long when he was summoned to come and play his harp for the king. This did not surprise him due to the king's countenance at dinner last night. It didn't seem to take much to disturb the king. Walking over to the table, David picked up his harp and followed the king's servant into the palace. They passed the main entrance, the dining area, and then they arrived at the king's chamber. As he entered the room, he immediately recognized the agitated look that was on the king's face. It was a look that David had become quite familiar with over the months prior to the Philistine war. The king had the same cold, distant face that David had seen every time he had been summoned. His countenance changed so drastically that he really didn't look like King Saul at all but someone else.

God taught David early on not to dread playing for the king during these times but to have compassion for him. A compassionate heart stopped him from judging the king or from pitying him. God was teaching David that the only true way to reach someone is by God's compassion. This was also the only way to keep his heart free from judging.

Regardless of what was wrong, the evil spirit or spirits had really upset the king today. His eyebrows were mostly gray now, but there was still a hint of black in them. Today, there was a heavy crease to them. His hair was very thick and now had more gray than black coloring. His hair was tousled like he didn't sleep at all during the night. His eyes had a glassy look and yet almost hollow, with heavy bags under them. Although hate and loathing are an emotion, he could see them seeping from Saul's eyes. Something had the king very upset indeed. Although this was not so unusual, David recalled last night and wondered if somehow this attack had something to do with him.

Upon entering the room, David sat down on a chair that was in the corner. Many times before, he had sat down in this very same chair. The king was usually in his bed. However, today he was sitting on a chair next to his bed. He had his javelin in his hand and seemed to be playing with it. His whole body looked rigid, almost cold, and as if King Saul was not the one in his body. Each movement that the king made was full of agitation and anger. Generally, the king stared straight ahead as though he was staring off into space, but today his eyes seemed glued upon every movement that David made. For a split second, a cold chill ricocheted through David's body. Calming his nerves down, he started to praise God. He found the king's actions rather peculiar indeed. The king seemed to be intensely watching his every move.

David was familiar with the javelin. However, he had only used one a few times. His family had viewed it as a sport rather than a weapon. He and Jonathan had thrown the javelin together a few times for entertainment. It looked a lot like a long fancy spear. It is a one-handed throwing tool with three main parts to it, the head, the shaft, and the grip. The head was made of metal, and King Saul's was decorated with an emblem on it. He could tell that a skilled craftsman had made the javelin. The shaft was made of solid wood. It had a cord grip and two loops of the cord, known as a thong. This was so that the king could put the tips of his first two fingers in the loose loops, one on either side. By using the two loops, it would fly toward the target when he released it. His hand would no longer be touching it, and yet he could still be pulling the javelin through his two fingers.

Today, David thought it would be wise to pray silently and to just play the soft, soothing music. He had not been playing long when King Saul stood up and started prophesying. Holding the javelin in his right hand, he stood up, stretching his arms out toward the heavens, and started speaking. His words came with such a deep resounding tone that they demanded everyone's attention within hearing range. David paused slightly in his playing, realizing that this was also new for King Saul. He was a little uncertain as of what to do.

King Saul had spent most of the night awake. He wanted to pray, but each time that he tried to, he found himself angrier than he was the hour before. Sleep did not seem to be an option at this time because he was being greatly influenced by the spirits. They were telling him to stand and prophesy. It was a plan to kill David and to justify the action. The prophecy would be interpreted as being from God. God would be blamed for giving the order to kill David. The king was proud of his perfect plan to end "this problem." Then he would continue to rule over his kingdom. Reasoning with himself, Saul was certain that no one would question his action *if* God gave the command.

Suddenly, David heard the words coming from King Saul's mouth, "...you are to show your dedication to me by being willing to sacrifice this shepherd boy to me. Take your javelin and use it as a tool to sacrifice this willing servant..."

"What's going on here!" Although David did not say the words audibly, he could not have been more surprised at the king's words. He could not explain everything, but he was certain of one fact, these words were certainly not from God. It was not God speaking at all! He knew the voice of God, and this was not God's voice speaking through King Saul. David would gladly lay down his life if he believed that was what God wanted him to do. But without a doubt, he knew this was not God! A force of authority started to rise in David. He wanted to tell this spirit to leave the king, but he knew that it was Saul's disobedience that had invited the evil spirit or spirits originally.

David prayed silently, asking God for wisdom and direction. Only now, his prayer was for protection for both himself and King Saul.

*Dear Father, please protect the king from this evil spirit that is harassing him. Help him to find You again. I know that he has already lost Your anointing as the king but help him not to lose his soul to this evil as well. Father, I am not sure what this prophecy is all about, but it appears that this evil spirit does not want me to live. I thank You for stopping the hands of my enemies and for protecting me with Your divine protection. I thank You that You protect us from evil and that You will protect me right now...*

Before David could pray any further, the king had finished his prophesying and had turned his eyes upon him. He was staring at him as if to pierce him with his eyes. Then, he turned slightly as if to adjust his stance. David had been watching the king's hands. It was as though God told him to focus and to watch. The king tightened his grip on the javelin, and David saw him. Just as if it were in slow motion, he realized what the king was about to do, and then he heard the words coming from the king's mouth, "I will smite David to the wall with it..."

With one swift action, the javelin that Saul had been holding on to came whistling right by David's head. He darted in the opposite direction. David was almost in shock. He turned and looked at the javelin; it was stuck in the wall not far from his head. The words that the king had supposedly prophesied echoed in David's head. "I will smite David to the wall with it..."

As quickly as the king had thrown the javelin, he was over retrieving it from the wall, and just as quickly, he threw it at David one more time. Again, God was with David, protecting him from the pierce of the javelin. It became quite clear to King Saul that God was protecting David. King Saul considered himself to be excellent at throwing the javelin. He could pierce the quickest of enemies, even when they saw him coming. However, twice David had been able to move swifter than his throw.

*Yes, God is protecting him,* the king thought. *So if God is anointing him and protecting him, he must be the one who has received my blessing.* Although all these thoughts were private, even more hatred and anger filled the king, festering like a large splinter working its way deep into his soul.

David darted out of the king's chamber after the second time he threw the javelin.

*I knew the king was crazy, but this is even worse than I expected,* David thought to himself.

Looking down at his hands, David was grateful that he had not dropped his harp. "Lord Jehovah, please don't ask me to go back in there, he may be the king, but he's crazy!" David was not certain what he should do next. Regardless of his next step, he was determined to put some space between himself and the king. Eager to leave the grounds, David went for a long walk behind the palace. He needed time to think, pray, and seek God's help and direction.

After a few hours had passed of worshipping God and resting in the woods, David had total peace about the attacks that had occurred that morning. He felt that God had shown him that things would get worse before they would get better, certainly not a comforting thought at all. He believed that God gave him peace to trust and to be patient and that He would have His way in taking King Saul out of his position. God also spoke to David about going back to the palace and that God would be his protection.

The sun was starting to cast a shadow as the afternoon wore on. Jonathan had been looking for David for some time before he found him.

"Hey David, how is it going? What has our king had you doing today?" Jonathan asked.

Debating on whether or not to tell Jonathan the truth, he realized that there was only one answer to that question. Their friendship was built on honesty. Consequently, he began to unfold the details of the morning. Jonathan's head dropped in deep thought. It was as though the ray of sunshine that had been in Jonathan was replaced with dark clouds of storm.

"David, I am sure it was just the evil spirits and that my father loves you just as I do. I can't believe he would do what you said with full understanding of his actions..." Deep in thought, Jonathan brought his hands to his face and started stroking his chin.

"In fact, are you certain that he wasn't just playing around and just trying to hit the wall...you know...target practicing inside? As king, he thinks he can do anything..."

A ray of hope glistened in Jonathan's eyes as he hoped that David misinterpreted his father's actions.

David wanted to give a sarcastic laugh but chose to guard his true feelings. However, he had to respond with the truth.

"He was target practicing all right...but I was the target. No, Jonathan. I heard the words of prophecy that he spoke as he threw the javelin at me. He knew what he was doing, and yes, he intended to kill me." Regret and remorse filled David's face.

As Jonathan stroked his beard, he looked up at David. Gently stroking down on it, he asked, "What will you do now?"

"God has shown me to stay here for the moment and to trust Him; He will be my protection from my enemies."

After a long pause, still stroking his beard, Jonathan softly repeated the word "enemies." "David, I do hope that you know that most people here are not your enemies... I love you like a brother and would gladly serve out my days here as the next king with you at my side."

The traditions held that the king's eldest son was first in line for the throne upon the king's death or at such a time as he could not lead the people anymore. David knew this and yet still found the words almost strange to his ears. Jonathan's words caused him to take a deep breath while considering his next words carefully. Of course, David knew that Jonathan was not aware of God's plans to ordain him as the next king. However, he still found these words almost surprising to hear, especially in the light of today's events. He was also confident that God would reveal His plans to Jonathan in time.

David turned toward Jonathan and gave him a big reassuring smile. Then, reaching over, he patted his friend on the back. "Of course, I know that. I have seven brothers, and I never felt as close to any of them as I do to you, Jonathan. Besides, I am still wondering about the rewards for killing Goliath. Actually, there is only one reward that I would like to have arranged currently."

Jonathan relaxed his hand from his beard, and a teasing smile spread across his face. Then, he said, "What reward is that...the king's daughter in marriage?"

"Very funny..." David replied. "How did I know that you would say that? No, I would like to see my father's house free from toll, tribute, custom, and service, just as was promised. He is coming along in age, and it would bless him greatly to know that this is one burden that he will not have to deal with from year to year."

"All right, since you are not asking about one of my sisters, I will prompt the king to write it on a tablet and have it sent over to him immediately," Jonathan replied, still ready to bait David and to tease him about his sisters.

# Chapter 10

*"Keep me free from the trap that is set for me, for you are my refuge" (Psalm 31:4, NIV).*

A few days had passed since King Saul attempted to kill David. Only a few people had heard about the attack. However, it was beginning to be rumored around the palace. In a short time, everyone would hear of it. The king thought long and hard about this situation with David. He ran many different scenarios around in his head, trying to decide the best way to handle things. Finally, he decided on poisoning. If poison was given discreetly enough, David's death would look like a "natural" death. Perhaps the people would think this was God's judgment upon David. He thought about using a spear to kill him, simple and swift, and then realized that the people might rise up against him. Then, as if falling into a trance, the king recalled the entry into the city, the beautiful women dancing and singing. As if sitting in an auditorium and the stage curtain was opening, he watched the scene play out. He saw the shocked, then hurt expressions on his own face, then he saw his expression turn quickly to raging anger. He recalled all the emotions behind the expressions. Then, his thoughts turned to how dangerous the war with the Philistines had been and how the people owed him.

*War...maybe that was the answer...* His thoughts played out a brutal battle death for the shepherd boy, including the fighting, his death, his burial, and a time of mourning. That would solve everything; the Philistines could be the "bad guys," and his kingdom could not find fault with him. It was a brilliant plan! *I have already promoted David into my army. Now I will make him a captain over a company of men and send them out to the most dangerous areas. Then, when they do battle against the Philistines, David will be killed. The people will see their hero fall at the hands of the enemy. Won't that be a shame...a real shame... Yes, that is the perfect answer! I must make sure that Abner gives him the advice that all new captains need, make sure he is the one leading the men into battle.* A captain should be right at the front where the battle is the heaviest.

An evil, almost sinister look came over the king's face. He called for his servant and summoned a messenger to go and get Abner. While he waited for Abner, he used the time to think about David. The king found it somewhat frightening to think about God being with David. He had seen God's power and knew that he could not fight God's strength. So the real question was whose strength was David walking in...a cocky youthful arrogance, or was it really the strength of Jehovah? The thought of this being Jehovah filled King Saul with a jealous rage. He was still angry that God had removed his blessings from him. He was certain that this David was the one that the prophet spoke of when he said, "The Lord has rent the kingdom of Israel from thee this day, and hath given it to a neighbor of yours, that is better than thou."[4]

His face wrinkled up with disgust as he thought of David. A nauseated feeling settled in the pit of his stomach. As he envisioned David sitting upon his throne, he saw a small boy with a staff as a scepter and the smell of sheep lingering through the halls. How could any God prefer the likes of a shepherd over a man as refined and distinguished as he had become? It was as though every bone in his body shuttered and ached with hatred at the very thought of David. The evil crept over his body and filled him completely. His eyes turned darker than normal, and there was a strong presence of evil taking over the room.

Jonathan had talked to his father and was satisfied to accept his father's answer about the attack on David. It was the illness. Of course, he loved David, just as if he were his own son. He would never intentionally hurt him. Jonathan placed his hand on his father's shoulder and reassured him that he would be fine and that everything would work out. "Trust God, and He will lead you. I know that it is God's plan to heal you." As the king thought back over his conversation with his son, he let out an arrogant laugh at the thought of God leading him again or healing him.

"How absurd... God has turned his back on me. He doesn't love me anymore. Just as I have dismissed soldiers, God has dismissed me." The hopelessness overshadowed the king's eyes. He became still and slipped back into his thoughts.

Abner had been trying to guess what the king wanted to see him about as he covered the distance from his house to the palace. He tried not to worry, but the king seemed so unpredictable these days. One moment, he was the best captain the king could have, and the next moment he was absolutely the worse, or at least, according to King Saul. One moment, he was being blessed with rewards, and the next, he was being threatened with prison. What would it be today? Would he be walking with God or tormented by evil spirits?

Abner couldn't help but remember the beginning years... He was there when his cousin was anointed as king. It was so totally incredible! The whole town came out for his anointing. The Prophet Samuel was the one who anointed him and placed him in the position of Israel's first king. So many days had passed since then. It had been a long while since Samuel had been around. Now, when the army is called in to rescue the king, it is from one conspiracy attack to another, and generally, the attacks are only in his mind.

Abner couldn't help to think about how much he loved his cousin Saul. But it was his opinion that the king was really starting to lose it! Now, suddenly, there is a new problem, and this problem came with a name...David. He was convinced that this David was out to take over his position. Maybe that's what the king wanted to see him about... Maybe he is already being replaced as the captain. Suddenly, his thoughts were overshadowed with fear and anger. He could feel his stomach tightening into knots, and his blood wanted to boil over with anger at the thought of losing his position. He predetermined this was why he was being summoned. *Yes, this David has been successful after all.*

Approaching the doorway to the king's study, Abner brought his thoughts back in to check. He flexed his eyebrows up and down to relieve the stress behind his eyes. Then, he opened his mouth wide as if to yawn to relax the muscles in his cheeks.

Abner approached the doorway to the king's study. It was a large chamber room, one of the largest in the palace besides the banquet hall. The king conducted much of his business here. It was a stately room, very well designed. It had a royal blue woolen rug that covered the front area for the people to kneel upon when coming before their king. He'd heard they used a massive number of blueberries to dye the rug. The lighting was torches carved of fine mahogany wood with roses carved into the handles. The holders for the torches were made from brass and embellished with layers of brass to fashion flowers all over the holder. There were two small tables up by the king's chair for his drinks and refreshments. The wall was lined with mahogany wooden chairs. Generally, two soldiers stood to attention outside the room, while two servants were handy and waiting for the king's next command. The servants were expected to be close enough to be summoned and yet far enough from the king to not hear the king's business.

As Abner approached, he could see that today was not a good day for the king. Perhaps his greatest fears were about to come upon him. He stood there waiting for the king to realize that he had arrived. It was not acceptable to approach the king without his invitation and could result in imprisonment or beheading. Therefore, he stood at attention, waiting to be invited in.

King Saul was sitting in his favorite chair, a chair designed for him as king. It was large, sturdy, and overstuffed for comfort. The legs and back were made of fine dark mahogany wood. The top was carved and had top-quality jewels attached to it. The seat and the back were covered with velvet material. It had been dyed to a beautiful deep red. The dye was taken from the plant, Papaver rhoeas, found between Jerash and Anjana, Jordan. The Papaver rhoeas was quickly being nicknamed the "poppy plant." On the back of the chair was a cushion made from goose feathers, and there was a small cushion inside the back cushion to provide additional lumbar support. Directly above the cushion, on the back, was an engraving that read, "King of Israel." Around the title were engraved flowers that held captivating jewels of rubies, sapphires, and emeralds. Around the base of the chair and the top was a gold casing. The legs had the engravings of lion feet. Yes, it was a very fine chair created for the king.

Abner addressed the king, saying, "Greetings, my king, I understand that you wanted to see me. How may I be of service to you?"

The king sat there for a few seconds, just looking at Abner as though he was deep in thought. Then slowly, almost methodically, the corners of his mouth changed from a non-expression to a slight smile. His eyes went from a blank stare to searching out Abner. Abner had learned to read the king's expressions over the years. Regardless of whatever was going on, the king was up to something; that was certain.

Giving a quick wave of his hand, he said, "Abner, I am glad you are here. Come, come, you may approach me."

"King, I understand that you summoned for me. How may I be of service to you?"

"I am sure that you have noticed that this 'shepherd boy' is becoming a problem."

A hint of irritation reflected in Abner's reply, "Yes...I have." There was a deliberate pause between his words.

The king continued, "I am sure that you must have heard how the crowds changed the words of my song upon entering the city. Did you not?"

"Ah... I did, and I found it very disturbing."

Continuing, the king said, "I spent most of the night thinking and have decided that this 'David' should be promoted."

"Promoted! Excuse me, king!" First, a look of shock seemed to surface on Abner's face, only to be replaced with a look of irritation.

"I think that you will agree with me once you have heard what I have to say." Saul continued on pausing between each thought, for he was still working out the details.

Continuing, King Saul said, "If he were promoted to a captain of...let's say, one thousand men...then we could send him out to war against the Philistines. The rest of the army, including certain leaders, such as yourself, would not need to go. Wouldn't it be a shame if the battle was so intense that most of the soldiers were taken over and sadly lost as casualties of war? Then, of course, the captain would also die while fighting. It would be so sad...so very sad indeed..." The king sarcastically pretended to show remorse.

While listening to him, Abner found a slight smile growing as he realized what the king was scheming. A coy look spread across Abner's face. His tone changed to one toying with a deceptive plan, "The men are tired, king; it would be good for many of them to stay here and to have time with their families."

His words were slowly spoken with deliberate emphasis on certain words, "are tired," "many of them." "It is a wise plan, my king."

A silence hung in the air as both men worked on the developing plans.

The king's words broke the silence, "These men that will assist '*Captain*' David, they need to be, shall we say, 'expendable.' I would like you to handpick these men, Abner. Oh, and make sure to include David's brothers."

"You have spoken well, my king. I shall be happy to oblige you. How soon do you want the men sent out? And shall I handle assigning David to the position?"

"Let's say, 'effective immediately.' It's been a few days now since we returned; the men have had a chance to return to their families. The Philistines are already challenging us and ready to do battle again. Tell the men to prepare to leave by the end of the week, and yes, I would appreciate you handling David's... promotion."

The king dismissed Abner and asked him to keep him abreast of the developing plans. Abner, of course, agreed and went on his way to set into motion their devilish plan. Abner knew why he didn't like David but wasn't certain as to the king's reasons. He had been so certain that it was his position that David had been after, but perhaps the king was feeling the same way. Anyways, this David was trouble. As Abner left the king's chambers, he felt a new wave of excitement. He found himself gently rubbing the sides of his head in humor to make sure that no horns were sprouting. He loved a good deception, and currently, Abner had one to work on. Abner mused to himself, "Maybe the king was doing better than he had originally thought."

# Chapter 11

*"Keep me as the apple of your eye; hide me in the shadow of your wings" (Psalm 17:8, NIV).*

The weeks were passing, and David had been assigned a regiment in the country. He took pride in the fact that he had been made captain over a thousand men. They went out against the Philistines and came back with victories. He was not sure of all that was going on, but he felt it was very important to walk in the highest honor possible before God. He held his head high and tried real hard to think before reacting. It was as though God had placed supernatural wisdom upon him. He could see God's hand was with him, and he could hear God's voice with every turn. He did not take pride in his own success but in God's success. In his quiet times, David found himself singing praises to God. When he took time to think about the attack that happened with King Saul, he began to wonder if Jonathan might possibly have been correct. Maybe King Saul had not been trying to do him harm, but then his heart would feel the sadness of realizing that he knew differently.

David would come and go before Abner. He carried out the business that he was given.

During the times that David was out fighting in war, the people fell more in love with him and praised him continually for his achievements. They took great pride in David's accomplishments. Quite often now, as David and the men approached a village or a town, the people would come out from their houses and line the roads to sing praises. They would wave at David and the men. The people's arms would be full of food, and they would be offering their services. Some of the farmers would offer to feed their horses and to fill their wagons with food. Others would offer to sharpen their knives and spears. The leaders of the towns would find the largest house and put together a feast for David and some of the weary soldiers. The maidens were always batting their eyes and dancing around joyously. When they thought no one could see them, they would pinch their cheeks for that rosy rouge appearance. The maidens were always hoping to find an available soldier that would find their beauty irresistible. Whenever there was a physician in the area, he would take the necessary time to treat any wounded soldiers. If there was a smith who forged iron available, he would be called to help them rebuild any weapons. All of this was summoned and organized by the elderly men and priests of that community. David felt thankful for all the help that they were receiving. It humbled him before God and yet filled his heart with gratitude.

*****

Not much time passed before King Saul found himself more worried than ever. It was obvious that God was walking with

David and blessing him. David behaved himself in a very wise manner. No matter what happened to him, he always came out a success and winning the people's favor. The situation was worse than the king could have anticipated. David was gaining acceptance with the community leaders. To make matters worse, David was quickly growing in fame with all the citizens in both Israel and Judah. It appeared to Saul that David was deliberately seeking favor with the leaders. This filled King Saul with even more fear as he realized that God was with David and blessing him. It was obvious that this plan was not going to work. No matter how great the odds, David came out the victor. It was time to devise a new plan...

Upon David's return, King Saul sent for him. David found himself slightly apprehensive, remembering the last time he had been summoned to come before the king. He took the time to put away his warrior garments and dress in attire that was more appropriate for approaching the royal court. He shaved and trimmed his hair. Then, after a few minutes in prayer to prepare his heart, David made the journey from his house to the kings' chamber. As he stood at the door waiting to be called in, he thought back to his first night at the palace. Jonathan had made it a fine greeting and a delightful evening. Jonathan seemed to make everything fun and enjoyable.

"Come in, David, come in." The king smiled and greeted him kindly. This was certainly different than the last time he had been here. Although the king was doing everything right by having a pleasant expression and talking friendly, David felt as though God was telling him to keep his guard up, "Beware."

"I have been watching you and the success you have had when fighting the Philistines. It seems that you, being so young, know how to handle yourself as if you were an aged warrior. I believe it is time to give you the next reward that you have coming for killing Goliath."

David thought back to killing Goliath. In fact, he remembered the very first moment that he heard about the king's rewards given to the man who would kill the giant. Once again, he could feel the atmosphere of Goliath's challenges and how it stirred righteous anger within him. He remembered all the men standing around talking about the king's rewards and how they would love to have them. Then he heard the words echoing through his mind, *The man who kills Goliath will receive great wealth from the king. King Saul will also give the man his daughter in marriage, and he will also exempt his father's family from taxes in Israel.* In his thoughts, he found himself wondering what great wealth he would receive. His father had been very blessed when he received the parchment signed and stamped by the king exempting him from paying taxes in Israel. Next, he found himself thinking about the king's daughters. Perhaps he was going to be given one of them in marriage. As if echoing in the far reaches of his mind, he heard his own thoughts as though they betrayed him, *Michal*... It was a soft thought as he realized that her beauty had undeniably touched his heart. His thoughts trailed off, and he was brought back to the present by the king's words.

"I want to give you my oldest daughter, Merab; she will be your wife. Only I expect you to continue to fight for me with valor. You have shown yourself to be strong in war to this point. I expect you to continue to fight the...battles by engaging in war against those who come against the...me."

Hearing the king's words, David felt as though he could fill in the pauses in the king's sentence, "I expect you to continue to fight the...*Lord's* battles by engaging in war against those who come against the...*Lord*." He had heard the king use these words many times before. David could not help but feel saddened by the hardness of the king's heart. It was obvious that the king did not wish to give Jehovah the due place in his life.

Saul stood and walked toward the window that overlooked the courtyard. He gloated at the thought of the Philistines being the ones responsible for killing David and not he himself. An evil smile crept over his face as his eyebrows arched down toward his nose. He thought to himself, *Let not my hand be upon him, but let the hand of the Philistines be upon him!*

As satisfaction for this new plan settled over King Saul, he put on the expression of sincere joy over his future "son-in-law." He then turned back around to face David and stretched out his hands to congratulate David.

David smiled at the king in response to his words. Merab... he thought that the king might offer Merab since she was the oldest and still unmarried. He found the words surfacing to his lips, *But what about Merab and Adriel...* Maybe the king did not know of the devotion that was developing between them. David decided against saying anything and that this was not really the issue at the moment.

As the reality of the situation returned to David, he asked, "Who am I? And what is my life, or my father's family in Israel, that I should be a son-in-law to the king?"

The king quickly reminded David that he had already earned this reward with the killing of Goliath. He also proceeded to remind David that he, too, had come from humble beginnings. When he still lived at home, he tilled his father's field. Of course, King Saul felt so much more superior than his father had ever been. *He* had been anointed to be Israel's first king. His father... well, he was just a farmer... It was his name that made a place in the historical scrolls for the tribe of Benjamin.

That evening, the king hosted a grand dinner for his daughter and David. It angered the king to have to do anything at all for David, but he must make this betrothal appear real, especially when he didn't intend for David to live through battle long enough to marry his daughter... What an absurd thought, the son of Jesse marrying either of his daughters...

The maidservants made King Saul aware of Merab's reaction to the betrothal. Although Merab didn't speak a word, anger showed strongly in her actions; she marched off as quickly as she could to her room. She was a lady of grace and humility. She knew well that women were the property of their fathers until they were married. Though she did not spout off, she was clearly not happy with this decision.

King Saul found his way to his daughter's room later that afternoon. With eyes red from crying, she pleaded with him to allow her to marry Adriel, the Meholathite. He was from a city in the territory of Manasseh and traveled regularly with merchandise to the king's palace. Almost a year ago, she had met him for the first time. She had been handling some of the household duties for her mother. His skin was dark, and he had an appealing smile that immediately caught her attention. All his travels kept him in shape, something that she could not help but notice. As he lifted the merchandise off his wagon, the sleeves on his halug, his tunic, came up just enough that she could see his muscular arms. Embarrassed that she had stolen a glance, she turned away, blushing. She hoped that he had not seen her embarrassment. Although all of their contact was around her purchasing materials and supplies from him, they had started to develop an attraction that she hoped would lead to marriage. Recently, they had talked some about marriage, but he always came back to not having a dowry... Now, her father was promising her to someone who was younger than her and someone that she was definitely not interested in, someone who was not...Adriel.

Merab thought to herself, David... *He is still such a boy! He is Michal's age; let them be married... After all, she has noticed him and already finds him appealing.* So many thoughts flooded her head that day, so many discouraged and predetermined thoughts about her future. She even entertained the idea of running away instead of submitting to her father's wishes. She concluded that she would rather not marry anyone than marry David. She didn't hate David...he...well...he just wasn't Adriel, and furthermore, he didn't have a dowry either! Tears streamed silently down her face as her father entered her room. She heard his footsteps but chose to keep her head buried in her quilt. Her father told her to sit up like a lady and to listen to what he had to say; she would do whatever she was told and that her marriage to David was best for the kingdom. Then, his words sounded a bit mysterious to her. He said, "Don't worry, things have a way of working out even when we don't think they will." Was it his words or the tone of her father's voice that made her wonder what thoughts lay behind his words? Either way, all she could see was a life of doom as she thought of Adriel's arms lovingly pulling some other woman to him... Adriel... Her heart was breaking at the thought...

David considered talking to Merab concerning this arrangement later that evening after supper but then decided to leave matters in God's hand. He could see how miserable Merab was at dinner that night. He could tell that she would attempt to paste on a smile when needed. It was obvious that she had been crying that day. Her eyes were red and puffy. Maybe he should talk to Jonathan about the situation. After all, David was confident that he could find his own wife; he really did not need to be married to one of the king's daughters.

*****

Over the next few weeks, David returned to his men and went back to the battle, fighting against the Philistines. Again, it was one battle after another, ending in victories for him and his men. Each night, he found time to get away from everyone and to enter into prayer and worship with God. He would withdraw to a secluded place, a safe distance from the men. He knew that his heart was not devoted to Merab, and he felt certain that God had the answers for all concerned. After this battle was won, they would be returning to the palace for his marriage to Merab. The men made jokes about their wedding night and asked if they too could be given a month off of going into battle. David would just smile and remind them that this is the king's daughter that they were speaking of and to keep their conversation honorable.

# Chapter 12

*"I waited patiently for the LORD; he turned to me and heard my cry" (Psalm 40:1, NIV).*

Upon returning to the palace, David entered the courtyard. Abner was there to meet him and asked him to come and find him in his quarters as soon as he had dismounted his horse and freshened up.

David was quite certain that the look in Abner's eyes indicated that something was wrong. He had that stern, distant look about him. It was a look that indicated that there was a problem or problems. David's thoughts trailed off to his family, but he was quite certain that if there was a problem at home, a servant would have found him and his brothers. Maybe it was the king again; perhaps his mental state was worse. *Maybe he is going to attempt to kill me again.* Then, there was his betrothed; had she taken ill? He prayed for God to guide him and to prepare him for whatever was ahead.

David dismounted and led his horse, Bedouin, into the stables. One of the servants assigned to the stables offered to take the horse, brush him down, and feed him. However, David loved taking care of his horse and declined the offer. He often found himself talking to his horse. Bedouin had become his closest friend while out on the battlefield. Other than his brothers, he had to guard his words with everyone. Therefore, David often found himself confiding in his horse. Bedouin always returned his love without question. He would often respond with a snort or a whinny sound as if answering David; he was a loyal horse. Bedouin loved to nudge David's leather pouch looking for fruit or some grain. A good snack made life a little more exciting for a horse.

David took a deep breath and said a silent prayer as he found himself standing in front of Abner's house. It seemed unusual that the guards were standing at attention. On the battlefield, they stood outside the tent, but this was in the city. Things were generally more relaxed here. There were soldiers that watched the entrance of the city and alerted them to danger. But these soldiers looked as if they were expecting an intruder...or some sort of trouble.

Just as David went to knock on the door, Abner opened the door and invited him in. He must have been watching for him, or else someone alerted him that he was approaching. Either way, David was invited in. There was an atmosphere of hostility that filled the room. David found himself wondering what was happening. He thought about asking what was going on but decided to let Abner lead the conversation. He had done nothing wrong to his knowledge, nothing that called for this kind of a hostile greeting.

As David entered his house, he looked around at the humble surroundings. The front door entered into Abner's study, perhaps because he was an officer in the king's army. There was a door at the back of the room that probably led into the rest of his house. He could hear faint sounds of others behind the curtain, probably his family busy with their daily tasks. There was only a small table for working at and a bench for sitting. However, on the wall to his left was a show of swords and knives. His armor hung on a makeshift chair. There were a few other items around the room, such as a fine pennant necklace and a few carvings. These were probably trophies of war.

Abner hesitated for a moment; then, as he pointed to the bench, he told David to have a seat. He looked at David rather sternly and took a slow, deliberate breath as he began to speak, "There have been some changes since you were here last..."

David wanted to ask if anyone had died. The way Abner was acting indicated that it must be some really big change.

Abner went on to say, "During your absence, the king decided to give Merab to Adriel the Meholathite as his wife. The king knows that you will not be happy with this decision. So he has asked me to prepare you with this news."

Silence filled the room as Abner gave him time to register the words that he had just spoken. Abner stood alert and eager, watching for any sign of anger that David might display. Maybe he would throw a fit or go into a jealous rage, and they would have to arrest him. If he pulled out his sword, they would be able to kill him...

David wanted to let out a big sigh of relief but thought better of it. A smile started to spread across his face at the reality of these words. Inwardly, David heard himself exclaim, *This was all that was going on... Jehovah heard both of our hearts after all.*

Abner started to get a little angry with David, "What are you smiling about? Don't you realize what this means? The king has

116

taken back a promise that he has made to you. This is wrong… Your betrothed has been given to another man, and you sit here with a smile on your face! What is wrong with you?" By this time, Abner was practically shouting at David.

David smiled and replied, "I am happy for both Merab and Adriel. I was aware that they had feelings for each other. I have actually been praying that Jehovah would work things out however He thought was best. Based on what you have shared, I would have to say that Jehovah's best plan was for the two of them to be together."

As if Abner had not heard what David had said, he continued to help David with devising a plan to regain his dignity and to get his betrothed back. "Maybe you should challenge Adriel for Merab. She was, after all, promised to you first. You could contest the king's decision. I am sure that the council would listen to you. I could speak to the king and tell him that you want to challenge Adriel, and by the end of the day, she could be your wife." Deception spewed from Abner.

With a calmness that totally irritated Abner, David said, "There is no need to challenge Adriel, and there is no reason to contest the king's decision. I have spent time praying for all involved. I knew that Adriel and Merab were attracted to each other, and I have been praying that Jehovah would have His perfect will in all our lives. I believe that he already has."

Frustrated, Abner grabbed for another way to provoke David, "What will your soldiers say about this? Aren't you concerned about losing their respect?"

Answering Abner, David replied, "No, when God is in our lives, we don't have to worry about such things. Besides, who I marry is none of their concern."

David seemed truly happy for the couple. Once again, the king's plan had been foiled. The king was certain that David would feel provoked when he returned and learned the news. In fact, the king had even imagined David getting violently angry and being fatally struck down while the soldiers protected themselves. King Saul would be more furious than ever to learn of David's response. Abner looked at him almost with an appalling look and then felt alarmed at the thought of what the king would say.

To reinforce his words, Abner said, "How can you take this so lightly? The king and Merab have betrayed you. Don't you think that you should challenge Adriel? After all, he has married your betrothed while you were at war. You could request that he be stoned to death for his actions."

Then, as if a light came on, Abner decided to demand action out of David. Practically hollering at David, he demanded an answer, "What do you intend to do about this?"

David could feel the manipulation in Abner's voice, but he refused to back down, "Why should I do anything? They are obviously happy together. I will offer them my best wishes when I see them next."

A sound of desperation rang forth from Abner's voice as he said, "He has stolen your betrothed. You should challenge the king and demand her back!"

David smiled at Abner, beginning to feel slightly irritated. He was extra cautious to guard his words. David wanted to ask him why this was so important to him, but he did not. It was beginning to become apparent to David that they were expecting him to react in anger. He had caught a look between Abner and his soldiers as if they had their own private conversation going on. There had been so much tension in the air. The soldiers were alert and ready for action. *So this was all a plot against me. The events may have even been planned, hoping for a negative reaction from me.* Speaking firmly to reinforce his words, David said, "I see no reason to question the king's decision. Merab and Adriel are together just as Jehovah has planned."

This was why the guards were standing outside the door. They had expected him to respond in anger. When Abner could not get David even slightly aroused over the betrayal, he stormed off toward the palace while mumbling under his breath.

David considered laughing out loud for just a second but thought better of it. Why provoke Abner? No, he better just keep quiet and let Jehovah continue to walk before him and prepare his path.

The next day, David had a surprise visit from one of the king's servants, asking him to once again come before the king's presence. He couldn't help but wonder if the king was going to ask him about his feeling concerning Merab and Adriel as well. Should he be just as honest with the king? Yes, he decided that he should be as honest. However, not everything needed to be spoken. He prayed, asking Jehovah to guide him in his words as he set out to come before the king's presence.

In David's absence, the king had tired of Merab's pleadings and decided that if she were to marry Adriel, then it might provoke David into anger. It had seemed like a good plan, but once again, his plan had failed to this "self-righteous shepherd boy." David's response had angered the king, but as if fate had stepped in, he learned that his younger daughter, Michal, loved David. King Saul found this to be very good news indeed! He could ensnare David with his daughter's love. He thought to himself, *I will give her to him, and she will be a snare to him and so that the hand of the Philistines may be against him.*

*Now, do I just send him out to war for a period of time prior to the wedding? That did not work before. How do we raise the stakes? The king meditated, The uncircumcised Philistines have to be the cause of his death... The uncircumcised Philistines... The uncircumcised Philistines... The uncircumcised... That's it!* As he treacherously sought for a way to make certain David's death, he devised another plan, another brilliant plan indeed. He beamed with pride that he would finally be rid of this "shepherd boy" for good. This plan was certain to not fail.

King Saul had always had a strong relationship with his daughter Michal. If all else failed, he was certain that she would see the need to rid their family of this David. Certainly, Jonathan should be able to see the dangers in letting this David get too close to the throne. But his son was too much like his mother. He always believed the best in everyone, even to his own defeat.

Then, suddenly, for just a split second, King Saul did not see this as the weakness that he had now invented it to be but as a humbleness of letting Jehovah be in control. For just a split second, he admired his son and desired to be more like him. And for just a split second, King Saul found himself wanting to cry out to Jehovah for help and beg for Jehovah's forgiveness. But just as quickly as the thoughts came to him, he found other thoughts filling his head with anger and bitterness. Biting his lower lip to control the anger rising within him, King Saul heard as clearly as if he spoke out loud, "No, it is a weakness that Jonathan has to overcome." Wondering to himself, he thought, *How could I ever have been so foolish as to have thought that God would walk with me?*

As David entered the king's study one more time, he looked around and wondered if he should be looking for something to hide behind in case he needed protection from one of those flying spears. Perhaps he should not get too far from the door. He pasted a cordial smile on his face while waiting for the king to speak.

Sitting in his chair, King Saul spoke, "I have decided to give you a second opportunity to become my son-in-law."

David felt a flutter in his heart. He clearly knew that the king only had two daughters... Michal... Although this intrigued David, he had learned to be very cautious and to move circumspectly in everything that he did. He focused his attention back on the king. As David stood there silently, the king said, "I can see that you need time to think about what I have said to you. Take your time. Michal will make a good wife."

David left the king's presence wanting to smile and be happy. He wanted to dance and shout, and yet a feeling of unworthiness accompanied by a feeling of hesitation. He determined to go to the Lord in prayer and to get Jehovah's direction.

As soon as David left King Saul's presence, the king called some of his key servants into the room. He then told them that he had just offered Michal's hand in marriage to David. He commanded them to speak with David privately and to say, "Look, the king is pleased with you, and his servants all like you... Now, become his son-in-law." So they left the room, all agreeing to do the king's bidding.

One by one, they found their way to David and spoke privately to him, repeating the king's words. One by one, David responded with what was in his heart, "Do you think it a small matter to become the king's son-in-law? I'm only a poor man and insignificant."

Saul's servants told the king of David's response. The king instructed them, saying, "Speak with David again, only this time tell him that the king wants no other price for the bride than a hundred Philistine foreskins to take revenge on his enemies."

Again, the servants found their way to David, and one by one, they spoke the king's words to him.

David meditated upon all that had happened, and he felt so humbled. He knew that he came from the honorable and ancient family of Judah. He saw himself as a humble man. He relived his accomplishments when defeating Goliath. He thought about being a soldier, and still, humbly, he bowed before Jehovah to seek His guidance. David knew that someday he would be the king, but he wanted it all to be in Jehovah's timing. He wanted it to be Jehovah's plan. He only teased about marrying a king's daughter. He was just a shepherd boy; he was unworthy to be a son-in-law to the king... Sometimes he remembered the Prophet Samuel's words that he spoke over him as though it was only a dream. How could Jehovah use him as a great person or a king? *Doesn't Jehovah know how unworthy I am? Doesn't Jehovah see the selfish thoughts in my mind? Surely, the prophet must have made a mistake...*

As David's thoughts whirled around within him, he found himself seeking Jehovah. He prayed for peace and that Jehovah would direct his path. He also prayed that Jehovah would make His divine word be a light upon his path. Peace started to fill David, and a new challenge began to rise within him. David realized that God was giving him a way to fill the dowry that was part of a long-established custom. Although it was a very unusual dowry for most, he could not help but smile at the thought of how it fit his situation. God started to fill him with new confidence and determination for defeating the allotted uncircumcised Philistines. If the king wanted one hundred foreskins, then he would give him two hundred foreskins. Yes, that was what he was going to do.

He ordered his brothers, the captains under him, to have the men get ready to go, "Tell the men to make sure that their horses are freshened and that they have all the supplies that they will need to be out for a few weeks."

Finding the Philistines was never hard. They had such a foolish notion that they were undefeatable. Still, after all the times that David and his men had come after them, they refused to admit that God was with the Israelites and still tried to take them on. Each time, it amazed David. But then that is the way people are when they have hardness in their hearts toward God.

The men found it rather humorous to be circumcising the Philistines. It would not change their hearts or their destination, but it would put an end to these particular men who were coming against God. They joked about circumcising them and how it would be a sign to the other Philistines. No one volunteered for the task of taking care of the foreskins, but David found a few soldiers who agreed to take the steps necessary. Since the skins could not be put into a leather pouch without rotting, it was important to dry them out before storing them. That took someone staying close to them to keep the birds away. Dried, dead skin was a bird's feast! They used the heat from some of the larger rocks around the desert to dry them. Next, they had to find someone to tally the number of foreskins accumulated. This was no easy task because not all of the men were educated enough to count that far. But once again, he found a few men who could keep track of the totals.

At night, around the campfire, the men found themselves reliving different stories that they could recall on circumcision. One of the stories that they found the most pleasure in was the one about Jacob and Leah. Leah's daughter Dinah had gone out to visit the women in the land, and Schechem, the son of Hamor the Hivite, saw her and took her, and as the recorded word said, he defiled her. Together the men recalled every detail of the story... Schechem mistook his feeling of lust for love. Acting on these feelings, he went to his father and asked him to speak with the girl's father, Jacob, and ask if he could take Dinah in marriage. Dinah's brothers were furious after hearing about how he had violated their sister.

Hamor went to speak to Jacob while he was working in the field and said, "My son Schechem has his heart set on your daughter. Please give her to him as his wife. Intermarry with us; give us your daughters and take our daughters for yourself. You can settle among us; the land is open to you. Live in it, trade in it, and acquire property in it."

As if to reinforce his earnestness, Schechem stepped forward. He had been standing at a distance behind his father. He stepped forward and spoke, "Let me find favor in your eyes, and I will give you whatever you ask. Make the price for the bride and the gift. I am to give as great as you like, and I'll pay whatever you ask me. Only give me the girl as my wife."

Not waiting for Jacob to answer, his sons replied deceitfully. They answered both men, "We can't do such a thing; we can't give our sister to a man who is not circumcised."

At that point, the men would stop and laugh and joke about what was ahead for these unsuspecting men. The Hivites chose to be circumcised as Jacob and his brothers had spoken. Three days later, while all the men were still in pain, two of Dinah's brothers, Simeon and Levi, took their swords and attacked the unsuspecting city and killed every male. They killed Hamor and his son Schechem with the sword and took Dinah from Schechem's house. Jacob's other sons came to the city. When they saw the dead bodies, they looted the city where their sister had been defiled. They seized their flocks, herds, donkeys, and everything else of theirs in the city and out in the fields. They carried off their wealth and all their women and children. They took everything that was in their houses too. Jacob was very distressed about what his sons had done. Being certain that his sons had brought great wrath upon them, he went before God and prayed for direction. His sons felt as though this retribution was their duty in protecting their sister.

This old story had brought a lot of conversation and amusement to the camp. The soldiers found it comforting to know that others had used circumcision as a means of war. Sometimes they would get carried away talking about the methods used in circumcision, as well as the pain being inflicted. Sometimes, David would find it necessary to remind them to keep their conversation honorable. It just seemed impossible for there to be this much circumcision and no jokes about the procedure. He used this time to remind the men that true circumcision takes place in the heart. However, since he was still a man, David could not help to find a little humor in some of their jokes. He had a heart to serve God but still understood that some issues had to be treated delicately. Often, he would find himself suppressing a smile while determined to keep himself in check. David used the stories of Abraham to illustrate how every male among them needed to be circumcised. It would be a sign of a covenant between Abraham and God. From that time on, every male born among them would be circumcised at eight days old. This was to include all of their household, those born in their houses, and those that were bought with money.

David recalled the words of God spoken to Abraham, "My covenant in your flesh is to be an everlasting covenant. Any uncircumcised male, who has not been circumcised in the flesh, will be cut off from his people; he has broken my covenant."

# Chapter 13

*"Teach me your way, LORD, that I may rely on your faithfulness; give me an undivided heart, that I may fear your name" (Psalm 86:11, NIV).*

King Saul had not expected David to return so quickly. In fact, he had not expected him to return at all! Feeling quite furious, he was certain that God's hand was upon him. What a totally nauseating and infuriating thought. What was it the messenger had proclaimed? "He has killed not one hundred Philistines but *two hundred* Philistines!" Of course...

King Saul knew then that more drastic measures would be necessary to assure David's death. As anger festered in his heart and caused darkness to settle over the king, he meditated upon a new plan. He thought about his precious Michal being given to this shepherd boy. The thought caused him to get sick deep in the pit of his stomach. In the same breath, a cold chill shivered down his spine. He was certain that his beautiful Michal would not let him down. She would help him to rid their lives and their kingdom from this David.

Then, without warning, his thoughts drifted back to another time. He recalled a precious moment when his Michal was only three years old. His wife and her maids took care of the children, but on this particular day, she had slipped out and found her way to her father's side. He was on his way to the stables when she caught up with him. She reached for his hand. He took her tiny little hand in his large rough hand. He still recalled how gentle and soft her hand was, just like her heart. Her black hair only hung shoulder-length at that time, but it bounced in curls around her tender little face. She smiled from ear to ear as she looked up at him. His heart filled with deep love and devotion as he smiled back at her. He reached down to pick her up and swung her into his arms. She was so small. He was sure that she was the right size for her age, though. Being such a big man, he was certain that it was his size that made her feel so extra tiny. He asked her why she wasn't at the palace with everyone else.

"I want you, Daddy," she replied with big eyes that grabbed his heart.

Her love tore its way deep into his soul. She would climb up in his lap in the evenings and tell him that she wanted to grow up and marry him, just like Mommy. Of course, she did not understand marriage at all. She was just a child that loved her daddy. He had always loved all of his children, but he had a soft spot in his heart for Michal. Merab had always been closer to her mother. She spent her time being groomed to be a true princess. Michal would spend her days riding out to war with her father if he allowed it. She did, however, accompany him on occasions when he could guarantee her safety. Michal was also a true princess, but she loved the outdoors...and her father.

\* \* \* \* \*

Michal was beaming as she approached the new day. The sun was shining in her bedroom window. She looked around at her bedroom. Everything seemed extra special today. Her maidservants had awakened her with the best news possible. David had returned. She curled the blankets up close to her neck and drew in a deep breath of fresh air. A smile beamed across her face as she thought of David. Her long dark hair flowed over the pillow. She brushed it back out of her face with her hand. She had so many questions and thoughts. She actually knew very little about David. They had only talked briefly on different occasions, but she knew that she loved him in her heart. She thought that he had feelings for her too, but she couldn't be sure of it. She took delight in the thought though that he met the required dowry double what her father had asked. The whole kingdom seemed to know about his success and anxiously exaggerated the story of this "doubled" dowry.

She sat up on the side of her bed and looked at her room. Would this be the room that she and David would share? She blushed as she thought about them being intimate. The ladies in the city would be envious of her. They would all desire her position as his wife. After all, they already desired her position as King Saul's daughter. She looked around her room, taking in everything as she found herself imagining the next few days filled with the excitement of the wedding, *her* wedding. Her eyes settled upon her small dressing table that stood near her window. It was full of perfumes, oils, fragrances, jewels, eye paint, nail paints, and lacquer. She looked forward to dressing as a bride. Glancing over her fragrances and scents, she thought about which one she would wear for David. Would he like a sweet scent reflecting her innocence or a spicy, more flirtatious fragrance?

How she loved it when the merchants brought treasures from Egypt. She'd heard many of the stories between the Egyptians and the Israelites. Michal had grown up hearing the story of Moses and the plagues, but it seemed as though they were imagined stories meant to be a part of her childhood. She was so removed from all "that." What mattered the most to her was the wealth of knowledge that the Egyptians had on personal hygiene and adornment. The Egyptians, both male and female, were vain about their personal appearance. She had heard many times that Egypt was full of shops where you could go to be made beautiful. Her mother had requested such a shop be set up on the palace grounds. Her father granted the request and bought an Egyptian slave named Nefatar to oversee it.

As she and Merab were growing up, they had taken classes regularly under Nefetar. Michal always thought of Nefetar as very beautiful with her dark skin. She was always showing them the importance of using the oils to protect their skin while keeping it soft and moist. Earlier in Nefetar's life, she'd been training to become highly skilled as a perfumer. She was learning the art of makeup too. She had come quite far in her studies when her father was killed and left a rather large debt. She was sold as a slave to settle his debt. It was a sad tale, but Michal was so glad her father had purchased Nefetar and brought her to the palace. At that moment, Michal decided to have Nefetar assist her when preparing for her wedding.

While training with Nefetar, Merab and Michal learned that her name was a derivate of the word "nefer," which meant "beautiful." As young girls, they envied Nefetar, thinking her to be the blessed one with all of her beauty and knowledge. Michal and Merab had learned much under the teaching of Nefetar. They learned the importance of ancient Egyptian perfumes and of the great variety of oils and fats, and the many different ways to use them.

She recalled how there were three main techniques of producing perfumes. Most perfumes come from flowers, fruits, or seeds. Enfleurage was the first way that they learned. It is saturated layers of fat with steeping flowers. The second technique was called maceration. With this step, the girls learned to dip flowers, herbs, or fruits into heated fats or oils. The flowers or fruits were then pounded into a mortar and then stirred into the oil. The mixture would then be sieved and cooled. The third technique was her favorite; it expressed the flowers or seeds in much the same way that they made the oils and the wines.

Michal made her way over to her table and sat down in front of it and now gently ran her index finger over the top of a small vase. Her eye paint was stored in it. The most popular colors were black and green. Nefetar introduced the red paints to them as well. She taught Michal and Merab how the green pigment or paint was made from malachite, an oxide of copper. Finally, it was prepared as a dried paste or powder. Upon finishing it, Nefetar stored it in shells or in segments of hollow reed wrapped in plant leaves. Michal recalled the time that Nefetar showed them how to carefully place it in the small vase. The black eye paint was called kohl and was made from galena, a sulfide of lead. This was used more to darken the rims of the eyelids. The Egyptians felt that this made the eyes appear larger and more luminous. Nefetar even shared how the green eye paint represented the eye god Horus, a potent amulet. She told the girls that the dark line around the eye stopped the glare of the sun. Michal looked down at her cheek color. It was stored in a small vessel that fit in her hand. It was filled with red ochre in a base of fat. She had a small brush that allowed her to apply it to her cheeks and an even smaller brush for her lips.

Nefetar spent a few lessons teaching the girls about henna. Henna is a colorant used on the hair, the palms of the hands, the soles of the feet, and their nails. Tattooing was used largely in the Egyptian culture, and Nefetar had also learned this art. Their father had, however, restricted Nefetar to sharing this art only with the dancers and the musicians.

Michal came back to the present as she dreamed of her wedding with David. By now, she had started to apply some of her paints to her fair skin. It was only early in the day, and yet there were so many stars in her eyes as she dreamed of her betrothed. She positioned her mirror so that she could look into it better. Most people had to use a reflection of water as a mirror, but not her nor anyone in her family. It was so grand to be rich! She admired herself in the mirror; then she admired her beautiful hand-crafted mirror and the wealth that it spoke. It was a highly polished bronzed disc. Nefetar said that the circular shape, brightness, and reflective qualities suggested to the Egyptians the face of the sun and its life-giving powers. The motif or theme used to decorate the handles of her mirror was of the papyrus plant. This plant was a symbol of vitality; it is the head of Hathor, the goddess of fertility and beauty.

Michal's father had also purchased fine jewelry from merchants coming in from Egypt. They were also blessed with it from the visiting kings. Nefetar had thought of this as a final element of dress. Although most Israelites wore jewelry for personal adornment, Michal had enjoyed learning the amuletic purposes for wearing it. She often wondered if her father would approve of them learning these truths. Michal was so intrigued by the underlying purposes. She'd reminded herself that it was her father who had instructed Nefetar to teach them. Nefetar explained that the Egyptians wore jewelry to be protected from both tangible and intangible evil forces, which might invade the vulnerable points of the body. Michal, having laid her mirror down, ran her finger over her jewelry. She had it stored on a silver tray made with a motif of roses and vines. She reached gently and touched her neck straps of lotus flowers, jewels, and fine metals. She wondered what she should wear. Of course, she would be covered completely with a badeken, her veil. David, her chatan or groom, would be the one who would place the badeken upon her as reminiscent of Rebecca covering her face before marrying Isaac. She snickered as she recalled that old, old tale. How differently Jacob's story would have been had he been the one to place the badeken upon Leah. Poor Leah... How sad it must be to have a large built for a lady and to be as homely as the story tells. A gleam of pride shone in her eyes as she admired her delicate features; of course, this was her gift from God to show her worthiness.

Michal decided that it was time to get Nefetar working on her head ornament. It would have a lace material base with flat strips of materials tying live flowers to it. Again, David would only see this as he was putting her badeken on her head...and later removing it. Her thoughts paused for just a second at the thought of him removing it...the tender thoughts caused her heart to pulsate. As a last touch, Michal fingered her limb ornaments, her bracelets, and anklets. Which one should she wear? She had a full selection. Some were made from shells, and others were made from ivory or beads. Michal had only one made from fine inlaid metal and jewels because this was a new art that the merchants were just learning. It was time for her to get dressed and check on the wedding plans. She must not, however, see David. It was customary for the chatan and the kallah, or the bride, to not see each other one week before the wedding. Since it had been a few weeks, they would not need to wait to get married.

"Oh, why must it always be customs and traditions? Why must she be the one sitting and waiting for word on the wedding plans?"

Then a smile spread across her face as she realized she could request an audience with the king, and he could inform her of the plans.

*****

David couldn't believe it; two days had passed, and now, he was standing in front of Michal, placing her badeken of soft silk over her beautiful face. He wanted to run his finger down the side of her face but decided to wait just a little while longer until they were alone. Her skin looked so soft, and her hair was so long. Thoughts of running his hands through it caused sweat to break out on his forehead. It was not sweat of nerves but of anticipation...which caused a heightening in his cheek color. David liked how he stood a few inches taller than Michal. He found it easy to look down into her face. He knew that he would treasure this moment forever. They stood there staring into each other's eyes with smiles so big that their hearts grew more in love with each passing second. They would be having the chupah or the wedding ceremony outside under the stars because this was a sign of the blessing given by God to the patriarch Abraham that his children should be as the stars of the heavens. The day had been full of traditions and customs of a Jewish wedding, as they remembered the patriarchs of old.

David stood under the chupah. The chupah was a symbol of the home to be built and shared by him and Michal. He held on to the plain gold ring he was about to place on her finger. He looked over to his two witnesses, Abinadab and Shammah. They were both smiling. He caught the glimmer of teasing in Shammah's ear-to-ear smile. They found great joy in teasing their little brother. Then David heard the words coming from his mouth as though he was somewhere in the background watching the events unfolding, "Behold, you are betrothed unto me with this ring according to the laws of Moses and Israel." Then, he placed the ring upon her finger.

Both Michal and David could hardly wait for the wedding festivities to pass. There was the festive meal, and soon...yes, soon they would be alone.

\*\*\*\*\*

Michal was in awe as she stood in front of "her" David. It all seemed like a dream. Everything was happening in slow motion as her heart worked overtime to catch up. David was covering her with the badeken. She had saved this material especially for her wedding day. It was of a fine-spun silk material that had been brought in from the east. It had been bought a few months back, and as soon as she saw it, she knew that it was the perfect material for her. David looked into her eyes as if he was about to kiss her this very moment. Her mind filled in anticipation; would his kiss be hard and filled with passion or soft and tender, stirring every fiber of her being? She filled with anticipation as she imagined feeling his lips upon hers, and yes, she imagined both kisses. Her eyes glimmered in eagerness. She couldn't help to think about his eyes...it felt as though they were penetrating deep into her soul as if he could read her thoughts... Could he? She wanted so badly to feel his tender touch against her face. What would it be like to feel his fingers sliding gently down the side of her face or touching her hair, or feeling his lips caress her? Soon, her heart told her. Very soon.

Nefetar had placed the head ornament upon her just prior to seeing David. It was beautiful with all of the fresh flowers tied around it. Nefetar had served her well. She had made the selection of the fine scents' fun. Merab had joined them as they dressed Michal for her wedding. They had laughed and giggled together, just like young girls who were good friends. Nefetar helped her to eliminate her fragrances and scents down to two different choices; a soft scent to accent her innocence and a spicier scent creating a more mischievous and flirtatious feeling. Then she encouraged Michal to follow her heart and to wear the one that created the mood that she was feeling. Merab had given her advice on how to treat a husband and all the what-to-dos and what-not-to-dos in marriage. Michal teased her about having so much more experience than she. "Let's see... How many weeks now have you two been married?" It had been such a fun day already. She would treasure this day forever, and it was only the beginning. There was so much more to be shared as the hour approached when she and David could excuse themselves.

Her father had the cooks prepare the seuah, the festive meal. It was a feast of many of their favorite foods. There were many different types of meat to enjoy, and many various fruits and vegetables, and bread and pastries to numerous to name. The musicians played their finest music for hours. The dancing and the feasting would go on for most of the night.

David decided that before they would retire to Michal's chambers, they would go for a walk around the palace grounds. The music flowed from the courtyard for miles. The breeze was so gentle that David imagined God carrying their wedding music for miles as a way to encourage those out there who were still praying for the love of their life. As they enjoyed walking, David reached down and took Michal's hand. He could not help but notice how his hands felt rough and calloused compared to her soft, dainty hands. Both David and Michal felt a connection in their hearts...like they belonged together. In fact, everything felt right and good for them. It was an evening to cherish forever. David stopped before her and asked if she would mind if they prayed together and committed their marriage to Jehovah. It seemed like a bit of an unusual request to her, but of course, she agreed. Wasn't their marriage committed to Jehovah by the priest already? Although she did not fully understand his motivation, she enjoyed his tenderness. She smiled as she looked into David's eyes and nodded her head in agreement. She wanted to speak but was so enjoying this moment that she feared words might ruin the mood.

Soon he would be hers; she would have his full attention in another way. His eyes were so incredibly brown and so full of love. She knew that he loved his God. She could not help but feel slightly jealous as she hoped that he would love her just as much someday. She also loved Jehovah, but there was something different about the way he loved Jehovah. She had seen it from afar as she admired him.

David uttered a soft prayer before her and the Lord while holding her hands. As he said amen, he reached down and lowered his lips over hers. She had longed for this moment; she felt a flutter in her stomach that made her knees feel shaky.

David loved the feeling of her soft lips against his. He felt her trembling and wondered if it was the night air, or was she feeling the same excitement down in her soul that he was feeling?

The couple made their way back to Michal's bedroom chambers. A guard had been placed outside the room to secure their privacy. The servants had already prepared her room. There was a tray of fine wine and cheeses waiting for them to enjoy. The bed covers had been cleaned and turned down. A vase of fresh flowers sat on the window ledge. There was even a fresh vase of water with clean towels and linens for washing. The room had been cleaned and filled with candles and fragrant oils to create a romantic setting. As they locked her door, they both let out a sigh of relief at the same time. They turned and looked at each other and started to laugh. They had both been slightly nervous about this moment and found much of the tension and nervousness that they had been feeling left in that quick moment of laughter. Although they had spent some time talking and communicating over the past few years, it had only been light conversation. David complimented the work that the servants had done and how beautiful they had made her as his bride. Then, he commented on the servant's preparation. At that point, he noticed that they had even moved his things into one of the corners of her room.

He suggested that they sit on the edge of the bed and just talk about more personal matters for a while. As they did, they found that they were both relaxing and breathing easier. The moon was a full moon as if to reflect all of God's love upon them. It shined in her bedroom window, giving so much light that they would not have needed candles had they not desired the romantic atmosphere they created. They talked briefly about their families and his relationship with her brother, but that was all surface distractions so as to not move too quickly. Their youthful desires kept bringing them back to tender moments. He took his index finger and traced the shape of her finger; then, he traced her wrist. He brought her delicate hand up to his mouth and kissed it ever so softly.

Michal cherished each tender kiss. She found herself closing her eyes and just taking in the feeling of David's kisses, *Would this be what it would be like to be loved by David?* Although he was a man of war, he was a very kind and gentle man. The love she felt for him seemed to be exploding in her heart. The passion was building, and she found her breath catching with each tender touch and each wave of emotion.

His hands gently embraced her cheeks; then, slowly and deliberately, his right hand moved ever so gently down to her shoulders; then, he traced her slender neckline. His eyes could not help but travel down to her breasts, the curves of her firm rounded breasts...they were tiny, matching her delicate features, but that only intrigued him more.

David guided Michal to a standing position, and with his masculine fingers somewhat fumbling, he started to take her jewelry off her. Such tender movements ignited a passion within her that she had never known existed. He untied her girdle, allowing it to fall around her ankles; then, with all the grace within him, he proceeded to lift her kesut from off of her shoulders. He slid his hand under her neckline, lifting her long flowing hair from off the back of her neck. He kissed and caressed her neck and her shoulders. So as to not scare her, although she did not look like she feared what was to come, he took his time, caressing her beautiful, youthful skin. Oh, she was as beautiful as he had imagined her to be. Her skin glowed with radiance. She smelled so good; was that myrrh that he smelled? It was a soft fragrance, not overpowering like some girls wear. Until now, she let him do all the leading, just taking in his caresses. She proceeded to undress him next. Now her hands were enfolding and sculpting his body as he was hers. As her hand slid down his bare back and down to his thighs, he felt his own passion was growing stronger and stronger. Suddenly their kisses were eager and full of passion. Suddenly they could not get enough of each other's lips... Suddenly they fell on her bed... Suddenly... And he heard her ever so softly whisper, "Oh David, I have dreamed of this moment with you..."

# Chapter 14

*"Then I will ever sing in praise of your name and fulfill my vows day after day" (Psalm 61:8, NIV).*

A few weeks had passed since Michal and David's wedding. They had been the talk of the palace. There seemed to be an air of youthful and carefree happiness that lingered in the sky. It seemed as if there was an increase of new couples courting as if the gift of love was catchy. The summer flowers were in full bloom, and so were the hearts. Newly married men were granted time off from war to consecrate their marriage, and although David had not intended to take more than a couple of weeks off, the time had passed rather quickly, totaling up to four weeks since he had been to war.

For David, it had been an incredible time. Most of their time was spent just with the two of them. They had so completely enjoyed each other's presence that they spent the time learning more about each other. They went for long walks daily. One day they had gone for a walk even though the sky threatened to rain. While they were out, it started to downpour; they were drenched. Instead of hurrying back to the house to get dry, they decided to enjoy the warm summer rain. It was something that he had not done since his shepherding days, but then those days did not compare to walking hand and hand with his new bride.

They talked mostly about their childhoods and how differently they had been brought up. David shared his strong faith in Jehovah God. It seemed to David that Michal would have to be discipled to learn of the true deep relationship that he experienced with Jehovah. He hoped in time that she would also share his love and admiration for the Lord Jehovah.

One of their favorite things to do was to go riding in the morning hours. It would get so warm during the day that they chose to ride their horses in the early hours. He rode Bedouin while she rode her stallion named Jewel. He'd inquired as to the reason behind her horse's name. She hesitated before answering but then went on to explain. She said that the reason the Egyptians wore lots of jewelry was not only for beauty purposes but to protect them from harm from dangerous creatures. It protected them from unseen evil forces that might enter the vulnerable points of the body. When he asked where she had learned that, she said from the merchants. David sought out ancient text to teach her that God protects us and that by following Him, we have a shield of protection, a covering that will protect us from all evil. Michal listened, but it was obvious to him that she did not have a clear understanding of the words he spoke.

They enjoyed a few dinners with Merab and Adriel, including a couple of picnics. They shared in Merab and Adriel's joy when they announced that Merab was in a "mothering way." However, these good times were coming to an end. God had started to speak words of warning to David, so he knew things would soon be changing. But at least, they had this time together before the realities of life set back upon them.

*****

Michal loved being married. She treasured their private times together. She had been raised well and knew that a woman must control her emotions and not show them around others. However, it seemed like an impossible task. How could you be quiet when everything within you knew that the gods of the heavens were blessing you? It was so exciting that it seemed like the earth itself was in full celebration with them. The grass was greener; the flowers were blooming; the trees were bringing forth their fruit. The young ones were being born to women and animals alike. All of nature seemed to be shouting with joy at their union. It had been a glorious last few weeks. It would have been perfect if it weren't for David taking off alone daily to pray to his God. When would he see that there doesn't have to be just one god? Oh well...she would just have to teach him the error of his ways. But it had been a good last few weeks...walks, talks, picnics, and time with Merab and Adrial. Oh, and how exciting that she was with child! She would make a good mother with all of her refined and gentle ways. The thought crossed her mind that maybe it was being married that she loved as much as David. But then she dismissed the idea because... Weren't they the same?

She treasured the day that they got caught out in the rain. That had been such a fun and carefree time. Her parents would not agree to such nonsense, but it had been a special moment for her. Yes, everything about David was perfect, or it would be if he could just concentrate a little more on her and a little less on praying or personal time. Oh well, things can't be perfect, can they? She loved the horse riding and remembered back to the day that he asked about Jewel's name. She knew that she had deceived him slightly by not telling him where she learned about the Egyptian ways, but she did not want him to find fault with Nefetar. She enjoyed learning about other cultures. It was just insight for her, and not like she worshipped their gods, although she was not sure that would be a wrong thing. Why did there have to be just one god? After all, if one god could protect you, couldn't two or three gods give you even more protection? She knew that David would soon be returning to war. Her father had been suggesting that it was time. That meant that David would be leaving her soon.

\*\*\*\*\*

As David returned to war, she worked on preparing a home for them. She could not help but flash her ring around when she was shopping for materials or merchandise to build their own home. She imagined her and David building their own palace behind her father's or adjacent to her father's. She dreamed of what it would be like to have their children. She would most certainly have a son. Maybe she would even have lots of sons, although the thought did make her a little nauseated. But it would make her the true envy of all the women in Israel. Her head swelled with pride as she thought about it. Not only would she be the king's daughter, but she would also be David's wife and then, to be blessed by God to have a house full of sons! Truly she knew that all women would envy her and desire her position.

Then her thoughts traveled back to holding their first-born son in her arms. He would grow up strong and courageous, just like his father. Who knows, there might even be a Goliath that he would kill to earn his own claim to fame. But then, she hoped that her son would never have to know war as his father had, although it did seem to be the way of men. She dreamed of nights around the fireplace while David played his harp. Then with a slight ping of jealousy, she remembered that David would retrieve in private for a while every evening. He said that he was praying, but how could anyone pray that much! Oh well, he probably is praying. Again, she felt a slight irritation at the love David felt for his God. She loved David. She would have to work just a little harder to win his full love. She could do it, and she was up to the challenge.

*****

Not much time had passed before the challenges started coming in again from the Philistine commanders. It seemed that their hearts were so totally hardened that they would never learn. They continued to go out to battle against the Israelites. Each time that they did, David was there to meet them. His success was even more than he could imagine. God protected his men and gave them great success. David listened to God and walked in His wisdom, something that the rest of Saul's officers had not yet learned. He did not preach to the men but would share with them when they would ask what his secrets were for so much success. His name became well known throughout the entire region.

During the weeks prior to David returning to war, the king stayed away from them. It made him sick to see what was happening to his daughter. It also caused him to become more fearful of David. He panicked as he realized God was with David. Everything that David did or put his hands to was blessed. Now, his daughter looked at David with that look in her eyes that spoke volumes of her love and desire for him. As the fear of David deepened within King Saul, he deemed that David was his enemy and would be for the rest of his days. This revelation caused the hatred and bitterness to become even stronger within him. It stirred up the evil spirits, and now, there was no "shepherd boy" to play his harp to quiet them. The results could only get worse.

# Chapter 15

*"The salvation of the righteous comes from the LORD; he is their stronghold in time of trouble"* (Psalm 37:39, NIV).

King Saul summoned Jonathan and all his servants to come to him. The king had prepared for this meeting by making up a list of charges against his new son-in-law. Once everyone was in attendance, King Saul handed the scroll to one of his servants and requested him to open the scroll and read the charges. Once the charges were read, King Saul proceeded to tell them of how David had broken his allegiance with him. He called David an outlaw and a coward, using the people of the land to build his popularity. He said that all of David's successes were devised as part of his plan to take over the kingdom, his kingdom. He referred to David's steps of popularity as his steps to stealing the throne from the line of King Saul. He looked directly at Jonathan and emphasized that David was out to take over the kingdom and desired to be the next king, emphasizing again that it was Jonathan's inheritance to the throne that David was coveting. Therefore, it was imperative that David be killed. He must be stopped from all of his treacherous ways.

Jonathan looked around the room at the servants and guards. He was filled with a very grievous sadness. It surprised him to see how many of the servants supported the king's position against David. They looked like they were getting pumped up and ready to go to war against a true enemy, like the Philistines. Some of the servants raised their voices in victory to express their hostility toward David. There were head nods in favor of the king's words. It all saddened Jonathan very much. Some of the men were hard to read. Their expressions did not reveal the intents of their hearts. He could not tell by their faces whether they agreed or disagreed with the king. Couldn't they understand David's heart? David was a man of integrity. However, there was one exception and one man he could clearly read. Jonathan had never trusted Doeg, and lately, it seemed as though he was always shadowing his father. There seemed to be a deceptive grin on his face. Jonathan never cared for the guy, and as a kid growing up, he'd get chills whenever the man came around. He stood a few inches shorter than Saul. He had the dark hair and features of the Edomites. He was his father's chief herdsman. Doeg was also on the hefty side, as though food was his main focus in life. He was a relative of his father's, but it never seemed to Jonathan as though he had his father's best interest in mind. *Did this line of thinking come from him?* Jonathan wondered. Either way, Jonathan loved David and delighted in everything about him. He would have to seek David out and tell him what had happened here today. There would be no time to spare either.

As the meeting ended, Jonathan went out immediately to find David. As he walked along the palace halls, he thought of all of the ways he delighted in David. He loved the way he was so devoted to the God of Abraham and Isaac. He loved David's devotion to others. He delighted in how David found happiness in everything that happened and how he appreciated the beauty of each day. He remembered how David made killing Goliath look so simple and then gave all of the credit to God. Why was this happening now? David and Michal were just finding their own happiness. He was sure that the evil spirits were stirred up within his father again. However, this time there were too many people lining up to come against David. He must find him and warn him.

After searching the palace, Jonathan found David in the armory sharpening his sword and knife. David knew that it was time to return to war. Jonathan came up alongside David and placed his hand gently on his back shoulder, "How's it going, Brother?" David smiled and looked up at him, answering, "It would be hard for things to be better..." His smile started to fade as he added, "God has been showing me that there is change in the air. He has been warning me of danger." Jonathan could not believe it! God had been warning David of the very thing he had come to speak to him about. Was there no end to the power of Jehovah! Seeing the puzzled expression on Jonathan's face, David asked him what was going on. Jonathan relaxed slightly and told David that he had come to warn him of danger, but it seemed that God had already done that for him. Jonathan asked if they could go for a walk. He did not want any of the king's servants to hear what he had to share with him. So David cleaned off his sword and put it away. Together, they left the armory. They headed off toward the acreage at the back of the palace grounds. This was a place where they had spent much time together practicing shooting arrows. David had taught Jonathan the art of slinging, although he was not nearly as good as David. They laughed together and enjoyed precious moments of friendship. Jonathan replied with laughter and bantering in his voice, "I guess it is a good thing then that they didn't have me fight Goliath. With my slinging skills, we would be serving the Philistines right now." They laughed and took pride in each other's abilities. Jonathan teased David by adding that he would never be as good at the javelin as he was. As quickly as the pleasant moments flooded Jonathan's mind, they slid back into his memory as moments from yesterday. He had much more pressing things to deal with right now. The pleasant times were about to end, and Jonathan knew it all too well.

"David, my father called a meeting this morning. I don't know how to say this, but my father is looking for a chance to kill you. Be on your guard tomorrow morning, go into hiding and stay there. I will go out and stand with my father in the field where you are. I'll speak to him about you and tell you what I find out."

It caused deep sorrow in David's heart. Logically, he knew what was happening in King Saul, but the convictions of his heart were very strong; he had done nothing wrong. He had always been loyal to his king. He had spent hours praying and playing his harp for King Saul. He agreed to Jonathan's plan. Then, David asked him to relay a message to Michal that he would not be coming in tonight, "Please make an excuse that I am out visiting soldiers and seeing what the current status is."

\*\*\*\*\*

The following morning, Jonathan went walking with his father, leading him to the field just as he and David had discussed. They were both so tall and full of stature. Their broad shoulders were almost of equal height as they strolled out across the fields. Jonathan's curly black hair fell in ringlets as it flowed around his shoulders. It seemed that the longer it grew, the shorter it got. The curls seemed to tighten more with each inch of length. King Saul's hair now had many hints of gray speckled throughout it. As they walked together, King Saul couldn't help but reflect back on the many walks he and his son had taken over the years. When Jonathan was young, this was a favorite tradition of theirs. Sometimes they would see a single doe or buck feeding. If they were quiet enough, occasionally, they would see a whole herd of deer feeding at the back of a field. The sudden flood of memories blessed his heart. Yes, Jonathan would be the next king. It was his responsibility to make sure that would happen.

Jonathan knew the task that was ahead of him. So many times lately, his father had been irrational, just as when he issued the order to have David killed. He wasn't worried, though. Jonathan had spent most of the night in prayer, asking God to soften his father's heart. The conviction of his own heart was so strong concerning David that he knew he must be direct and yet careful in his approach to his father. It was so obvious to Jonathan that his father was wrong. His thoughts then shifted to the days when he had been a council for his father. They had been very close back during the days of his father's early kingship. Of course, King Saul sought the council of the prophet and the council of his military leaders. But he would seek out Jonathan often when something was troubling him. Together, they would discuss the matter on a long walk. During those talks, Jonathan's father would talk to him and listen to what he had to say. Perhaps today would be like that. Perhaps God had heard his prayers during the night and was preparing the king's heart to listen to him. Maybe this would be one of those father and son moments once again.

They spent a few minutes catching up on the new cook from Egypt and discussing what they thought of the new herbs he was using. Then, they talked about the Philistines and how they were building up for war again. As their conversation paused from small talk, Jonathan uttered a silent prayer asking the God of Abraham to help him speak the words that were in his heart. As he opened his mouth, it was almost as if God was giving him the words to speak. Jonathan found himself listing the many accounts of David. As he named each one, he could see the events unfolding in his mind.

He said, "Please, Father, do not do any wrong to David; he has not wronged you, and what he has done has benefited you greatly. He took his life in his hands when he killed the Philistine."

Jonathan heard the Philistine's words ringing out in challenge once again. Then he saw David, just a young shepherd boy standing on top of the giant swinging his head in the air in victory.

"The Lord won a great victory for all Israel, and you saw it and were glad. Why then would you do wrong to an innocent man like David by killing him for no reason?"

Saul listened to his son and was moved by his son's compassion for David. So he took an oath, "As surely as the Lord lives, David will not be put to death."

Yes, God prepared his father's heart, and once again, things would be right in the kingdom for all of them. He uttered a silent prayer of thanks to God.

As quickly as he could get away from his father, Jonathan found David and told him the whole conversation. Smiling from ear to ear, Jonathan was full of delight at the change of heart his father had expressed. He took David to King Saul, and for the moment, David was restored to a place of honor before the king. For the moment, he found his position again as Michal's husband, as Jonathan's brother-in-law, and as King Saul's son-in-law.

King Saul could not help but feel lighter in his heart. He had just sworn an oath to his son Jonathan. Feeling peace with his new decision not to have David killed, he returned to the palace to spread the word to the guards. He thought about all the things that his son had said. He thought of all the times David had played his harp for him, the victory with Goliath, and how he was sure the people would see him as the greatest king they could have. He also thought of the many times that David had gone out in war for him. Yes, God's hand was upon him, but he was still the king, and that made him the hero of the hour. No matter what David did, he still worked for the king. Because of Jonathan's love for David, and as an afterthought, Michal's love for him, he agreed not to have David hurt. He just hoped that he would not live to regret this decision.

\*\*\*\*\*

Although David was happy about the change, he also knew that God had spoken very clearly of the upcoming danger. He had to guard his heart and listen to the voice of God. Only then would he be really able to relax and to enjoy the moment.

\*\*\*\*\*

Within just a few weeks, David was headed out to war against the Philistines. He never ceased to be amazed over how the Philistines were certain that they could and would defeat the Israelites. Once again, he and his men went out with the hand of Jehovah upon them. David was getting tired of these little battles, though, so being filled with the confidence of God, he and his men attacked the Philistines with such fury that the Philistines all ran away. This brought much laughter and excitement to the men. They were learning about the power of Jehovah through David. They were starting to feel Jehovah's supernatural leading. The men were so exhilarated that David could not stop smiling! Their joy and excitement showed as they sang songs of praise all the way back to town. David could not help but savor the moment. His greatest joy was in seeing others learn to draw their strength and victory from God.

# Chapter 16

*"Every morning I will put to silence all the wicked in the land; I will cut off every evildoer from the city of the LORD"* (Psalm 101:8, NIV).

A few more weeks passed before David felt God's warning strong in his heart again. It did not cause fear in his heart because he was totally confident that God's plan would be done in his life. In fact, he almost felt a little smug about the danger. He had God's assurance that God had a plan for him. He was called to be the next king, and he was still a long way from that petition. Therefore, he had an added confidence that he would live a long life. However, he knew to heed God's warnings and to keep a watchful eye. Since King Saul was his most obvious enemy, David would appear to be relaxing when in his presence, but he would keep one eye always focused on his enemy. There were a few others in the king's palace that David didn't trust. One key person was a man named Doeg. Doeg was actually the head herdsman for King Saul. So why did he always seem to shadow the king? Maybe he should ask Jonathan his opinion of this man.

This morning he had been summoned by King Saul to come and to play his harp for him. The evil spirits were tormenting him once again. This was never a good sign. He felt a little smile cross his lips as he recalled how just a few months back, he found himself dodging for his life as a spear came swiftly toward his head. He wondered if today would be a repeat of that scene, regardless of his confidence in God's protection.

He walked into the king's chambers and started to play soft, gentle worship sounds. These often worked the best. He felt his heart quicken just a bit when he saw the king pick up his javelin and start to play with it. If he were a betting man, he would have had fun placing bets as to what was going to happen next. However, he was not a betting man, and this was not a funny situation. David never questioned God's ability to totally surround him with His protective shield. With one eye, David carefully watched the movements of King Saul's hands. After a few minutes of playing the harp, as if it were all in slow motion, King Saul hurled his spear hard and fast at David. David was sure that if it had not been for God's protection, he would be a wall ornament this very moment. Just as quickly, David dodged once again for the doorway and escaped into the palace. Glancing quickly, he saw the spear stuck in the wall, right where he had been sitting.

King Saul was up stomping around the room before David had even fled out of the doorway. He was cursing and shouting at the God of Abraham. Anger seethed from his lips and from his heart. He would never forgive Samuel the prophet for taking away God's blessings from his life. He was almost spitting each word as he relived how he had thrown the spear perfectly. It should be in David's head this very moment. What was it going to take to be rid of him?

\*\*\*\*\*

David was so thankful to God for His protection. Although his blood was pumping, he felt jubilant as he thought of God's protection. A smile grew on his face as he ran as far and as fast as he could from King Saul. It had been King Saul's intention to kill him this very day. No matter how many times King Saul promised not to kill him, David knew he could never trust him. Yes, it was time to leave. He had to get away...far, far away. But he had to go and see Michal first. She was his wife, and she would be hurt if he just disappeared. He stayed away quietly until the sun had set. Then he quickly found his way to his house. Michal was in their room waiting for him. She had already heard the news as it spread through the palace. A reward had already been posted for the one who killed David. Her heart was breaking as she took David into her arms. She knew that it was no longer safe for him to stay by her side at the palace. She also knew that if she helped him, she was putting her own life in danger. David was being charged with treason against the king. If she assisted him, she could also suffer the predetermined fate of beheading. As angry as the king was over David escaping, he was bound to have her arrested and killed. She determined that it was a chance she'd have to take. She loved David and could not allow her father to hurt him. She hoped that she still knew her father, and since he was still her father, she could sweet-talk him.

Michal was not sure how long they would be apart, but she pledged her love to him always. Michal promised to be his ears and eyes to know when it was safe to return to the palace. She had her own servants. She would find a way to get information to him. They discussed the few servants that they thought they could both trust. Then, they discussed all of the uncertainties of their future.

David talked about leaving early in the morning; however, Michal warned him that it would not be safe, "David, if you do not leave tonight, you will most certainly be dead by the morning." David felt as though God was speaking to him through her words.

Knowing that she was correct, he packed a few things that he would need. Michal helped him to climb out through a window and escape into the night. Then, she looked around the room, trying to decide what to do next. Should she just go to sleep and wait until morning? She was confident that the king's guards would be knocking at her door soon. As she looked around her room, her eyes rested upon the wooden teraphim. The teraphim was a family idol. This image was thought to bring about healing. Although they came in different sizes and shapes, this one was almost the size of a man. It had been given to her as a wedding gift from Nefetar and some of the other Egyptian servants. Nefetar knew how she was interested in their ways and thought she would enjoy it. It would give her comfort and healing, as she needed it.

Michal took the teraphim and placed it in her bed, where David would normally sleep. She wrapped it in a blanket and placed it in a sleeping position, bringing the blankets up slightly over his head or the teraphim's head. Then, being wise to the ways of deception, she took a cushion of goat's hair and placed it where David's head would be. This might not buy him much time, but it should give him a little time to escape and to get clear of the palace.

*****

Jonathan talked his father into waiting until morning to launch a full-scale attack against David. He pleaded for him to give Michal and David this one last night. As morning approached, the troops were sent in to arrest David. The soldiers knocked loudly on her door. She casually strolled to the door as if she had not a care in the world. Although the soldiers wanted to push their way inside the room, they showed restraint. They told her that they were there for David.

Her eyes glanced over toward the bedroom as though she was looking in David's direction. Giving her best regretful look to the soldier, she told them that David had awakened very sick that morning. He was still in bed and too sick to get up. Every time that he tried, he found himself running to the window. Some of the men appeared squeamish at this suggestion and turned away from her as if this action would put time and space between this illness and themselves.

The soldiers reported back to King Saul. His fury was increasing as he became frustrated with their incompetence. How much wisdom did it take to know what to do next! His cheeks turned bright red as his blood pressure started to rise. He was losing patience with these men. His voice came out in a loud and clear command as he shouted, "Then bring him to me in his bed..." pausing only long enough to catch another breath of air, he belted out, "...so I can kill him as he lies there!"

Fearing for their lives, the soldiers quickly exited the king's room and hurried down the hall to David and Michal's house.

Michal heard the soldiers approaching, so she pulled out her best acting skills and pretended to be a man vomiting. Grunting from deep inside her, she made the awful, gut-wrenching sounds that accompany vomiting. She knew that it was not ladylike and wanted to laugh as she imagined their faces. She might have laughed if not for the seriousness of the situation. Her time of deceiving them was running out. They would quickly know that David was not here. She was thankful that she did not know where David had fled. She had done her part; it would quickly be up to David's God to protect him. She knew that she could not stall them much longer.

As the soldiers pounded upon the door, they threatened to bust the door down if she did not open it at once! She paused to catch her breath, making sure that her voice would sound genuine and sincere. She told them that she had to help David get back to bed and she would be right there.

She wanted to laugh as she opened the door. Some of the soldiers had their hands over their mouths, and they looked rather green. She could tell that her acting skills had worked. Allowing only a worried look to cross her brows, she moved slowly and carefully, emphasizing the sickness in the room. Michal hushed them and pleaded with them to keep the noise down. Then in a slightly irritated voice, she asked them what was going on and then threatened to report all of them to the king, her father.

Assuring her that they were following the king's orders, the soldiers surrounded the bed. Most of them were being careful not to get too close to David. They reached down to lift up David and quickly discovered the teraphim and the camel's hair. A few soldiers appeared to sigh with relief, while a couple appeared to be stifling a laugh. A couple of men were looking around the room for David. Giving a very displeasing look at Michal, the soldiers in charge stormed out the door. They reported everything back to King Saul.

Michal felt her knees shaking slightly as she stood before her father. She was rather sure of herself that she could talk her way out of anything, but still...standing before her father as the king was never fun. Saul's look was strong and very angry. She would have to choose her words carefully. It was getting harder and harder to reason with this man. She loved her father, but wasn't it right for her to love her husband more?

King Saul could not help but feel betrayed by Michal. She had been his favorite daughter. He let her have her way as often as he could. He always bought her the finest jewelry and fabrics, and here she was protecting David...the very person who needed to die. Wasn't it obvious to everyone else that David coveted the throne? Couldn't they see the truth with clarity as he could? What was wrong with his children? At least Merab had not been drawn into this situation. Determined that his daughter was wrong, shame and reproach accompanied his words, "Why have you tricked me and let my enemy escape?"

Michal clouded up as if she was going to cry, feeling her father's anger. How could he be so mean to David...to *her* David? There was nothing else to say to her father but the truth. "I had to..." as she paused, she thought quickly of how to get out of this mess, "...he threatened to kill me if I didn't help him." The king's face softened at the turn of events. Perhaps his daughter was still loyal to him. Perhaps she had acted out of fear from David.

His eyes softened slightly, and he opened his mouth to speak, "Then this only confirms what I already believe to be true. David must die!"

# Chapter 17

*"...my God on whom I can rely. God will go before me and*
*will let me gloat over those who slander me"*
*(Psalm 59:10, NIV).*

David was walking northeast into the morning sun. The
sunrise was beautiful. Under other circumstances, it would be
nice to share it with Michal... *My beautiful Michal, how long will it*
*be until I see you again?*

When he climbed out the bedroom window, all he could think
of was to get away as quickly as he could. David was running and
almost out of town before he realized that he didn't know where
to go. As quickly as the prayer was on his lips, Samuel came
to his mind. Panic struck David as he realized that he would
endanger his family if he went near them. The old prophet was
the one who got him in this mess; maybe he would have an
answer from Jehovah. This was now another attack from the
king. If God wanted him to be the next king, perhaps he could
think of a better plan than the one he now had. Obviously, he
was not going to walk into the kingship through marriage. No,
it would take a supernatural intervention from God. Normally,
David found himself confident and encouraged, but he felt

tired and weary from all of the weeks of being on his guard and watching King Saul. How long had it been since he saw the old prophet? Had it only been less than two years?

His mind saw the old prophet, his long grey beard, and his loving face. His hair was long and almost as white as snow as it flowed down his back. Such authority flowed from this man of God.

*Samuel talks to God, and maybe God has given him a word for me. Regardless, maybe he can protect me. I know Saul is going to send men after me this time. Such hatred in his eyes...how does a man like that become king?*

Many thoughts whirled around in David's head, just like the sands in the desert picked up by the strong southern winds. David felt tired and like he could just lie down on the ground and fall asleep. He had been traveling most of the night. David could tell that he was getting closer to Ramah with each step he took. His steps grew heavy as he continued walking. Ramah was on top of a hill. The constant uphill grade was wearing on him. He knew he was getting close now because Ramah consisted of a cluster of separate dwellings. Ramah was where Samuel's parents had lived, and as an adult, he returned to his home area. The houses were getting more frequent, and he started to see olive trees and various other crops. The olive trees brought back memories of home. He hoped his family was fine; he missed them very much. Sometimes, David could not help to miss the "simple" life of being a shepherd.

The dew on the morning leaves turned his thoughts to Michal. He could see her hair draped around her on the pillow as a sea of endless curls. David felt a slight bit guilty for not being concerned for her safety. However, he had seen Michal manipulate her father on many occasions and was certain that she would come out on top in this situation too.

*****

It was good to see the old prophet again. David's heart embraced the peace that surrounded Samuel. David knew this peace; it was the constant indwelling in the presence of God. It reminded him of when he was a young lad. He'd run to his mother's arms for comfort; it was a protective comfort, one that could only really come from God Himself. When David saw Samuel, he started to tell him what was going on. He didn't stop talking until he had told him all that King Saul had done. It felt good to actually complain to someone about all he had been enduring. Samuel led David up to Naioth; Naioth is what he called his home. David still had many questions to ask the prophet, but now he had some assurance that God would direct his every footstep.

*****

Over the next few weeks, David stayed at Naioth with Samuel. On the walks around Palestine, Samuel took time to tell him about the history of the city. He told how Naioth had become known as a prophetical college town and how he was the one who started the school. The men who came were often referred to as "sons of the prophet." Samuel laughed about all the sons he had. David found comfort in listening to the old man's words; it made him forget his own situation for a few minutes while he listened to someone else's life's story. Each morning David took time to seek God's direction for his life. He prayed for King Saul, although this felt a little tough at first. He prayed for Michal and, most of all, his friend Jonathan. He missed Jonathan the most. He was a true friend—someone David would always cherish.

*****

The wind had picked up as a storm moved in. The sand was swirling around Saul and his men, making it hard to breathe. The sun was hidden behind a thick layer of clouds, causing the midday sky to be as dark as the evening dusk. King Saul hardly noticed the storm surrounding him and his men due to the storm that was raging inside him. The events of the past few days played over and over in his mind, similar to when the people practiced for the theater performance.

Upon hearing that David and Samuel were together, King Saul almost went mad with jealousy and hatred. He ordered a group of soldiers to bring David back. The next day, he received word that when his men entered and saw the prophets prophesying and Samuel as the one leading them, the Spirit of God came upon them too, and they started prophesying.

Although he found this incredibly disturbing, Saul sent a second group of soldiers to bring David back. The following day he received the same report as before. So he sent up a third group, figuring this could not possibly happen a third time. When word came back that now a third group of his men had

THE RISE OF A KING

fallen under their influence, Saul decided that his men were just too weak for the job. He now knew that he'd have to go himself and show his men what he expected of them. The great cistern at Secu lay approximately halfway between Gibeah and Ramah. When King Saul arrived there, he asked where David and Samuel were. Upon being told Naioth at Ramah, he gave the command for his men to keep going. The Spirit of God came upon King Saul without a moment's notice, and he started prophesying. He continued prophesying, not just for the journey to Naioth, but for an additional twenty-four hours! He wouldn't have believed what his men reported to him about stripping off his robe of royalty if it were not how he found himself when he came too. It angered the king greatly to find that he stayed in a naked state during the entire process.

With each step his horse took, he felt Samuel and David's betrayal and their mockery. Anger churned and built within him as he thought of how God stepped in and delivered David every time.

The king's thoughts tortured him, *Who is this David anyways? Does he really think he can just step in and take everything from me?* Saul vowed that David would pay with his life! His hatred thickened, allowing confusion and strife its full place in the King's heart. He had already heard the rumor that was circulating, "Is Saul also among the prophets?" What atrocities, how could they ever think he'd want to be!

\*\*\*\*\*

Relief came upon David when he realized that Saul's men couldn't capture him. Three sets of men came for him, and all three had started prophesying when they entered the prophet's presence. They were telling details of each other's lives to one another. Sometimes they had a word in the future as the Spirit of God spoke through them.

David found it interesting when one of Saul's men came up to him and prophesied that King Saul was on his way and that he would not be able to touch him. The words he spoke sounded like they were from God Himself, "Watch and see what I do..."

Not knowing where exactly to go, David returned to Gibeah and found Jonathan. Much of the frustration of the past few weeks flowed from David as he started to tell Jonathan everything that had happened. Jonathan was his closest friend, and yet David could hear his words as he expressed his anger and hurt.

"What have I done? What is my crime? How have I wronged your father that he is trying to take my life?"

Jonathan emphatically replied, "Never! You are not going to die! Look, my father doesn't do anything, great or small, without confiding in me. Why would he hide this from me? It's not so!"

Jonathan couldn't believe his father intended harm to his best friend. David had to be exaggerating the severity of the situation... He had to be. Besides, David knew how sick his father had been...

So determined was David in what he was sharing that he made an oath with Jonathan, "Your father knows very well that I have found favor in your eyes, and he has said to himself, 'Jonathan must not know this, or he will be grieved.' Yet as surely as the Lord lives and you live, there is only a step between me and death."

Seeing David's determination, Jonathan said, "Whatever you want me to do, I'll do for you."

Although David wasn't really watching anything, his eyes focused on a tiny sparrow pecking at the ground while looking for a meal. He found himself shuffling the toe of his sandal into the sand, making a small mound while he gave the matter some thought. He had to determine Saul's intentions. As a plan started unfolding in David's mind, he said, "Look, tomorrow is the New Moon festival, and I am supposed to dine with the king, but let me go and hide in the field until the evening after tomorrow. If your father misses me at all, tell him, 'David earnestly asked my permission to hurry to Bethlehem, his hometown, because an annual sacrifice is being made there for his whole clan.' If he says, 'Very well,' then I am safe, but if he loses his temper, you can be certain he is determined to harm me!"

David knew the New Moon was a festival day, and the king would observe it by burnt offerings and sacrifices, as well as banquets. It was a public time before the people, and those who normally dined at the king's table were expected to be there; to not attend was a major insult to the king!

David's words had been directed to Jonathan concerning his father, but now he paused, and for a brief second, he looked down to the mound he had made and moved it with the toe of his sandal. Then, very seriously, he looked at Jonathan, "As for you, please show kindness to your servant, for you have brought me into a covenant with you before the Lord. If I am guilty, then kill me yourself! Why hand me over to your father?"

Jonathan's cheeks turned red as anger rose up in him at the very idea. "Never! If I had the slightest thought that my father was determined to harm you, I'd tell you!"

David wasn't trying to offend his best friend, but he had to make sure that Jonathan was being completely truthful. Dread of anticipation caused David to look deep into Jonathan's eyes as he asked, "Who will tell me if your father answers harshly?"

"Come," Jonathan said, "let's go out into the field."

David knew what field he was talking about because it was the field that they had set up for archery. They loved practicing and honing their talent as a sport as much as a skill. They had practiced many times over the past couple of years. David found a smile coming to his face as he remembered some of their competitions between them, "The one who wins gets to serve the other for the evening..."

They had a special bond between them that they were unable to explain to anyone else.

Upon reaching the field, Jonathan turned to David and said, "By the Lord, the God of Israel, I will surely find out my father's intentions by this time tomorrow. If he is favorably toward you, I will send you word and let you know. But if my father is intent on harming you, may the Lord deal with me, be it ever so severely, if I do not let you know and send you away safely. May the Lord be with you as he has been with my father. But show me unfailing kindness like that of the Lord as long as I live so that I may not be killed and do not ever cut off your kindness from my family...not even when the Lord has cut off every one of David's enemies from the face of the earth." His father's words had begun to sink in and make sense to Jonathan, and now he had no doubt that David would be Israel's next king. God had made it as real to his own heart as he had to David's, but he believed that they would always work side by side to rule the kingdom. Jonathan thought of his children and their future generations to come and hoped that God would keep them all safe.

So Jonathan made a covenant with the house of David, saying, "May the Lord call David's enemies to account."

Then, Jonathan had David reaffirm his oath out of love for him because he loved him more than himself.

# Chapter 18

*"Help me, LORD my God; save me according to your unfailing love" (Psalm 109:26, NIV).*

It seemed like months had passed since David had last seen Jonathan. So much had happened since the New Moon festival. David couldn't help but relive much of the past few weeks. The fire kept him warm as he looked around at his new home...a cave. Somehow, he didn't feel as though he was on any fast-track to kingship. Here he was, anointed to be king, and he was sleeping and living in a cave. Determined to not look at the circumstances, David would encourage his heart by communicating with God. He wrote poems to God. He sang praises to God. Sometimes, he complained about his enemies in the poems. He spoke, almost in a prophetic way, of how God would deliver him from his enemies. These poems nourished his soul like food nourished his body. These times kept David from giving in to the discouragement that threatened to swallow him alive. As he thought of King Saul, words filled his heart to sing.

Give ear to my words O Lord, consider my sighing. Listen to my cry for help, my King, and my God, for to you I pray. In the morning, O Lord, you hear my voice; in the morning I lay my requests before you and wait in expectation.

Not a word from their mouth can be trusted; their heart is filled with destruction. Their throat is an open grave... But let all who take refuge in you be glad; let them sing for joy. Spread your protection over them, that those who love your name may rejoice in you. For surely, O Lord, you bless the righteous; you surround them with your favor as with a shield.[5]

Deliver me from my enemies, O my God; protect me from those who rise up against me... Oh my strength, I watch for you; you, O God, are my fortress, my God. God in his steadfast love will meet me; God will let me look in triumph on my enemies. ...Then it shall be known to the ends of the earth that God rules over Jacob.[6]

The righteous cry out and the Lord hears them; he delivers them from all their troubles. The Lord is near to the brokenhearted and saves those who are crushed in spirit...the Lord redeems his servants; no one will be condemned who takes refuge in him.[7]

David recalled the last time he'd seen Jonathan while he lay there watching the firelight dancing on the ceiling of the cave. It was the second day into the New Moon festival. Just as they agreed, Jonathan and a young lad came out to the field to shoot arrows. David waited anxiously in anticipation of which way he'd shoot the arrow. Jonathan ordered the boy to "Run and find the arrows I shoot." Then he hollered, "Isn't the arrow beyond you?" Jonathan paused, then continued, "Hurry! Go quickly! Don't stop!" The boy picked up the arrow and returned to Jonathan. Handing his weapons to the boy, he said, "Go, carry these to town."

Jonathan had not told the boy anything about what was really going on. Once the boy was out of sight, David got up from the south side of a large rock. He bowed down before Jonathan three times with his face to the ground. David was presenting himself as a servant rather than as a friend. Jonathan reached down, and with his strong hands, he reached for David's arms and lifted him up until they both were standing upright. They both wept as Jonathan shared the events that had led them to this moment. Tears streamed down both of their faces as they kissed each other goodbye. It was a sad moment in each man's life as they hugged each other around the neck. They were not sure when or if they'd see each other again. David found himself grieving for Jonathan upon recalling how his own father had nearly pinned him to the wall with his spear. Deep hurt cut into Jonathan as he recalled his father's words. David had seen the depth of his pain in his eyes as they talked. Jonathan had shared how his father had asked him, "Where is the son of Jesse?"

Jonathan shared with his father how David had asked his permission to go to be with his family for a sacrifice in town. As he did, anger flared up in Saul. With a deep, loathing voice that grew in volume with each word, he growled, "You son of a perverse and rebellious woman! Don't I know that you have sided with the son of Jesse to your own shame and to the shame of your mother who bore you? As long as the son of Jesse lives on this earth, neither you nor your kingdom will be established. Now send and bring him to me, for he must die!" His insults were degrading and meant to shame him.

Jonathan could not believe his father's words, and he challenged his father by asking, "Why should he be put to death? What has he done?"

At these words, Saul hurled his spear at Jonathan to kill him. At that precise moment, all doubt left. He knew beyond a doubt that his father did intend to kill David.

With anger seething from every fiber of his being, Jonathan got up quickly and stormed out of the feast. He was very grieved at his father's shameful treatment of David.

Upon reaffirming their friendship and the covenant between their descendants forever, David turned around and walked off into the distance.

# Chapter 19

*"Have mercy on me, my God, have mercy on me, for in you
I take refuge. I will take refuge in the shadow of your wings
until the disaster has passed" (Psalm 57:1, NIV).*

The firelight danced off the walls of the cave as though putting on a show for David. It offered enough light to perform some tasks but not enough for studying or writing. He stared at the firelight as though watching a theater show. He listened to the crackling of the fire as he lay there, and soon, his thoughts trailed off. David recalled how he headed for Nob to see Ahimelech, the priest, after saying goodbye to Jonathan. He knew that Ahimelech came from a strong family line and that Eli was his great grandfather and believed to be a direct descendant of Aaron. Nob was located northeast of Jerusalem on the eastern slope of Mount Scopus; the name means "high place."

David had hoped to find protection and succor from the priest. Ahimelech greeted him with a slight trembling to his hands and a look of fear upon his face, revealing to David that Ahimelech must have heard something of what was going on. Ahimelech asked David where his men were, his equipment, and his provisions. When David had stopped by in the past, he always had a brigade of men. David assured the priest that he was sent on a "secret" and very urgent matter for the king. Because of the urgency of the king's business, he hadn't had the time to assemble things as normal. He assured the priest that the men were already directed to a specific place. Then he asked Ahimelech for five loaves of bread or whatever he had to eat.

The priest said, "There was no ordinary bread available, only consecrated bread, providing that the young men have kept themselves from women."

David answered him, "Indeed, women were kept from us as is usual whenever I go out on a mission, and the equipment of the young men is consecrated even when it's an ordinary journey, so how much more is their equipment consecrated today?"

The priest's questions didn't bother David because he knew that this ordinance came from the giving of the law during Moses' time in the wilderness. Ahimelech gave him the consecrated bread that had been pulled from the altar that morning.

All the while David was talking to Ahimelech, he kept an eye on the man standing off to the side of the priest. David recognized him as a servant of King Saul and as his head shepherd. His name was Doeg, the Edomite. David was trying to decide if the man could be trusted or not. He was a rather short man with a shifty appearance. He had a tooth broken in front, giving him an even more questionable look. Remembering what he knew of him, David recalled that he was a man more concerned with himself than others. David was certain that his presence would be reported back to the king.

Next, David asked Ahimelech for a sword or a spear. He knew he needed some form of weapon. He knew that the priest might not have much protection available to give to him but felt as though he had to ask.

The priest replied, "The sword of Goliath the Philistine, whom you killed in the Valley of Elah, is here; it is wrapped in a cloth behind the ephod, the priestly garment. If you want it, take it; there is no other sword here but that one."

David said, "There is none like it; give it to me."

Upon receiving the sword, David could not get out of there fast enough. He didn't trust Doeg and wanted to be as far from there as he could get. Feeling the sword handle in the palm of his hand brought back memories...what a victorious moment that had been, not only for God but for himself and all of Israel. So much had changed since that moment, including the way the sword fit into his adult hand. He recalled how he was considered "just a youth" by almost everyone at that time. In the few years that had passed, he gripped the sword again, only this time with a man's hand. He was amazed at how much lighter it felt now that he was a man. Yes, he would be king, and he welcomed the sword for the days ahead. As he left, David found his thoughts trailing back to the moment he stood on Goliath's chest with the sword raised high above the uncircumcised Philistine's head. Once again, he relished in the victory. The words he spoke that day were forever a part of him. "You come against me with sword and spear and javelin, but I come against you in the name of the Lord Almighty, the God of the armies of Israel, whom you have defiled. This day, the Lord will hand you over to me, and I'll strike you down and cut off your head. Today, I will give the carcasses of the Philistines army to the birds of the air and the beasts of the earth, and the whole world will know that there is a God in Israel. All those who are gathered here will know that it is not by the sword or spear that the Lord saves, for the battle is the Lord's, and He will give all of you into our hands."

Yes, the birds of the air and the beasts of the earth had a feast that day. Then, he recalled the thrill of fighting alongside his brothers in battle and how he had gained some approval in their eyes that day.

# Chapter 20

*"Taste and see that the LORD is good; blessed is the one*
*who takes refuge in him" (Psalm 34:8, NIV).*

The temperature was quite hot that day as David made his way down the mountains in the direction of Ashdod. Feeling desperate for help, David reasoned within himself and was certain he could find help from Achish, the Philistine King of Gath. Since King Saul saw him as an enemy, then surely, he could join ranks with the Philistines. He had hoped to go unnoticed among the men. It seemed like such an easy solution to his problems. Maybe he could hang out in the Philistine camp for a while. Feeling dirty and dusty from all his travel, David thought about how good a fresh cup of wine would taste about now. His father was always teaching him and his brothers that names had meanings behind them. He knew that Gath meant "winepress." Having fought the Philistines, David knew that Gath was the closest of the large Philistine cities to the Hebrew province.

Upon reaching Gath, there was no welcome as David had dreamed. In fact, fear immediately came upon David as he heard the men saying among themselves, "Saul has slain his thousands, and David his tens of thousands."

As fear gripped his heart, he prayed instantly for God's help, dreading the fact that he had not prayed more prior to his own brilliant plan. As the soldiers escorted him to King Achish, David started to drool, creating saliva to run down his beard. He started to thrash his arms and act insane. With God's help, he might actually be viewed as a madman. He did not make eye contact but stared wildly at everything. He hoped this would allow him to appear insane to all that were around him. He dug his nails into the doors of the gate and made marks upon them. Anything he could think to do to be found insane, he did. He swung his head wildly to mess up his hair and to appear angry and mad.

King Achish was almost furious with his men as he realized that David could not possibly distinguish between reality and fantasy, "Look at the man! He is insane! Why bring him to me? Am I so short of madmen that you bring this fellow here to carry on like this in front of me? Must this man come into my house?"

One of the soldiers tried to tell the king that David had asked to speak to him only minutes prior and had been acting quite normal, but the king cut him off at each attempt. At the king's words, they drugged David outside the city gates and dropped him face-first in the desert. David worked his way up to a standing position. Then, thrashing his arms and hollering, he ran off in the distance like a madman. David continued his thrashing about until he was confident that he was out of the Philistines sight. Thankful for his very life, David praised God for protecting him. He found himself walking toward

Jerusalem, and as he did, God brought the cave of Adullam to his thoughts. Yes, a cave would give him protection from the elements and allow him to make some plans of what to do next. This cave was considered a "stronghold," meaning that it had become known as a place that was fortified, a place designed to protect against attacks. It was located near the town of Adullam, and David found it to be a long exhausting walk to get there. That night, he took time to pray and comfort his soul with songs of praise unto God. Looking down at his harp, David was very thankful that he had thought to hide his few belongings prior to going to see King Achish. Of course, he knew it would have been suicide to take Goliath's sword into the city, but he had not foreseen how drastic the situation could turn on him. As David sat by the firelight singing praises to God, there was an owl off in the distance hooting. David was certain that it was also singing praises to God. These words flowed to the music his fingers played on his harp.

> I will extol the Lord at all times; His praise will always be on my lips. My soul will boast in the Lord; let the afflicted hear and rejoice. Glorify the Lord with me; let us exalt His name together. I sought the Lord, and He answered me; He delivered me from all my fears. Those who look to Him are radiant; their faces are never covered with shame. This poor man called, and the Lord heard him; He saved him out of all his troubles. The angel of the Lord encamps around those who fear him, and he delivers them. Taste and see that the Lord is good; blessed is the one who takes

refuge in him. Fear the Lord, you, his saints, for those who fear Him lack nothing. The lions grow weak and hungry, but those who seek the Lord lack no good thing. Come, my children, listen to me; I will teach you the fear of the Lord, whoever of you loves life and desires to see many good days, keep your tongue from evil and your lips from speaking lies. Turn from evil and do good; seek peace and pursue it. The eyes of the Lord are on the righteous, and His ears are attentive to their cry, the face of the Lord is against those who do evil, to cut off the memory of them from the earth. The righteous cry out, and the Lord hears them; He delivers them from all their troubles. The Lord is close to the brokenhearted and saves those who are crushed in spirit. A righteous man may have many troubles, but the Lord delivers him from them all; He protects their bones not one of them will be broken. Evil will slay the wicked; the foes of the righteous will be condemned. The Lord redeems his servants; no one will be condemned who takes refuge in Him.[8]

David knew just how important it was to give God praise, no matter what. But beyond anything else, he loved God completely. Together they talked, and God seemed to personally teach David of His truths. Praising God was as natural as breathing air. A wave of humility flowed over David as tears of gratitude trickled down his cheeks. He humbly thanked God for delivering him. As he recalled the fear that overtook him, he thanked God for delivering him from them all. Suddenly, the firelight dancing off the cave walls allowed him to envision angels encompassing around him with divine protection. This was how it had been just hours before when he was in the presence of his enemies. A smile started to form in the corner of his mouth as he thought of the Philistines as the lions, which grow weak and hungry. But praise filled his heart as he thought of how he would use this song and this story to teach his children someday and all others who would listen to him. David felt as though God outlined the keys to all success.

*I will extol the Lord at all times... His praise will always be on my lips... I will glory in the Lord...and as I seek You, Lord, You will answer and deliver me from all my fears. Thank You, Lord.*

As David drifted off to sleep, he meditated upon how good God was and how He protected him this very day. David might not be sure of all that lay ahead, but he was sure of God's love and his divine protection. He was also confident that angels encamp around him and those who fear the Lord. As David reflected on the Lord, he heard God say in his heart, "Taste and see that I am good; blessed is the one who takes refuge in Me." With a warm heart, David drifted off to sleep.

# Chapter 21

*"They repay me evil for good, and hatred for my friendship"*
*(Psalm 109:5, NIV).*

Within just a few days, most of David's family started to show up. David asked how they knew where he was, and his brother Shammah, smiling and winking, said, "You're not the only one who talks to God."

Taking in a welcomed breath of fresh air, David couldn't believe how good his brother's bantering felt. He also noticed how much he had grown since killing Goliath. At that time, he used to look up to Shammah; now, they were eye to eye. David's brothers informed him that he was the talk of the area and that word was other men were finding their way to join his army. David couldn't believe the support he was finding. Had it only been a few days since God spoke to him and said, "Taste and see that I am good..." He turned his eyes to heaven and, in his thoughts, said, *Thank You, Lord!*

Joab, David's nephew, had been among the first to find David in the wilderness and to join him. Joab was very loyal to his uncle and determined to fight alongside him. He even offered to steal into the camp and kill King Saul for David, but

David would have no part of such a plan. He always took the time to speak of the respect for leadership that God had put in his heart. Joab reminded David of himself; he had that same teen youth look that he had when he killed Goliath. Just as he had, Joab would grow into his body and probably very soon. Joab had his mother's eyes, and David could see his sister Zeruiah each time he looked at him. His hair was the same dark brown that ran through their family, but it had a tint of red in it that made David favor him a little. His hair was thick and curly, just as his mother's. What a sense of humor the kid had; he smiled just thinking of all the practical jokes that Joab was constantly trying to pull on someone in the family.

As the men sat around and talked, they dreamed up many different battle plans and often asked David, "What is next?" It seemed like a funny question to David because none of this was planned, let alone the next step. So they discussed plans to bring in food and supplies that were needed to prepare for war and to keep them going. Since Joab was so eager to help, David asked him to count and see how many men had joined their ranks. To their surprise, the total was around four hundred men. Just a few days ago, David had felt alone; now, he was surrounded by a small army. Obviously, God had a plan. He just had to listen and talk to God to find out what that plan was. As David looked around, he wondered if God knew that besides his family, a lot of the men who had joined him were in distress, in debt, or discontented with King Saul or those in authority over them. Oh well...he recalled how he started out..."just a shepherd boy"...now the ruler over four hundred men...and already called of God to be the next king...

As David spent time in prayer, urgency arose within David to find a safe place for his parents. Sorting out all of his options, he decided to call upon another "enemy" of King Saul's and join an alliance with them. Although things had not worked out well with King Achish, he was certain that it would work this time. He decided to call upon the kinship that he had with the Moabites. His grandmother Ruth had been a Moabite from Moab. David was certain within himself that they would assist him and keep his parents safe as long as he swore to protect them. David went to Mizpah in Moab and spoke with the king about his parents staying there until he could see what God had planned for him. The king agreed to take care of them and to protect them. David asked, or rather assigned, four of his brothers to go get their parents, anything of value, and to take them to stay among the Moabites. They were to all stay, or some of them stay with them to make sure they were protected. He believed he could trust this king but felt it wise to have some men there who could protect them also.

Before he left Moab, the Prophet Gad found David and said, "Do not stay in the stronghold. Go into the land of Judah."

David and his men traveled back to Judah and went to the forest of Hereth. They found a good location in the mountain country southwest of Adullam. The forest was filled with lots of pine trees. Although it was thick, it was not so thick that you couldn't watch and spot people coming. The brown, dry ground was a good contrast to the bright green trees making spotting people an easy process. There were a few natural paths that people and the animals used. They tried to avoid these so as to not be detected when Saul sent out his search parties.

David had a handful of men going behind them with pine tree branches used as brooms to eliminate their tracks. He also sent men on ahead to scout out an area for them. He even set up a few decoys in case they tracked them that far. The clear blue sky above was beautiful, and from the top of the mountain, the view was breathtaking. There were some jagged rocks to work their way around as they went up the mountain. These would be a good ally as they found a place to camp.

The men got excited when they saw tracks from some wild goats called Nubian ibex. There was either a family or a small herd. They were certain that the largest was a bull, and then there was a smaller one, probably a doe, and then some kids. The horns are what made these goats unique; their long horns curve backward. The ibex's coat was a light sandy brown with the hindquarters lighter. David decided that he would have to send a hunting party out to bring in a few for a good meal. Then the corners of his mouth curved up as he found himself smiling at the thought of a "few," realizing it would take more than a few to feed this crew! In fact, it might be wise to organize a couple of hunting parties with this many men to feed.

Every once in a while, they would come to an area where the ground was wrapped in flowers. The Anemone coronaria wildflower was a true sign of spring. The coronaria is a beautiful flower that grows very well in the mountains. They love getting some of the shade of the trees, although they could be found in full sun areas as well. It reminded him of how he'd pick a bouquet for his mother when he was a young boy. His mother had taught David and his brothers that the Anemone coronaria was an herbaceous plant. The flower had a rosette or a cluster of leaves in crowded circles. It had spirals starting from a crown. The base of the stem had a few leaves, and it grew in a variety of colors, purple, red, blue, and white. The white flower was also known as the Snowdrop Anemone. David recalled how his mother would work the plant during the early spring months to prepare the fluids that ran through the plant for medicinal purposes. He recalled how she taught them that it could be used for snake bites by chewing the tops of the plant and applying it to the bite. It was also used for skin diseases, eye infections, and much more. It would be a help to have these plants. He would have to assign some men to work on gathering the plants and putting the fluid away in jars for emergencies that might arise. *Are there any physicians in the camp?* he thought to himself. *If not, then some will have to be assigned to become physicians and learn to attend to the men's needs.*

After a few more days passed, the men were sitting around a campfire eating when a man came running over the hill toward the cave. Although they did not know who it was, everyone could tell that something had to be wrong, terribly wrong. There was an urgency in each step the man took as he rushed toward them. Joab took it upon himself to be David's protector and rushed out to find out who this was and what the urgency was. The men in the camp started rising to a standing position and reaching for their weapons. Although they did not have much in weaponry, they grabbed something close by for protection. Some had homemade makeshift knives, and some had bows and arrows. Many of the men had at least a spear. Some of the men fashioned themselves to be slingers after David and had a pocket full of stones and a slingshot. Some of the men had a club and not much more, but they all looked for something for protection. A few men had a large rock the size of the palm of their hand. They figured, if necessary, they could always protect themselves by using it on someone's head.

As the man approached, he slowed down his step. It looked as though he might have traveled a long distance on foot. He looked ragged and worn out and yet frantic.

David watched the man approaching and thought he had the appearance of a priest. Was he wearing an ephod? What could be so urgent to cause a priest to run out to them? Yes, it had to be a priest; he had a priestly girdle tied around his waist of blue, purple, and scarlet linen. He also had the breastplate of twelve stones representing the twelve tribes of Israel. He wore the miter as well. Yes, this was a priest.

Quite curious, David started walking toward the man, cutting the distance down quickly. As he approached David, he couldn't talk. He inhaled deeply, trying to catch his breath. Bent over, he placed his hands above his knees and exhaled, trying to calm his breathing. As he started to talk, his speech was broken, "I...am...Abiathar..., son...of...Ahimelech..., son...of...Ahitub..."

He stood up straight as he started to catch his breath, "I have escaped...and fled...to join you."

David was quite anxious to hear the full story. "Escaped from who or what?"

With a horrified look on his face, he told the most crucial elements of what had happened, "King Saul has murdered Ahimelech and his whole family."

Utterly filled with grief, Abiathar appeared ready to collapse. David ordered one of the men to find some water for the man to drink and told him to take a moment and, as soon as he could, tell him everything.

After a few minutes and a full cup of water, Abiathar started to relay the horrifying events.

"Doeg the Edomite told King Saul that he had seen you come to Ahimelech, son of Ahitub, at Nob. He also said that Ahimelech inquired of the Lord for you and that he gave you provisions and the sword of Goliath the Philistine. At that, King Saul called for my father, the priest Ahimelech, son of Ahitub, and my whole family, or all the priests that were at Nob. He called them to come to him. As they arrived, King Saul was sitting under the tamarisk tree on the hill at Gibeah, and all of his official men were surrounding him. When they arrived, King Saul accused him of conspiring against him by helping you. He accused him of joining you in plotting to kill him. My father answered him by saying, 'Who of all your servants is as loyal as David, the king's son-in-law, captain of your bodyguard, and highly respected in your household? Was that day the first time I inquired of God for him? Of course not, for your servant knows nothing at all about this affair.'

"The king was so angry that he was almost spitting with each breath. With a hatred deeper than I have ever seen, King Saul looked directly into my father's face and said, 'You will surely die, Ahimelech, you and your father's whole family.' A cold chill crept over my whole body."

"King Saul's face turned red as the anger grew uncontrollably. With such loathing in his voice, he turned to his guards and ordered them to kill the priests. Hateful words filled the air as the king sentenced them to death. Saul was practically shouting now as he said, 'Turn and kill the priests of the Lord because they too have sided with David. They knew he was fleeing, yet they did not tell me.'

"I could see shock come over the guards' faces. They could not believe King Saul had said to *kill* the priests...the holy men of God...the men chosen from the line of Aaron to lead the people...those who pray for forgiveness for our sins..."

For a second, Abiathar couldn't speak. A small pool of tears started to form in the corner of his big dark brown eyes. A lump formed in his neck as if he tried to swallow his grief away. After a few seconds, he started to relay the events that had forever changed his life.

"Seeing that the king's men would not kill the priests, he ordered Doeg too, 'You turn and strike down the priests.'

"Doeg did just that. My father was the first to fall under his *filthy* sword. What was worse was that he didn't even have the decency to face him. He had been standing behind him, and walking up behind him, he shoved his sword into my precious father from the back. His white linen ephod was suddenly covered with his own dear blood as his body fell to the earth. Then he continued going right down the line, killing one of my kinsmen after another until eighty-five of them lay dead in that area. I could not find the strength to just stand there and let them kill me. As I saw what was going to happen, I snuck off and hid behind the houses until I could get away. It was horrifying... Blood was everywhere... The sounds of those crying out to God for help as they lay on the ground breathing their final breath will haunt my memories forever..." His voice trailed off as tears formed in his eyes; Abiathar took a breath

There was a somber atmosphere in the camp that night as each man thought about the priests and what they had learned that day. They knew then that they could not leave David, for their own lives would be just as easily snuffed out.

# Chapter 22

*"...how long shall my enemy be exalted over me?...But I have trust in thy mercy..." (Psalm 13:2b, 5a, KJV)*

After a few weeks had passed, the men were settling into somewhat of a routine. They had hunting parties that went out to bring in their daily food. They organized scouting parties that watched the area for signs of King Saul's army or other enemy armies. They even had designated runners, men who went into the towns to get the local news so that they could know what was going on in the area surrounding them. Abiathar assumed his role as the priest. One afternoon, the men brought word to David that the Philistines were fighting against Keilah and were looting the threshing floors.

Keilah is located in the Judean foothills southeast of Adullam. David had been taught that the history of Keilah went back to the dividing of the land to the twelve tribes during Joshua's time. The name Keilah means "fortress." It was built up with gates and bars to protect the people from outsiders. Obviously, it was not working against the Philistines. They were stealing all the harvest that the people had in their barns.

David went to the Lord in prayer and asked if he should go down and attack the Philistines. The Lord answered David and said, "Go, attack the Philistines and save Keilah."

David's men said to him, "Here in Judah, we fear for our lives, how much more, then, if we go to Keilah against the Philistine forces!"

Hearing their arguments, David went back to God to seek confirmation. Once again, God answered him and said, "Go down to Keilah, for I am going to give the Philistines into your hand."

David told his men to prepare for battle. Leading his men down to Keilah, they came against the Philistines. Upon defeating them, they carried off their livestock. David and his soldiers inflicted heavy losses on the Philistines and saved the people of Keilah.

While David was fighting and cleaning up the Philistine's spoils, King Saul learned of David's location. Excitement filled King Saul as he took in what this meant. Keilah was a fortress of bars and gates, and he knew David had entered into an area that offered no escape. Saul called his people to come together for war so that they could besiege David and his men.

Word quickly reached David that King Saul was coming to Keilah to destroy the city because of David, and he would soon be there. David called for Abiathar and asked him to put on the ephod, the colored shoulder-cape. It was woven of gold, blue, purple, scarlet, and linen threads and ornamented with gems and gold. He asked Abiathar to enquire of the Lord as to whether the people of Keilah would deliver him and his men into the hands of Saul. The Lord answered and said, "They *will* deliver you and your men up."

David's men had grown to almost six hundred by now. He told them to prepare to depart; they were leaving Keilah. Later, they received word that King Saul did not go to Keilah, not once he learned that they had departed.

They did not go back into the forest of Hereth. Taking his men, David went into the desert strongholds. They went into the hills of the desert of Ziph, a wilderness four miles southeast of Hebron. Moving from place to place, they proceeded to use the natural fortresses in the woods and mountains. He used the places that were difficult to access as his base to set up camp.

Word continued to come daily to David of King Saul's relentless search for him. But God... Yes, but God protected him and did not give David over unto Saul's hands. David found much comfort in the words "But God..." King Saul could have no authority over him as long as God continued to protect him. David had to remind himself of this truth when he found worry and doubt coming upon him.

It was hard to find private time in such a setting, so he had to do more praying in the midst of his men. David was thankful for his tallit, which was also called prayer shawl. He found such comfort from it. As their tradition stated, a Jewish boy of thirteen received a prayer shawl. His felt extra special since it was made for him by his mother. She had taken a lot of time to make one for each of his brothers, as well as himself. Their prayer shawl was made from the fine wool from their sheep. Sometimes he'd bring it up tight to his nose and take in a deep breath, and for a few fleeting seconds, he could almost smell his sheep and slip back to his childhood days.

He had always wrapped his harp in it before putting it in his canvas bag. He smiled that he still had three items from the home of his youth, his harp, his tallit, and his sling. Then with an even bigger smile, he realized he had four things from home, his heritage.

He loved how it reminded him of the law his father taught them. It reminded him of Jehovah God as he recalled how it spelled out "One Jehovah." Prior to receiving it, he learned there were six hundred and thirteen laws that gave them six hundred and thirteen coils on the tasseled end. These represented three hundred and sixty-five laws that were probations, "Thou shall not..." and two hundred and forty-eight affirmations, "Thou shall...!" His father taught and passed down all six hundred and thirteen laws. This is something he would do with his sons...whenever he had sons. The white wool represented righteousness, and during Moses' time, they were instructed to wind a blue, conspicuous thread among coils that symbolized heavenly origin. The name "tallit" came from two words, "tal" means "tent," and "ith" means "little." Often, people would just call their tallit their "little tent." It represented the holy place that they could escape to and pray alone with God.

During the time David was at Horesh, he fought anxiety. It seemed hard to fight it because of how determined Saul was to take his life. He knew better than to give in to anxiety because God's hand of protection was upon him, but he still found it hard on occasion not to give in to it.

One afternoon, David had a special visitor come and offer support to him. Jonathan found his way to David. Jonathan had dressed down to look like one of David's soldiers instead of a soldier in the king's army or the prince. He snuck into David's camp, pretending to be one of the men, and worked his way to

David. Seeing the look on David's face told him that David was worried for his life. Jonathan said, "Don't be afraid; my father Saul will not lay a hand on you. You will be king over Israel, and I will be second to you. Even my father, Saul, knows this."

Jonathan came to encourage David. The two men rejoiced at seeing each other again, giving each other a big hug. Upon talking for a few minutes, they took time to renew their covenant to each other. Then, Jonathan slipped back out and returned to the Israelite camp. Joy filled both men's hearts at seeing each other again. David couldn't believe that it had only been a year since they last saw each other. What a long and eventful year it had been. Seeing each other was a joyous occasion. Jonathan pledged his love and devotion to David forever and talked of their ruling the kingdom together. There was no doubt in David's mind to the sincerity that ran through Jonathan. It would be fun to rule the kingdom with Jonathan at his side, but still, David wondered if that was what God had planned. Time would tell them both.

# Chapter 23

*"Rescue me from the mouth of the lions; save me from the horns of the wild oxen" (Psalm 22:21, NIV).*

A small group of men traveled to Gibeah from Ziph with a single purpose in mind. They intended to plot against David, for they were certain this would gain them favor with King Saul. The king was sitting upon his throne as they entered his presence. The men bowed lowly to show their respect. His closest soldiers were surrounding him as if to protect him from some enemy. He had a crown upon his head that sparkled with gemstones, and the light from the windows caught the gold, causing it to shine brightly. King Saul commanded the men to come forward, asking them what news they brought. Rising to their feet, the men proceeded to move closer to the king. One man stepped forward a full step and bowed his head slightly to show his reverence. Speaking for the group, he gauged his voice to show genuine concern for the king's safety. Then he proceeded to say, "Is not David hiding among us in the strongholds at Horesh, on the hill of Hakilah, south of Jeshimon? Now, O king, come down whenever it pleases you to do so, and we will be responsible for handing him over to you."

The rest of the men shook their heads in agreement while smiling to show their union with the man speaking, as well as their loyalty to the king.

Saul, in a very clever manner, replied deliberately slow and methodically, "The Lord bless you for your concern for me." Saul paused slightly as if he was showing respect to God; then, he gave them a command, "Go and make further preparations. Find out where David usually goes and who has seen him there."

Pausing while gently stroking his beard, he started to describe David's personality to them, "They tell me David is very crafty..." Pausing so as to not appear too eager, King Saul continued, "Find out all about the hiding places he uses and come back to me with more precise information. Then I will go with you; if he is in the area, I will track him down among all the people of Judah."

The men closest to the king could see the contempt on the king's face when he said the name "David." Such plotting, such hatred, such an evil heart reigned within this king, no matter how anointed he was at the beginning. A few of the men surrounding the king cared about what was right, whether that included David or not. But most of the men found pleasure in doing the king's bidding, even if that meant to kill someone like David. After all, what was David to them?

Besides, their loyalty was to King Saul and his family. Maybe David really was plotting against their king, and where did Jonathan fit into the picture? Many such thoughts echoed through the king's palace. But of course, never when the king was near.

Upon receiving the king's instructions, the men left and headed back to Ziph to gather more information. They also discussed plans to prepare for the king's visit. They discussed their sources and planned different strategies to gather more details concerning David.

*****

David and his men made their way to the wilderness of Maon, a town of the tribe of Judah. It is located approximately seven miles south of Hebron, in the mountains of Judah. It was named after the Maonites. The founder was Shammai, the great-grandson of Judah. As David looked around on his journey there, once again, he was led to praise God. He looked out over the landscape. He firmly believed that all creation was designed to cause men to worship God, "How glorious are thy works, oh Lord..."

As David rode his horse, he enjoyed worshipping God. He had noticed that his patterns were changing. Before the men joined him, he would take time in the evening alone to praise and worship Jehovah, but now, it was not so. Now, he took the early morning hours to be alone and found himself leading the men into worship each evening as the weather permitted. Either he or Abiathar would teach the men the truths of the God of Abraham, Isaac, and Jacob. In the early mornings, while they were camping, he'd find some quiet time. He'd sing songs and praises to God. He wrote still more songs to God and found his strength in communing with the Father. There was an anointing upon God's words so that he could tell when they came from the Father. Sometimes it was like they were talking in a conversation. David would tell the Father what was going on or all of his woes and trials; then God would speak words of protection or love or both to David. He could tell when his words changed to God's words of encouragement or direction. One such song he titled "Rejoice in His Salvation":

How long, O Lord? Will you forget me forever? How long, will you hide your face from me? How long must I wrestle with my thoughts and every day have sorrow in my heart? How long will my enemy triumph over me?

Look on me and answer, O Lord my God. Give light to my eyes, or I will sleep in death; my enemy will say, "I have overcome him," and my foes will rejoice when I fall.

But I trust in your unfailing love; my heart rejoices in your salvation. I will sing to the Lord, for he has been good to me.[12]

A few days later, after seeing Jonathan, David woke up particularly full of despair as word came to him of Saul's army getting closer. Crying unto God was all David could think to do. His heart felt broken at King Saul's continual pursuit of him. If a person looked closely, they could see a glistening tear or two upon his tanned cheek. The despair that was in David's heart flowed into the strings of his harp, filling the surrounding area with the same hopelessness. As David played his harp, these words flowed from his lips:

My God, my God, why have you forsaken me? Why are you so far from saving me, so far from the words of my groaning? O my God, I cry out by day, but you do not answer, by night, but am not silent.

Yet you are enthroned as the Holy One; you are the praise of Israel. In you our fathers put their trust; they trusted and you delivered them. They cried to you and were saved; in you they trusted and were not disappointed.

But I am a worm and not a man, scorned by men and despised by the people. All who see me mock me; they hurl insults, shaking their heads: "He trusts in the Lord; let the Lord rescue him. Let him deliver him, since he delights in him."

Yet you brought me out of the womb; you made me trust in you even at my mother's breast. From birth I was cast upon you; from my mother's womb you have been my God. Do not be far from me, for trouble is near and there is no one to help.

Many bulls surround me; strong bulls of Bashan encircle me. Roaring lions tearing their prey open their mouths wide against me. I am poured out like water, and all my bones are out of joint. My heart is turned to wax; it has melted away within me. My strength is dried up like a potsherd, and my tongue sticks to the roof of my mouth; you lay me in the dust of death. Dogs have surrounded me; a band of evil men has encircled me, they have pierced my hands and my feet. I can count all my bones; people stare and gloat over me. They divide my garments among them and cast lots for my clothing.[13]

The entire song had a different anointing upon it as David said the words and wrote them. He could tell they were not just how he felt but served a greater purpose, but what was the purpose? That he didn't know. He felt like God spoke to his heart that they concerned the future Messiah. How breathtaking to think of the Messiah.

As David asked God about these words, God said, "I will establish the line of David forever."

> But you, O Lord, be not far off; O my Strength, come quickly to help me. Deliver my life from the sword, my precious life from the power of the dogs. Rescue me from the mouth of the lions; save me from the horns of the wild oxen.
>
> I will declare your name to my brothers; in the congregation I will praise you. You who fear the Lord, praise him! All you descendants of Jacob, honor him! Revere him, all you descendants of Israel! For he has not despised or disdained the suffering of the afflicted one; he has not hidden his face from him but has listened to his cry for help.
>
> From you comes the theme of my praise in the great assembly; before those who fear you will I fulfill my vows. The poor will eat and be satisfied; they who seek the Lord will praise him—may your hearts live forever!
>
> All the ends of the earth will remember and turn to the Lord, and all the families of the nations will bow down before him, for dominion belongs to the Lord and he rules over the nations.

All the rich of the earth will feast and worship; all who go down to the dust will kneel before him—those who cannot keep themselves alive. Posterity will serve him; future generations will be told about the Lord. They will proclaim his righteousness to a people yet unborn—for he has done it.[14]

Having put his harp down, David lay prostrate upon the ground. With an open heart, he started to worship God and seek Him. He blocked out the sounds of the men throughout the camp. He shut out everything, including the animal sounds that he found so comforting. His heart was set on one thing, reaching the throne of God.

Save me, O God, by your name; vindicate me by your might. Hear my prayer, O God; listen to the words of my mouth.
Strangers are attacking me; ruthless men seek my life—men without regard for you. Selah.[15]

In his song, he called the Ziphites strangers because they were treating him like one. However, they were Israelites.

Surely God is my help; the Lord is the one who sustains me. Let evil recoil on those who slander me; in your faithfulness destroy them.
I will sacrifice a freewill offering to you; I will praise your name, O Lord, for it is good.
For he has delivered me from all my troubles, and my eyes have looked on triumph on my foes.[16]

Later, when David wrote this song, he titled it "God Is My Help." Upon perfecting the words of these songs, he would take the time to script them down on parchment paper. Sometimes, when he had nothing to write on, he'd use the back of tree bark, or he'd say it over and over, committing the song to memory.

Later that day, the fight became critical for David, as Saul and his men were only a valley apart. David and his men were on one side of the mountain, and King Saul and his men were on the other side. He prayed hard and knew the men were looking to him for protection. As the words flowed from his mouth, Saul's men started to turn around and leave. Unsure what had happened, David learned quickly of a Philistine attack. Some of his men heard King Saul's messenger as he hollered, "Come quickly! The Philistines are raiding the land."

They named the place Sela Hammah-lekoth, meaning "the rock of division" or "the rock of parting" because it divided between David and Saul. The mountain was an emblem of God's divine providence coming between Saul and David.

He knew he should see only the glory of God, but David couldn't help but wonder why Saul was allowed to pursue him in the first place. Why were they able to get so close? Was there a lesson for him to learn? Was he to give his men some real insights that he didn't feel he had? He tried not to be filled with anxieties or to allow his thoughts the freedom they wanted. He concentrated on seeking God and praising him.

While Saul and his men were busy with the Philistines, David and his men went up and lived in the strongholds, the natural wilderness protections of En Gedi.

Later, when David took time to praise and worship God, one sentence came out over and over from the depth of his heart.

This one sentence, he repeated for well over an hour as his heart meditated on the depth of its meaning.

"'Behold, God is my helper, and then all shall be well…' Behold… Wow, yes, behold… God, no, not any God, but *my* God, the God of Abraham, Isaac, and Jacob, *my* God, *my* protector, *my* Savior, *my* friend, *my* Lord… He is *my* helper, and then all, not some, but all shall be well!"

Later, as he thought about their being on one side of the mountain and Saul and his men on the other, a little laughter swelled up in David as he heard these words, "David now flees as a bird to his mountain…and finds God to him as a shadow of a great rock."

"Yes, that is just about how it was too! You have a great sense of humor, Lord, but please let all this foolishness stop…please, please!"

# Chapter 24

*"Who are you pursuing? A dead dog, a single flea?*
*May the Lord be our judge*
*and decide between us"* (1 Samuel 24:14b–15a, NIV).

David looked out over the valley as he climbed the mountain. King Saul and his men had reached it and were now off fighting the Philistine army.

David knew he should be shouting victory. But God... Yes, but God...protected him and did not give David over into Saul's hands. Once again, those words echoed of God's divine providence to David. They built him up, but he was still shaken by the continual chase and how close they were able to get to him.

David couldn't help but think, *If only King Saul were as the bear or the lion or as the uncircumcised Philistine, this battle would have been over a long time ago! But King Saul is an anointed servant of God.* Although David was not around when King Saul was anointed, he heard all the details surrounding it. Saul was anointed as Israel's first king. The old Prophet Samuel had anointed them both. Visions of God's presence refreshed David as he recalled the holy oil running down his face...such an incredible moment.

For a few minutes, he found himself basking once again in God's awesome presence.

No...King Saul was not the uncircumcised Philistine, nor the lion, nor the bear; he was the anointed king of Israel. David determined in his heart that it would be God who took Saul out of leadership and installed David as Israel's new king. He just hoped he had the strength to hold on for however long that would take.

*****

At the top of the Mountain, David's heart leaped at the beauty before his eyes. There were miles and miles of cascading Limestone Mountain ranges. Big rocks and boulders surrounded each mountain, providing both obstacles for them to go around, as well as a natural refuge from King Saul and his army. He knew well that there were various caves scattered throughout the ranges that would provide a safe haven. As David headed for En Gedi, his heart felt God's reassurance of divine protection. He would lead his men into the natural wilderness protections and live in the wilderness fortresses of this incredibly beautiful land. He had been close to this area before but never actually to En Gedi. He knew that the name meant "fount of the kid." It was named for its springs and the ibex that live in that area. He had heard of it many times throughout his spiritual training. Under a different name, Hazazon-tamar, the Moabites, and the Ammonites joined themselves against Josaphat. En Gedi was counted among the cities of the Tribe of Judah. David loved recalling his historical teachings. He'd spend hours dwelling upon what he knew. Often while the men were sitting around the campfire or just relaxing, they'd talk about the area and share their insights and knowledge. David considered himself a bit of a "historical enthusiast." He loved learning about the area in which God had called him to live. Each mountain contained its own unique array of colors throughout it. One of the men shared how some of these mountain ranges were formed by volcanic eruptions many years ago, creating the steep cliffs that overlook the Hula Valley. Others said it was formed during the flood. The men continued on to the southward region. They found it to have areas of craters, craggy peaks, and rock-strewn plateaus. In these areas, the weather was dry, and the mountains were higher. One look at these mountain ranges, and you knew they were cut deeply out of the earth's crust by the one true creator because of the broad range of colors that ran through them, a whole range of browns, reds, and grays. There were also many different types of rocks.

As David's eyes beheld the wonder, he could only think one thing, *Only our Creator could fashion such wonder!* One of the men passed word to David that he knew the way to one of the freshwater springs. Most of the springs in that region were saltwater, with only a few freshwater springs. David told them to bring him to the front and allow him to be their escort for the journey there. Occasionally, they'd find a natural trail that the ibex traveled, and their path was a little easier, but for the most part, they had to climb and wind their way through the boulders and mountainous region.

Thinking about the freshwater spring brought a renewed step to David and the rest of the men. Often, there would be an oasis of green grass and vegetation surrounding a natural water spring. David could not help but think how refreshing the water might taste...at least before the men dived in. He thought about how hot and sweaty he felt. Their travels the past few months offered little refreshing moments. A bath would feel real good, and some of the men were getting pretty foul in their odor. With a light chuckle, a little humor lifted his soul.

Yes, the natural beauty of God's creation was made to draw us unto the Father. David had no doubts about that.

They continued their descent down the mountain and only looked forward to several more ascents and descents. However, it would be nice to put some distance between where he last saw King Saul's men and him.

When they finally reached the freshwater spring, they spent a full day playing in the water, drinking the freshwater to their hearts' content, splashing, and throwing each other in for sport. Actually, David wasn't certain about a few of the men, if they were being thrown in for sport or because they were afraid of the water, but they also needed to bathe. Those who knew how to float on top of the water floated for what seemed hours. Their hands and skin wrinkled, their toes looked clean for the first time in a very long time, revealing how desperately some of them needed to cut their toenails. Because of the Philistine war, only a small amount of men needed to keep watch and were able to switch off early, allowing everyone water time. Some of the braver men, who knew how to swim, stood under the waterfall, feeling the exhilaration of the free-falling water totally immersing their bodies. Some men found a rock formation they could jump from and send water splashing everyone as they hugged their legs to their chest to emphasize the extra-large splash. A few men found a long thick rope and then a solid tree to tie the rope to, creating a swing for them to go further and higher before dropping into the water. All kinds of shouting and hollering took place before the men dropped into the water, everything from "Watch out below" to "Get out of the way, you uncircumcised Philistine!" They all loved that expression the most. David knew the words "uncircumcised Philistine" would follow him his whole life. That didn't bother him at all but established the difference between themselves and others who didn't serve God. It also established why Goliath had to die. Pleasure and true enjoyment radiated through the camp. David wondered how far their voices traveled through the mountainous terrain or if their voices were trapped in this little oasis valley or covered by the waterfall. He didn't know but was certain that he could give such a task to Joab to figure out.

Due to some of the men hunting ibex on the way there, the cooks prepared a good meal. One cook even took time to gather some salt at one of the saltwater falls they passed. Slight humor filled David as he remembered how some of the men tried to drink the water and the expression on their faces as they quickly understood what others had tried to tell them.

A silent prayer went up to God from David, "Oh, it takes so much for us to listen to those before us... Lord, help me to always listen to You and those who have gone before me with a humble heart."

That night, as David ate his food, he observed the small inner circle of men that was forming. He was building his core of people and realized that it was time to think of an armor-bearer as he recalled how he had been appointed to be King Saul's armor-bearer years earlier. As David looked around, two of his older brothers, Abinadab and Shammah, were relaxing and eating their food. He was glad to have Shammah with him. They had a special bond between them. He trusted him, especially with his very life. Abinadab was lying back now and chewing or sucking on a reed of grass; he wasn't certain which. He had done such things while taking care of the sheep. It seemed to relax the mind to have something to chew on. Then there was the overzealous Joab, his nephew. He thought of his sister Zeruiah. He'd have to remember to tell her some of the funnier moments he'd experience with him...like one time when Joab was certain King Saul's army was coming. All the men were on full alert, only to have a herd of ibex come running over the terrain. Wow, did he get heckled about that for days, "Hey Joab, is that King Saul's army I hear?" David actually had to give a talk to some of the men about Joab's sincerity and that it was time to move on. It is also better to err on the side of caution than to be caught off guard. On another such time, Joab was taking some personal time to relieve himself and got attacked by fire ants. As much as they understood his pain and sympathized with him, they could not help but laugh at the antics and the dance that followed Joab as he fought off the army of fire ants! Laughter filled the camp for days as different ones felt the need for banter.

If he were to call Joab his favorite nephew, it would also mean the most annoying one. Joab's zeal put him almost constantly in his face. He had one idea after another but was always the first to volunteer to do the task at hand. He was still praying about

Joab's position but knew Joab saw himself as David's captain over the army. Lord, would he be a good armor-bearer? Would he see it as a worthy position? Would he take it seriously?

*****

A few weeks passed when word came to David that King Saul's army was approaching. He had around three thousand men and was prepared to capture David and all those who followed him. Some of the men panicked and wanted to run far and fast. David was prepared. He had a team of men scouting out the caves. They found one large enough to hold all of his men. It had sections that gave the appearance of individual rooms that separated off behind the large entrance.

Cautiously, the men continued scouting the cave for a back entrance out until they found one. They had gathered enough material to tie ropes continually so that the men could follow it in the dark if need be. David took his men safely to the cave, and as the king's army approached, word was passed back to be absolutely quiet, not even the faintest whisper! This would stop the king from hearing them. It would also allow them to hear his command of attack if necessary, although they were ordered to stay armed and ready. It was here at this cave that David and King Saul's paths would meet once more. Only this time, David would control the outcome.

The majority of men were further back in the cave. Everyone was prepared and ready to attack upon command. Commands for total silence came with the approaching army. David and a handful of men were close to the front of the cave, waiting and ready to defend themselves. He was prepared to give the orders as needed.

Instinctively, he prayed a silent prayer to God for direction and wisdom to know what to do, "Father God, I need Your wisdom that comes only from above."

To David's surprise, although he could see the feet of a whole army of horses and men, only one man came walking into the cave. David couldn't believe it! King Saul walked in without any soldiers checking the cave for safety. There could have been a wild animal, a bear, a mountain lion, anything, including an army of men they considered their enemy! Anger rose within David at the total incompetence of the king's armor-bearer. He couldn't remember a time where he felt more justified in righteous indignation. Someone, either the armor-bearer or his captain or both men, should be taken out in the field and given severe lashes for not protecting their king.

The men right next to David whispered in his ear, "Now is your chance..." "God has given your enemy into your hand..." "Kill him! Now is your time..." "In just seconds, you will be the next king..."

Each man said something different, but all of them brought David back to the reality at hand. They urged David forward. Uncertain as to what he would do, he inched quietly forward.

King Saul entered far enough into the cave that his men could not hear him or see him. The king stood with his back to David, totally unaware of his presence as he pissed against the cave wall. *What a perfect opportunity,* he thought.

David's love and devotion to King Saul ruled in his heart. He could not harm the king, nor did he believe it to be God's will. David took his knife and cut a piece out of King Saul's skirt.

One key thing about being in these mountains, there is always sandstone close by for sharpening weapons. One quick and easy slice and a piece of the king's skirt lay in his hands. David quietly slipped back to his men.

Joab couldn't believe David. God brought King Saul right to David, and he was letting him walk out unharmed. Disapproval and reproach clouded Joab's face as he looked at David.

"A piece of his skirt...what good will that do!" Joab's words were primarily to himself but voiced just loud enough that those standing immediately around him could hear his complaint. He tried so hard to get his uncle to listen to him... Joab could not help but to shake his head, causing his thick dark curls to encircle his face.

David gave Joab a look, telling him to control himself. Even in the dark, Joab could see those eyes of authority. Joab knew to shut up and wait.

David recalled the last few minutes of all the thoughts that flooded his mind, *Kill him and stop all this foolishness! Take him hostage... Make him a prisoner... Throw a spear and pin him to the wall of the cave; we'll see how he likes that! What an opportunity to humiliate the king... If I made a loud cry right now, all the king's men would come in and find the king exposed...*

As quickly as all these thoughts flooded David's mind, one other thought prevailed first: the love and devotion he felt for King Saul as his armor-bearer.

When David became armor-bearer, he committed a lifetime of devotion, loyalty, and love to King Saul. How could he now be the one to take his life from him? David recalled how he committed his life to protect the king, even if that meant he would have to die for him. David knew the very word "armor-bearer" came from two different words; the first is "nasa." It means "to lift." The second word is "keliy," and comes from the root word "kalah," meaning "to end." David knew that his job as the armor-bearer was to stand beside his leader, King Saul. He was to assist him, to lift him up, and to protect him against any enemy that would ever attack him. Besides, David had been taught his whole life the importance of showing respect to those in position over you.

No...the love of an armor-bearer...a son...a son-in-law...runs deep... *Lord, I do not believe Your plan is for me to raise my hand to him or to kill him.*

All of David's men surrounding him looked at him. Expectation of his next move ran deep in their faces. In a voice filled with sorrow, David said, "The Lord forbid that I should do such a thing to my master, the Lord's anointed, or lay my hand on him, for he is the anointed of the Lord." He whispered to them so softly that had they not anticipated his speaking, they would have missed his words altogether.

King Saul left the cave and mounted his horse. David let them get a very short but safe distance away and stepped out of the cave. Giving a nod of his head, all his men joined him and surrounded David. Anticipation of what would happen next filled all the men. David's men clutched their spears and swords in their hands in preparation for a battle.

As David cleared the cave, he raised his voice loud to be heard by the king and called out, "My lord, the king!" He said this, filled with determination as he demanded the king's attention. Saul stopped and turned around and saw David.

He bowed down and prostrated himself with his face to the ground. Raising his head back up, he said, "Why do you listen when men say, 'David is determined to harm you'? This day, you have seen with your own eyes how the Lord delivered you into my hands in the cave. Some of my men urged me to kill you, but I spared you; I said, 'I will not lay my hand on my lord because he is the Lord's anointed.' See, my father, look at this piece of your robe in my hand! I cut off the corner of your robe and did not kill you."

At this, King Saul slid from his horse and inspected his robe. He brought each side up and turned it around until he found the missing piece David held in his hands. At this, sorrow and regret filled his eyes, and he listened as David continued speaking.

"See that there is nothing in my hand to indicate that I am guilty of wrongdoing or rebellion. I have not wronged you, but you are hunting me down to take my life. May the Lord judge between you and me, and may the Lord avenge the wrongs you have done to me, but my hand will not touch you. As the old saying goes, 'From evildoers come evil deeds,' so you can be sure I will never harm you. Against whom has the king of Israel come out? Who are you pursuing? A dead dog? A flea? May the Lord be our judge and decide between us. May he consider my cause and uphold it; may he vindicate me by delivering me from your hand."

Saul asked, "Is that your voice, David, my son?" Tears of regret filled the king's words as he started weeping out loud. Through broken words, he said, "You are...more righteous... than I... You have treated me well, but I...have treated you badly."

King Saul's head dropped down in shame at the reality of what just occurred.

After a short pause, King Saul continued, "You have not just told me about the good you did to me; the Lord delivered me into your hands, but you did not kill me. When a man finds his enemy, does he let him get away unharmed? May the Lord reward you well for the way you treated me today. I know that you will surely be king and that the kingdom of Israel will be established in your hands."

Pausing to take a deep breath, the king continued, "Now, swear to me by the Lord that you will not kill off my descendants or wipe out my name from my father's family."

Speaking with sincerity that flowed from his every fiber, David gave his oath to Saul. Saul and his men returned home, and David and his men went back up to the stronghold.

# Chapter 25

*"For in death there is no remembrance of thee; in the grave who shall give thee thanks?" (Psalm 6:5, KJV)*

So much had happened since David had his encounter with King Saul, but the biggest event was the passing of the Prophet Samuel. The whole country felt the pain of losing one of their greatest prophets of all time. All of Israel grieved at Samuel's death, and it appeared that the whole country came to his funeral. Had David not had the encounter with King Saul where he spared the king's life, he doubted he'd have gone to the funeral, at least without specific direction from God. Samuel was buried in his hometown, Ramah. They had the funeral in his home. David took a small army of men for protection. He joined in with those paying tribute to the old prophet.

As David sat by the fire that evening, he recalled the joy of seeing lifetime friends and the council from his hometown. His heart ached that his parents had to miss so much, but it was still necessary to keep them safe. He recalled the stories that were told as the men sat around the feast prepared to celebrate Samuel's life. Many of them talked of one tale or another where the prophet walked the circuit from town to town, issuing directions from God. Some told of words of judgment to keep them on the path of righteousness. Some people told of words spoken so directly from God that they felt God's presence in the very words. But the miracles that people encountered due to obedience were the most exciting part of the conversation. David even found some pleasure mixed with sadness when Abner gave a detailed account of the prophet anointing Saul as the first king. They all laughed at the story as he made it sound like a wild goose chase looking for the donkeys. Abner was a good storyteller if nothing else. He added such humorous comments that everyone roared in laughter. David thought his side would burst at laughing so hard. They were always one step behind the donkeys. You would have thought they had wings and could fly. Then they learned that the donkeys were found shortly after wandering off. But Abner tied it all together with the honor bestowed upon Saul by the prophet. He used it as an opportunity to emphasize how Saul was about to begin the greatest adventure of his life.

The image of the old prophet lying on the bier ever so peacefully would stay with him forever. His face had a touch of peace that no one could question. David was certain that his face was showing the moment Samuel saw heaven or the Messiah or God's glory. There was sadness in losing someone with so much wisdom, but David found his peace in God, just like the Prophet Samuel. He recalled standing in front of the prophet as he looked down at him, and in an instant, he relived the entire day Samuel anointed him to be Israel's next king. He saw the love that flowed from Samuel's eyes, the way he respected his Lord, the way he talked; yes, he relived it all as though it was only yesterday.

The priests had arranged the prayer shawl appropriately over Samuel. David reached down and gently ran his fingers over the prayer shawl, whispering a silent prayer to God, "Please Father, let his words be fulfilled. Let Your anointing be upon me, or I don't want to be the next king. It is Your love and Your mercies that I seek. Dear God, what good is there in death? We are cut off from You in death..."

Next, David recalled the singing and dancing that took place to celebrate his life. Some of the ladies had tambourines and ribbons tied to them. Their gowns flowed around their ankles. Yes, laughter filled the air as they told one heartfelt story after another. Some people took pleasure in telling how he had rebuked them in the most amazingly loving way. Yes, even in the midst of sadness, it had been a glorious time celebrating Samuel's life.

David could not help but dwell upon the fact that the dead do not praise God. They are forgotten and cut off from His hand. Yes, he would celebrate Samuel's life, but he grieved over the loss of his death. He knew the prophets' duties of guiding the people were being replaced by the kings, but he could not fathom a world without the prophets to turn to for specific direction and words from God. At that moment, peace flooded David's heart as he thought of his personal relationship with God. He knew God's voice. He had talked personally with Jehovah. David was confident that he would never be alone in any decision that he would make. During their personal time, God would share how he is righteousness. God would teach him about finding his favor and how to walk in his protection. David found himself shaking his head as a smile flooded his entire face. How could he think of his loving God and not have joy flood his soul? The psalms he had written and the ones he was currently working on came quickly to the forefront of his thoughts. Each psalm was a divine-inspired moment between God and himself. However, David knew each one was meant to be shared. They were to be used for teaching and direction. Therefore, David carefully took time to write each one down on parchment that could be kept. They were zamars meant to be sung and to sing forth praises to music. The music part might be the part David loved the most. He enjoyed the feel of the harp beneath his fingers, together with his head and heart; he could feel the music in every way. The music would take on the feeling of the words he sang. When he was in desperation during the time Saul sought to kill him, the tunes were often sad or violent or desperate in their melody. Although, they turned victorious as he saw God as his protector. When he thought of God as his fortress, the music took on a fortified strong, victorious sound. Sometimes the men would try to direct the focus of the music to David and his talents, but David just kept his eyes on the God that rules the earth and the God that rules over Jacob. He sometimes smiled when he would write a deceptive part, such as the words from the zamar he had written when Saul tried to kill him in the palace.

*"Not a word from their mouth can be trusted; their heart is filled with destruction. Their throat is an open grave; with their tongue, they speak deceit. Declare them guilty, O God! Let their intrigues be their downfall. Banish them for their many sins, for they have rebelled against you."*

The music spoke so clearly the words, causing you to feel the full effect of each word. Oh, and lightning bolts, those were so fun to add sound effects too, and reverence to God, now that took on such a holy and amazing feeling. Often the music was so light that you could actually feel God's presence.

\* \* \* \* \*

After returning to his men, David moved everyone to his mountain stronghold in the wilderness of Paran. It was located close to Maon, a town in the mountains of Judah. It is north of Palestine and south by the desert of Sinai. David so loved the history lessons he'd received growing up. It allowed him to teach the men concerning each area as they visited it, and then, together, they'd share even more insights and knowledge. The city of Maon was founded by Maon, the son of Shammai and a descendent of Caleb. Maon means the "habitation" or "dwelling of God." David couldn't help but imagine the Israelites being led by Moses and wandering around this area for forty years. Wow! He prayed that he would always stay soft and tender before God and never be given such a dreaded job of wasting away in the vast wilderness. During that time, God had used the words over and over, "a stiff-necked generation." Gratitude and thankfulness filled David as he silently said, 'Thank You, Lord, for a tender heart that You can always guide, a heart that always shows You how much I love You and appreciate Your love for me."

# Chapter 26

*"He delivered me from the strong enemy, and from them which hated me: for they were too strong for me"*
*(Psalm 18:17, KJV).*

As provisions ran low, David called ten young men to him and commanded them to go to a wealthy man in Carmel named Nabal. He knew of the man's reputation but hoped that since he was a descendent of Caleb, the man would show kindness and appreciation to David with some provisions. He was very careful to pick a time of harvest and celebration, hoping this would add to the man's generosity. Just hours later, he would learn that although the man was of Caleb's descent, he clearly didn't have his character. Nabal was mean and a very selfish individual. He had a reputation of always complaining and hurling insults at everyone around him.

David sent the men and gave them specific words to say when they greeted Nabal. Putting an emphasis on the word "my," David said, "Greet him in my name. Tell him that I have sent you and that you represent me. Say unto him, 'Long life to you! Good health to you and your household! And good health to all that is yours! I hear it is sheep-shearing time. When your shepherds were with us, we did not mistreat them, and the whole time they were at Carmel, nothing of theirs was missing. Ask your own servants, and they will tell you. Therefore, be favorable toward my young men since we come at a festive time. Please give your servants and your son David whatever you can find for them.'" Having received their instructions, the men were quickly off.

Plunderers were always a threat for all shepherds and herdsmen when out on the fields. However, in this region, the Philistines and others were attacking, killing, and stealing the people's flocks. David's men would ride around and protect the people. Already, David was training his army to watch over the people of their kingdom. More than once, David's men would be riding up over a hill and see the Philistines attacking or ready to attack different herdsmen. Sometimes, they would guard the shepherds from a distance, and they never knew they were watching out for them, but usually, they camped right with them and got to know the men they were protecting. David was not sure how Nabal would respond, but he was sure of one thing, when the men talked of Nabal, three key topics surfaced very quickly. The first being how rude Nabal was; the second was how beautiful his wife Abigail was, and the third thing was how rich he was, for he had inherited the bulk of the property. It had come down through the line from Caleb.

Not much time passed when the men returned without any provisions and gave David a detailed account. They had arrived just as they were told and spoke the words David gave them to say. Nabal's men were sheering the sheep just as anticipated. There was a huge pile of sheep fleece. The smaller boys would pick it up and pack it in sacks, but they would delay because it was fun to see the huge mound of woolen fleece. One of the men smiled and added, "You could tell by the look on those boys' faces that they would have jumped in the fleece and rolled around in it because of its softness had they thought they dare."

David wondered if the man was remembering his own son at home. Then, someone added how humorous it was to see how some of the sheep acted mad or embarrassed that they had their coats cut off, especially the male sheep. Another man added, "But one thing was certain, each sheep would *baah* as it escaped its capturers with a most certain sound of complaint."

This started a humorous round of *baahaas* coming from the men. David gave them a stern look of disapproval, and the sounds died down.

Nabal was of medium stature and had gained much weight over the years from too much drinking and partying. He was as hard and obstinate as his reputation indicated. Nabal not only refused to give any provisions, but he insulted David and accused him of being a runaway slave. The men had talked much about this man; he kept his beard short around his face. He was so stuck on himself that he changed outer garments as often a day as was necessary to always look clean and prestigious, although it was rumored that he was so hasty in his drinking that he was always slopping his wine down the front of his robe. His servants would often walk around with a clean robe draped across their arms. He liked to wear a head covering that was fashioned after a kingly design with a costly gem directly above his forehead. The people talked quite highly of his wife, however, saying how beautiful and very thoughtful she is. One can only ask why her father gave her to such a hard man as Nabal; perhaps it was Nabal's wealth that caused him to "purchase" her.

David questioned his men to make sure Nabal's insults were not the response of a misunderstanding. He asked what Nabal's men had said; they agreed that David's men had only ever protected them. They referred to their protection as a "wall built up around them." But this seemed to mean nothing to Nabal. As the men talked and each one added his own version of what happened, anger rose up within David. Reaching for his own sword, David took time to wrap or gird his sword belt three times around his waist to assure it would not come off in battle. This was the sign that they intended to shed blood. He shouted a command to prepare four hundred of his men for battle, "Put on your swords!" He gave orders to Joab to select two hundred men to stay behind and protect their camp.

The men enjoyed a good ruckus, but they wholeheartedly believed in protecting David. They believed that he would be their king, so in many ways, they already treated him like one. Honor was one of the most necessary things to show a king and a man who would not show that honor needed to be destroyed.

Had the man just hoarded his riches, David might have let the insult go, but to accuse him of being a "runaway slave." That insult would not be allowed to stand. What a narrow-minded man he must be. After all, the people had called him the slayer of ten thousand Philistines. Does this man really not know who he is dealing with? David found himself repenting of having kept this man's herdsmen and flocks safe. How could Nabal be so unappreciative? David didn't know, but Nabal would live to regret his hasty rude behavior. Was it possible that anyone would not realize that if they were an enemy to him, that they were an enemy to the almighty God? This man was obviously evil, and circumcised or not, he was no friend of God.

Mounted and descending the mountain, David was surprised to be greeted by an incredibly beautiful woman. She had her face mostly covered with a veil, but her eyes radiated with sincerity and kindness. As David and his men approached, she climbed down off her donkey and bowed low before David. Then, she introduced herself as Nabal's wife and quickly apologized for her husband's rude behavior. She raised her head only enough to look for understanding in David's eyes. David found himself wanting to chuckle at the humorous way she went about it. "May my lord pay no attention to that wicked man Nabal. He is just like his name—his name means 'fool,' and folly goes with him. But as for me, your servant, I did not see the men my master sent."

Abigail went on to explain that one of her servants came to her quickly after David's men departed. He told her of their arrival and request. The servant had used the words, "They, David's men, were a wall to us night and day, all the time we were with them keeping the sheep."

Abigail could not help but speak of the wise advice that this servant had given her. He made her aware of how rude her husband had been and added, "So know this and consider what you will do, for evil is determined against our master and all his house. For he is such a wicked man that one cannot speak to him."

Immediately, Abigail set out to rectify the situation and to pay tribute to David. She was not just taking care of her husband, the "fool" that he is, but she had heard of King Saul's pursuit of David and the rumors that King Saul believed he was to be Israel's next king. Only the story she had heard was why King Saul feared him...because God's anointing had left him as king and had been placed upon David.

Abigail quickly ordered her servants to prepare foods for her to bring to David and his men. After briefly sharing this series of events with David, she gave an account of what she had brought. She told him she had two hundred loaves of bread, two skins of wine, five dressed sheep, five seahs or five bushels of roasted grain, a hundred cakes of raisins, and two hundred cakes of pressed figs. They loaded them on donkeys, and she told her servants to go on ahead and explained that she would be right behind.

The men closest to David could see his admiration for Abigail. A few thought there might have been more than admiration on his part. Perhaps he, too, thought her to be as beautiful as they had all heard. David climbed down off his horse and walked up right in front of her. He reached out and took her hand and raised her to a standing position in front of him. Humbly, she received his hand and stood up. She kept her head bowed in reverence and respect, avoiding looking him directly in the eyes. He listened to the words of regret and apology that flowed from her lips... His eyes seemed to take in her whole face. He accepted her generosity and escorted her back to her donkey. As he assisted her back up, he let her know that he had just spoken prior to seeing her that "It's been useless—all my watching over this fellow's property in the desert so that nothing of his was missing. He has paid me back evil for good. May God deal with

David's enemies, be it ever so severely if, by morning, I leave alive one male of all who belong to him."

At this comment, Abigail grabbed her chest, and a tear swelled up in the corner of each eye. David was taken aback by her tender emotional response. She dropped her head down toward the ground. David reached out his fingers and gently lifted her chin up until their eyes met. Her eyes, though not pleading as in a beggar begging for his life, they still yearned for assurance of her husband and all that is theirs. David assured her that he was grateful for her intervention. As if to emphasize everything, Abigail added these words, "Now, since the Lord has kept you, my master, from bloodshed and from avenging yourself with your own hands, as surely as the Lord lives and as you live, may your enemies and all who intend to harm my master be like Nabal. And let this gift, which your servant has brought to my master, be given to the men who follow you. Please forgive your servant's offense, for the Lord will certainly make a lasting dynasty for my master because he fights the Lord's battles. Let no wrongdoing be found in you as long as you live. Even though someone is pursuing you to take your life, the life of my master will be bound securely in the bundle of the living by the Lord your God. But the lives of your enemies he will hurl away as from the pocket of a sling. When the Lord has done for my master every good thing, he promised concerning him and has appointed him leader over Israel; my master will not have on his conscience the staggering burden of needless bloodshed or of having avenged himself. And when the Lord has brought my master success, remember your servant."

There was a rather prophetic sound to her words that stunned David. Was it wisdom this woman had, or did she have a prophetic anointing upon her life that would only come from a relationship with God Himself? He didn't know, but he hoped he'd have a chance to encounter her again.

David answered Abigail, "Praise be to the Lord, the God of Israel, who sent you today to meet me. May you be blessed for your good judgment and for keeping me from bloodshed this day and from avenging myself with my own hands. Otherwise, as surely as the Lord, the God of Israel lives, who has kept me from harming you, if you had not come quickly to meet me, not one male belonging to Nabal would have been left alive by daybreak."

Placing his hand gently on her arm, he said, "Go home in peace; I have heard your words and granted your request."

David gave the command to head back to camp. Joab had already assigned men to receive the food supplies and to start turning the men around. It would take a few minutes for all four hundred men to get turned around and head back up the mountain pass. David used these few minutes to take in the sight of perhaps truly the most beautiful woman he had ever seen. Her hair flowed down below her veil, allowing him to only see a few inches. His breath escaped him. He didn't expect that and quickly thought to himself, *But she is married...*

The next day word came to David of Nabal's misfortune.

Nabal went to the banquet table to start feasting as soon as he woke up. When he saw much of the food was gone, he asked Abigail where it all was. Shortly after Abigail told Nabal about her encounter with David, Nabal grabbed his heart and fell down as though he was dead. He was not dead; however, he could not speak. His eyes were closed, and when they forced his eyelids up, he looked as though he was in some sort of a trance. Nabal would stay that way for the next ten days, upon which time he died. David saw this as God's judgment upon Nabal for treating him so cruelly. Upon word of Nabal's death and feeling no loss for the man, David shouted praises to God.

# Chapter 27

*"He gives his king great victories; he shows unfailing love
to his anointed, to David and to his descendants forever"
(Psalm 18:50, NIV).*

Wasting no time, David called a handful of servants and told them to go to Abigail and ask her to be his wife. David waited anxiously to see his new bride approaching, for he knew he would bestow his love upon this beautiful lady. He could only imagine that her life had been unbearable with a man like Nabal. He imagined his hands sliding over that long beautiful black hair... He recalled the softness of her hand...small, but not tiny...delicate, yes, but not too tender. She had all the refining qualities of a woman of royalty but none of the spoiled, selfish behavior of a princess, or at least that was what he picked up from this woman.

One of the men came back early with word that David's new bride was on her way with five of her servants. David had the men busy preparing a feast for the occasion and preparing him a bridal chamber, which was not too bad for being out in the wilderness. Another man prepared her a nice tent of her own.

It was to be close to David's, but not too close, for a king must have many wives to raise up a true prince to rule after him.

The men had already designed a nice tent for David as their king. Therefore, between skin rugs and makeshift furniture, it was a very luxurious dwelling indeed. This day, however, some of his men would bring in different dainties and make a comment like, "My wife would want our future king's wife to have this," and present him some fine material that their wife had sent with them for whatever purpose they might find. A couple of men even prepared flowers and incense for the occasion. One man made it his responsibility to prepare candles for his king and his new bride. These were placed in both tents, her dwelling and his.

The talk around the camp that day varied. Some men complained that a female would ruin their time together, and some men were excited. Many men missed their families, their wives or girlfriends, sisters, mothers, aunts...they just missed the routine of regular life, and having a lady in the camp might just bring in a touch of regular life.

Abiathar was busy preparing for the wedding ceremony. He was certain that it would be a simpler ceremony than what took place between David and Michal, but it would include the traditional customs. Some of the men were extra good at whittling dishes and cups out of the finer hardwoods in the region. So Joab had them prepare an extra nice wine cup and plates and hand utensils for the feast.

David stood at the edge of his tent, looking out with anticipation for his new bride. Although everything appeared ready, many were still busy with preparations around him.

Finally, his gaze caught sight of the donkeys loaded down, coming his way. In the front were his bride and a host of other women with bright, colorful gowns flowing around their ankles. None of the women were walking. They were all being led up the mountain pass by a few servants that had worked for Nabal. David's breath caught in his throat at the thought of seeing her. He felt a little like the young shepherd boy again, slightly embarrassed at the thought of the unveiling before them and yet with great anticipation. Having been married to Michal, he couldn't believe that he could still feel such excitement and nervousness all at the same time. He was never certain if his mother would have really enjoyed Michal, but he was certain that she would love Abigail. He was certain that his mother would see her as a woman of great understanding and certainly not just beauty. Soon they would be alone...soon, she would be his...soon.

What a full afternoon it had been, Abiathar prepared a very nice ceremony, and the men worked hard on the wedding feast. They had prepared enough food to have leftovers for a week if it were not for the hardy eaters in the group. Now, it was time; the servants were preparing them both for their evening together. Her hair was being untied and brushed out as he entered her tent. Another servant turned down their bed. A washbasin was prepared for the bridal couple. There was a tray of fresh cheeses, fruits, and nuts. A wineskin was prepared and sat out for them. Finally, a guard was posted outside the tent and given strict orders that under *no* circumstances were there to be any interruptions. He didn't care if King Saul himself showed up; Joab, Abinadab, and Shammah were in charge. They could handle anything that could possibly arise. Tonight, well, tonight was theirs... Anticipation built as David imagined how beautiful her hair would flow around her hips; her breasts were so full and inviting. Her eyes...so round and full of life. Her lips... He had not yet seen her lips, but he knew her kiss would be like her heart, devoted and tender. Her nose, so slender and straight, not long but just perfect. Her eyebrows raised with her every word, but not as in anger but as expressions of her integrity. She smelled of every beautiful fragrance in the area. What was that fragrance? He couldn't place it for sure but would enjoy trying. There was a confidence and a devotion that came from this woman. She understood her position and respected it in Nabal's home. David had no doubts that she would do the same in his house.

\*\*\*\*\*

A little routine settled into the camp over the next few weeks as David spent time with his new bride. Word came to him concerning the wife of his youth...Michal. King Saul had given her to another husband, Phalti, son of Laish, who was of Gallim. Certainly, Saul's plan was to punish him. David knew that someday, he would be king, and he would get Michal back. He was more determined than ever to succeed and walk in God's righteousness.

\*\*\*\*\*

A few months later, David took another wife. Her name was Ahinoam. She lived in the valley of Jezreel and came from the

Issachar clan. Issachar was the fourth son of Jacob and Leah. The Issachar clan settled there after entering the Promised Land. David had grown up knowing Ahinoam. They had seen each other one to two times a year until he went to live with King Saul. Her father was a merchant. He traveled south regularly to Bethlehem for buying and selling. They lived in the fertile Jezreel valley near the river, having an abundant amount of land. Her father became good friends with David's father. They exchanged goods with every visit. David's father used to rave about the wine her father made. Many men made wine, but her father had an extra good way of processing it. Perhaps it was the specially aged barrels. David didn't know, but lately, David's memories had gone back to this time. She was pretty as a young girl. Recently, he wondered how she might look now as a young lady. After four months, Abigail was not pregnant yet, and he needed a son or several sons to carry on his birthright. David felt like another wife was in order. The entire time she was married to Nabal, Abigail had not had children. Perhaps she could not bear children. Perhaps there was a reason God had not opened her womb. David sent some men he could count on. He also sent Shammah, for he trusted his brother's opinion. He knew that he would only bring her to be wed if she was of their family's standards. He knew Abigail would not be happy about this, but he also knew she would accept any new wife. Abigail already treated him with respect of being Israel's next king. The real question was where to place Ahinoam's tent. He'd let Joab figure that out. Within himself, he had to admit it was kind of fun delegating responsibilities.

Shammah and the other men were gone for a few weeks, but as he anticipated, they brought back Ahinoam to him. Yes, she was beautiful. She reminded him a little of Michal in the aspect that she too was small framed. She had a tiny frame and didn't really change in looks since that of a little girl. She wore her hair a little shorter and pulled back in ribbons. It was only halfway down her back, or was it the massive curls that pulled it up? She had a tint of red to her hair, just like his. He thought they might have a red-haired baby together. She had a touch of freckles that highlighted her cheeks when she was out in the summer sun. He loved teasing her about them when they were young; he hoped they were still there. She was a good runner and could come close to outrunning him when they were children.

He was pleased to find out she had never married and was not betrothed. God had kept her for him. In fact, her father gave Shammah proof of her virginity according to their law. He also included a barrel of wine for the bridal couple, as well as an abundant dowry. David found pleasure in knowing his parents would be pleased to personally know his newest bride. They didn't just know her, but they knew her father and how she was raised. She had that teasing way that they'd shared when they were little. As children so often do, they'd play together, teasing and chasing each other. David was shocked to find that familiar feeling of wanting to chase her and tackle her to the ground. Only this time, instead of tagging her or pinning her down, he desired to kiss her. Wrestling with her was taking on a whole new meaning. David remembered her eyes. When she looked at him, it was as though she could see deep inside him. It seemed to him that she knew his thoughts before he framed them with words. He was pleased to see that same "full of life" look in her eyes. How he would have teased her back then if he'd known how their lives would go. But then it was good that he didn't know. Ahinoam had always enjoyed his poetry. She loved sitting with him as he tended the sheep; that is when he was close enough for her to join him. Now, she was a full-grown lady. She knew the Hebrew ways, she shared their history, and she was raised serving the God of Abraham, Isaac, and Jacob. Yes, she was a good choice for a wife, and as long as her father lived, they'd be sure to have an abundant supply of outstanding wine each year.

*Of course, as king, I'll be able to buy all the wine we'll ever need, but it is fun to think of 'in-law' privileges... It is also fun to think of having an 'in-law' that will not, will not treat me as an outlaw.*

It sounded humorous and funny, but he was actually quite serious about these thoughts.

*It will be fun to invite all of our parents to my palace for the Jewish feasts... Yes...that will be quite fun indeed...* As these thoughts flowed across David's mind, he smiled to himself.

A few months later, Ahinoam came to David while he was worshipping God. He was singing a new psalm to God. Even now, the women were not to come to David unless he called for them, but she took a chance that he would understand. She almost felt like these rules didn't apply to her, oh, not because of her presumption, but because of the childhood history they shared. David never said they didn't apply, but he never strictly enforced these rules with her. She was careful not to take advantage of them and to appreciate the added relationship it gave her with him.

He was sitting on a large rock that was extending beyond the mountain. She took time to listen to his words as she walked up close to him.

He was singing, "The Lord is my rock, my fortress, and my deliverer; my God is my rock, in whom I take refuge, my shield and the horn of my salvation. He is my stronghold, my refuge, and my savior." He paused to play music for a few minutes. Then she heard, "From violent men, You save me. I call to the Lord, who is worthy of praise, and I am saved from my enemies."

His song went on to include waves of death swirling about him...torrents of destructions overwhelming him...cords of the grave coiled around him...and snares of death confronting him. Sorrow filled her heart for him, but as quickly as she felt his pain, she felt his victory in the words that followed.

"In my distress, I called to the Lord; I called out to my God. From His temple, He heard my voice; my cry came to His ears."

She sat down quietly, just off in a visible distance. He had not seen her because his eyes were closed in worship to his Lord. She admired David and was so glad to be bringing him the news she had growing inside her. She knew he would be excited. He'd asked her midwife to let him know when she thought she might be pregnant, but she'd kept this information secret; she wanted to be the one to share her news with him.

As she listened to his words, Ahinoam decided that God must speak to David personally. He knew truths about God that others didn't seem to have insight on, things that spoke of God's personality and His attributes. Her family had taught her about Jehovah, but David sounded like he knew Him personally... "To the faithful, You show yourself faithful; to the blameless, You show yourself blameless; to the pure, You show yourself pure; but to the crooked, You show yourself shrewd. You save the humble, but Your eyes are on the haughty to bring them low.

You are my lamp, O Lord; the Lord turns my darkness into light. With Your help, I can advance against a troop; with my God, I can scale a wall. As for God, His way is perfect; the word of the Lord is flawless, He is a shield for all who take refuge in Him."

Excitement filled David completely as he concluded his song, "The Lord lives! Praise be to my rock! Exalted be God, the rock, my Savior! He is the God who avenges me, who puts the nations under me, who sets me free from my enemies. You exalted me above my foes; from violent men, You rescued me. Therefore, I will praise You, O Lord, among the nations; I will sing praises to Your name. He gives His king great victories; he shows unfailing kindness to His anointed, to David and his descendants forever."

Joy filled her completely at this last line. David laid his harp down and came over to Ahinoam and asked what brought her out here. Smiling, she looked into his eyes and said, "I brought you news, but perhaps the Lord has already told you my news."

David looked a bit confused and asked, "Why would you think that?"

Smiling sweetly as she looked into his eyes, "It was the words you sang last..." she let her words sink in.

David recalled the last line and slowly recited it, "He gives His king great victories... He shows unfailing kindness to His anointed...to David and his *descendants* forever." Descendants...

Joy flooded David's face as he excitedly asked her, "Are you... Are we... I mean, are you with child?" She beamed as she smiled at him excitedly, shaking her head, "Yes."

That night in his tent, David held Ahinoam as they talked about the child they were going to have. They talked of what their son's name would be. David had prayed for a son, in fact, many sons, so he had no doubt that it would be a boy. She talked of all the sons she would give him. Finally, after discussing many names from both their family lines, they settled upon Amnon. They liked this name because it meant "faithful." The name came from Shimon, from Caleb's clan. David especially loved it because he would raise his son to be a faithful follower of the Lord. It would be fun to teach him and to raise him as his father raised him.

\*\*\*\*\*

Eight months later, Ahinoam gave birth to a son, and they named him Amnon as they had planned. Amnon's name came from "aman," which means "faithful." David beamed with complete joy at the birth of his firstborn. Not long after that, Abigail gave birth to a son also. They agreed to name him Daniel, for it meant "God is my judge." Abigail had been pregnant with his second son during his last encounter with King Saul, and his name represented David's self-control for not killing King Saul.

# Chapter 28

*"To the faithful you show yourself faithful, to the blameless,*
*you show yourself blameless..." (Psalm 18:25, NIV)*

What a day it had been... It was nighttime now, and David left the camp for some peace and quiet. A smile spread over his face as he thought of his boys. He loved his baby boys, but there was never a quiet moment now with babies around. Often, David used his prayer shawl to pray within his tent, but he'd always found God the quickest in a quiet setting. David positioned himself with some rocks to sit on and lean against. Gazing up at the stars that shined above him, he recalled the story of Abraham. He envisioned God telling him that his seed would be as the sands of the shore or as the stars in the heavens. He imagined all the Israelites that Moses brought out of Egypt and saw them as stars. Sometimes, as a star would dance across the sky, he'd imagine it was Moses leading the Israelites through the wilderness, and the other stars were following, with still others trailing behind. He loved to worship God anytime, but especially tonight. He was exhausted just hearing the fussing and crying babies. Worshipping God and spending time with Him built David up. He felt exhausted just thinking about his boys. It seemed as though when one baby was happy, the other was upset... How exhausting!

He found it a little humorous as men who had their tents closest to David were one by one moving them further back into the group of men. They were always quick to explain that David needed more room for his expanding family. He knew they weren't getting good sleep either and smiled slightly at the humor of it all. Some men would make light of the situation by sharing some of their own infant or toddler stories. The things they'd tell... One guy was lying on the bed holding his baby above his face, talking to his son. He was slightly bouncing him above in the air when suddenly the baby vomited in his face and, of all things, in his mouth. David couldn't be sure why the man shared that unless it was to make him sick to his stomach.

It had been a good day, a day with the life and excitement of his two sons in camp. He smiled as he recalled Daniel spitting up milk all over Joab when he held him earlier. It had been a while since Joab was around little ones, but he handled it well. Momma pulled out a cloth and cleaned the spot as well as she could, then took Daniel away so that the men could talk.

One time throughout the afternoon, Amnon tried to crawl over to his daddy and grab his leg. He then pulled himself up. He was not walking yet, but all the signs were there that it wouldn't be too terribly long. Both boys had the dark brown Jewish eyes that ran through his family. Amnon took after his momma, Ahinoam, and her father more than his side. He was a small frame, slender hips, even for a baby. But his rib cage fanned out slightly at the bottom, indicating he would be of a good size built when grown. The only chubs he had were the tiny bit on his thighs. He had his momma's black hair, and it appeared wavy but very fine. His hair was just starting to thicken. As he had hoped, Amnon had hints of red in his hair like both his parents. He had eyes like his mother's father, the cut of his eyes was slender, and yet he had Momma's sparkle for life in his eyes. He could wrap David around his finger just by giving him that tearful look that said, "Daddy, ou fix it..." or "Daddy, I need ou..." It was a real joy interacting with his boys. They both had the dark Jewish skin.

Even as a baby, Amnon loved to throw. How he could throw rocks or his toys and especially a fit when wanting his own way. David was certain that he'd be good with a javelin when it came time to learn. Even as a baby, though, he was soft-spoken, so David wondered if he'd find his voice as his successor, but there was plenty of time to mentor him and to raise him as a prince. Besides, as he'd learned with Jonathan, not everyone in succession makes it to the throne. The best thing he could do as their father would be to teach the boys how to yield to God. For in surrender and reverencing Him, then and only then, would they find their way to the throne. David chuckled at that thought because of its dual meaning, the throne of God and the throne as king of Jerusalem.

Daniel reminded him of Abigail. He has many of her features, but David felt like he had eyes like his own father, Jesse. David saw his father's expressions every time he looked at his son; it made him homesick to share his children with his parents. He remembered when his sister Zeruiah brought his nephews over to his parent's house. He recalled how his mother rocked Joab by the hours when he was little. He could see his father bouncing him on his knee. It was always fun and noisy when she brought the babies over. This brought to his thoughts one of David's favorite memories. David was around twelve at the time. Joab was around two years old and was determined he was going to herd sheep with his uncle David.

"Me go Un...Da-bid! Sheep..." As far as Joab was concerned, he was going. He had Grandma, who he called his savta, pack his lunch. He had Grandpa, or his saba, help him find a staff that would work for him. They'd done it all in good humor while assuring him that he couldn't go. However, he was completely upset when he learned he really couldn't go. The temper tantrum he threw... Such disappointment!

Both of David's parents said, "You're not old enough."

"Me to...ou-d...nuff!" He said those words over and over through his tear-stained face as he watched Un-Da-bid leaving. David recalled how he wanted to take him just because he was so resolved. Joab's determination and words stayed with him all day long. Disappointments... The very idea caused David's thoughts to take a turn, bringing with it words of comfort from God.

It had been a day of instruction; his men had asked questions and allowed him to teach them. But there was a heaviness that came with the day. A report came that King Saul was chasing and pursuing him once again. Some of the men of Ziph, the Ziphites, went to Saul while he was at Gibeah and said, "Is not David hiding on the hill of Hakilah, which faces Jeshimon?"

Questions of dishonesty, of men not following God, came to David's mind all day. He knew God would protect him, but why did men fall so easily to corruption and turn their faces so far from Him? It was truly a mystery that he could not and never wanted to understand. It seemed utterly abominable to David that people could think there was no God or that Jehovah was not the one true God. He just couldn't comprehend it. Words concerning these men came to David's heart. He looked around at his candles and lantern to make sure he had enough light to pin the words.

> The fool says in his heart, "there is no God." They are corrupt, they do abominable deeds, there is none who does good. The Lord looked down from heaven on the children of man, to see if there were any who understand, who seek after God. They have all turned aside, together they have become corrupt; there is none that does good, not even one. Have they no knowledge, all the evildoers who eat up my people as they eat bread, and do not call upon the Lord? There they are in great terror, for God is with the generation of the righteous. You would shame the plans of the poor, but the Lord is his refuge. Oh, that salvation for Israel would come out of Zion! When the Lord restores the fortunes of his people, let Jacob rejoice, let Israel be glad.[17]

David didn't often add a title, but he heard the title while writing it, "The Future of the Fool." Looking up at a stirring in the bushes, David watched a hyrax rustling around. It was a furry little creature, probably looking for some food. Then, back to back with the words of that song, another song came. It borrowed some of the same words. He called this one "No One is God, but One."

> The fool says in his heart, "There is no God." They are corrupt, doing abominable iniquity; there is none who does good. God looks down from heaven on the children of man, to see if there are any who understand, who seek God. They have all fallen away; together they have become corrupt; there is none who does good, not even one. Have those who work evil no knowledge, who eat up my people as they eat bread, and do not call upon God? There they are, in great terror, where there is no terror! For God hath scatters the bones of him who encamps against you: you put them to shame, for God has rejected them. Oh, that the salvation for Israel would come out of Zion! When God restores the fortunes of his people, let Jacob rejoice, let Israel be glad.[18]

David gave thought to the word "fool." It represented so many people he'd met so far in life. The word meant "foolish, a person who is morally deficient." David found it difficult not to smile when he thought of how that represented Nabal. "My Lord, help me to keep my heart pure before You."

David's thoughts turned to the Ziphite men as he stared off into the darkness. With a heavy heart, David said, "Now these Ziphite men are coming against me..."

Would these people ever learn that God was at the heart of everything he did? David saw the attacks of the Philistines and other evil men upon the local people as "them eating up God's people as they eat bread" by taking all their provisions and stealing from them.

*The Lord looks down from heaven on the sons of men to see if there are any who understand, any who seek God. All have turned aside... As a whole, this country seems evil. They've turned away from God. Lord... oh that salvation for Israel would come out of Zion! When the Lord restores the fortunes of His people, let Jacob rejoice, and Israel be glad! Bring Your salvation, bring Your hope for Your people, then Jacob will rejoice, and Israel will be glad! And together, we'll praise Your name.*

David had men watching King Saul, looking and listening for information. He'd learned that King Saul was coming with three thousand of his best men from Israel. He was on his way to the wilderness of Ziph.

David knew God gave him a promise of being Israel's next king, and he prayed over and over that he would not be asked to kill King Saul. That it would not come to that, but he had some fear in his heart that it could. His time in prayer allowed him to turn the situation over to God and to commit his worries to God and turn it into prayer. David would have to encounter King Saul again, but tonight he'd concentrate on encountering his Father God instead.

# Chapter 29

*"Let Your face shine upon Your servant; Save me for Your mercies sake" (Psalm 31:16, NKJV).*

David had spies who knew King Saul's whereabouts at all times. They told him that King Saul had set up camp and then continued to watch his activities. He was troubled at the thought of Saul coming after him...again.

Standing a safe distance off, David looked at where Saul had set up camp. It had been such a beautiful day. He still felt the heat of the sun shining down on him.

He knew his men had not lied to him, but he hoped that somehow the information was incorrect. It dampened his spirits to see their camp, even though David put his faith in God. He took careful assessment of where Saul's campsite was located and where Abner, the son of Ner, was set up. Saul had the men and the carriages encircled around him, offering him the best protection. Abner was close by him, as a first officer should be. He was his personal protection.

That night David asked Ahimelek, the Hittite, and his nephew Abishai, son of Zeruiah and Joab's brother, "Who will go down into the camp with me to Saul?"

Abishai was quick to answer, "I'll go with you."

The sun was setting, and dusk was now upon them so that David couldn't see Abishai's face clearly, although David could hear too much delight in Abishai's voice. He'd have to keep a close eye on him. David, however, had full assurance that all of his men would obey his orders, especially when it came to King Saul's life.

Overwhelming loneliness flooded over David as he stood looking out over the desert. For miles and miles, as far as he could see, all he saw was a vast and sparsely populated land made out of more little tiny grains of sand than one could imagine counting. David looked over at King Saul's camp. They were camped on a plateau, one of the peaks of the long ridge of el-Kolah, running out of the Ziph plateau on the south of Jeshimon. Many of the men shuttered when looking at the plateau; it was considered dark and uninviting. The name Hakilah means "darksome." Some said that an evil presence resided in the hill. Still, others joked that King Saul would feel right at home. David didn't know how true the evil "thing" was. What he did know was that King Saul was an exhausting individual...and he had no peace... No peace... What a destitute place to be.

Darkness had been upon them for a few hours. There was no sign of anyone being awake. David and Abishai had been watching the movements of the king's men for a while now. After spending time in prayer earlier while it was still daylight, David had felt like God was directing him to go into the enemy's camp. A little unsure as to what he would do when he got there, David prepared to go. Together they climbed down to the bottom of the mountain they were on, crossed the valley, and started up the front of the plateau. The plateau had looked rather peaceful as the sun set with the sun giving the last few rays of light. David found it rather fascinating as he watched the shadows grow so long and beautiful, eventually disappearing into the darkness of night. Abishai tripped over an unsuspecting rock. Though not falling completely, David was concerned about the sound he'd made. Both men crouched low and stopped silently, waiting to see if they would hear the sound of arrows raining down upon them. After a few minutes of total silence, they moved on. Both men were watching their steps much closer. Abishai had insisted on leading the way, but David knew God had shown him how to climb the front of the plateau. So David led the way. He thought Abishai's nobleness was impressive, though. A smile turned the corner of his lips as he remembered the chivalry he had shown. David smiled when he thought about him tripping and how he was slightly clumsy for his large frame. David slid each foot into a small foothold on the side of the plateau. He kept a firm handgrip on the rocks above to pull himself up. He had looked for a path, but the path was still rough and needed some hand climbing techniques. The animals must reach the plateau from behind. The front was too steep for most animals. When they reached the top, they carefully crept over to where the men were sleeping. All of a sudden, David stood up and started walking. He turned around and smiled at Abishai and asked him why he was still crouched down close to the ground. Abishai was surprised by his candor. He stood up, shocked and terrified that all the soldiers would wake up. David turned toward the soldiers, and with a sweeping hand motion, he said, "God is protecting us." Then, he recommended that Abishai not trip on anyone, though... At that, he told him to follow him. David knew right where King Saul was sleeping, so they headed that way. As he walked through the camp, David saw Doeg, the Edomite. For a fleeting second, thoughts filled David's mind of taking revenge for the priests. Just as quickly, David made God his judge and dismissed his actions. Next, David passed other men he'd known working for King Saul. Memories of days past flooded his mind. As he looked at the men, many looked peacefully sound asleep with the moonlight shining down on them. Abishai almost dropped to the ground when a soldier stuck out his arm as if wakening and grabbing his ankles. Placing his right hand on his chest, he patted it as if to calm down his heart. David smiled and turned back to his task at hand. Next, he saw Abinadab and Malchishua, two of Saul's younger sons. Thoughts of all of them around the king's table flashed through David's mind. He recalled one time when Malchishua told of a funny event that had taken place. He had them almost rolling on the floor in laughter as he recalled Malchishua's descriptions of everyone. He told of a time when he and his friends drank too much wine. Quickly, David prayed that God's will would be with these men who were now his enemies. Jonathan's brother, Abinadab, was not very old, too young for war and fighting, in David's opinion. He was around the age David had been when he began fighting, but there was a difference. David knew God and knew He'd protect him. Both of them, unlike Jonathan, had many of their mother's features, which included worshipping idols. Jonathan was built like his father. Looking at Jonathan,

David knew King Saul had been a very handsome man in his younger years.

There he is, David thought to himself. His closest and dearest friend. How he wanted to wake Jonathan and go off and talk, but those days were past... He had been brought here by the hand of God. As if he felt David's presence, Jonathan rolled over toward David. He wondered if he'd wake up, but he didn't. They moved around a few other soldiers and soon were close to Abner. As David approached King Saul, he felt instructed by God to take Saul's spear and water bottle. It had been King Saul's tradition every since David had known him to stick his spear in the ground just above where his head was positioned.

Not knowing David's intentions, Abinadab inched himself as close to David as he could. Talking softly, he said, "God has delivered your enemy into your hand this day. Now let me pin him to the ground with one thrust of my spear; I won't strike him a second time."

Whispering, but in a very assertive tone, David told Abishai, "Don't destroy him! Who can lay a hand on the LORD's anointed and be guiltless? As surely as the LORD lives," he added, "the LORD will strike him; either his time will come, and he will die, or he will go into battle and perish."

David then added, "The LORD forbid that I should lay my hand against the LORD's anointed. Now, get the spear and the cruse of water that is near his head, and let's go."

As they distanced themselves from the camp, Abishai asked what had just happened. He was certain that the men should have woken up, at least some of them. David told him the Lord put a deep sleep upon them. Abishai was kind of disappointed that he didn't know about that sooner. He was daring enough and would have danced around the camp making a bit of a scene had he known. David laughed at Abishai as he talked on, "I could have had some real fun. I could have mixed up their personal items and moved things from one place to another. That would have created some real fun when they woke up…"

David never had a dull moment when any of his nephews were around. Abishai had a good heart. He was just glad that Abishai had listened to him and not tried to take matters into his own hands with King Saul's life.

Once the men were back up on the other side of the mountain a safe distance away, David called out to the army and to Abner, son of Ner. There was teasing in his voice as he played with him, "Abner, son of Ner…"

"Abner…son of Ner, wake up!"

Adding more of a mocking to his voice, he asked, "Aren't you going to answer me, Abner?"

Abner replied, "Who are you who calls to the king?" He was still waking up; his voice sounded raspy and as though he was trying to figure out what was going on.

Mocking Abner, David asked, "Aren't you a valiant man? And who is like you in all Israel? Why haven't you guarded your lord the king? Someone came to destroy your lord, the king. What you have done is not good. As surely as the Lord lives, you and your men deserve to die because you have not guarded your master, the Lord's anointed. Look around you. Where are the king's spear and water jug that were near his head?"

Recognizing David's voice, Saul spoke loudly and said, "Is that your voice, David, my son?" Suddenly, emotion gripped David's heart as he heard the tender voice he'd once known.

The voice that allowed him access to the king's chambers and mostly his heart.

Guarding his heart from emotions, David replied, "Yes, it is, my lord, the king." Then, David said, "Why is my lord pursuing his servant? What have I done, and what wrong am I guilty of? Now, let my lord, the king, listen to his servant's words. If the Lord has incited you against me, then may He accept an offering? If, however, men have done it, may they be cursed before the Lord! They have now driven me from my share in the Lord's inheritance and have said, 'Go, serve other gods.' Now do not let my blood fall to the ground far from the presence of the Lord; the king of Israel has come out to look for a flea...as one hunts a partridge in the mountains."

With a humbled voice, Saul said, "I have sinned. Come back, David, my son. Because you considered my life precious today, I will not try to harm you again. Surely, I have acted like a fool and have errored greatly."

Stretching his arm upward, David lifted the spear high in the air. Then with a strong voice, he said, "Here is the king's spear. Let one of your young men come over and get it. The Lord rewards every man for his righteousness and faithfulness. The Lord delivered you into my hands today, but I would not lay a hand on the Lord's anointed. As surely as I valued your life today, so may the Lord value my life and deliver me from all trouble."

At that, David thrust the spear into the ground, so they could see it.

Then, Saul added with sincerity, "May you be blessed, my son David; you will do great things and surely triumph."

David turned away. Abishai asked just one time if he could stay and take vengeance upon the man who came over to get the spear. David didn't answer him with words but gave him a look that told him "definitely no." They didn't wait for the man; they headed off into the woods and out of sight. Abishai was sure he heard the men asking King Saul if they should take off after David, but he answered, "No...it is as I have said, I have errored greatly. I will not go after him again." Sadness filled King Saul's heart as he yearned for God's favor again. That was the problem. He didn't yearn for God; he yearned for the favor he'd known. However, even that would only last for a few minutes. There was an unyielding hardness that he'd allowed to consume his heart that left no room for love and tender emotion.

Another song or zamar was birthed in David's spirit; only this one was filled with the anguish he had experienced when his enemies were after him. This one was filled with despair.

*In You, Lord, do I put my trust and seek refuge; let me never be put to shame or disappointed, deliver me in Your righteousness! Bow down Your ear to me, deliver me speedily! Be my rock of refuge, a strong fortress to save me! Yes, You are my rock and my fortress; therefore, for Your name's sake, lead me and guide me. Draw me out of the net that they have laid secretly for me, for You are my strength and my stronghold. Into Your hands I commit my spirit; You have redeemed me, O Lord, the God of truth and faithfulness. I abhor those who pay regard to vain idols, but I trust in, rely on, and confidently lean on the Lord. I will be glad and rejoice in Your mercy and steadfast love because You have seen my affliction; You have taken note of my life's distresses, and You have not given me into the hand of the enemy; You have set my feet in a broad place.*

*Have mercy and be gracious unto me, O Lord, for I am in trouble; with grief, my eye is weakened, also my inner self and my body. For my life is spent with sorrow and my years with sighing; my strength has failed because of my iniquity, and even my bones have wasted away. To all my enemies, I have become a reproach, but especially to my neighbors, and a dread to my acquaintances, who flee from me on the street. I am forgotten like a dead man and out of mind, like a broken vessel I am. For I have heard the slander of many, terror is on every side! While they schemed together against me, they plotted to take my life. But I trusted in, relied on, and was confident in You, O Lord; I said, "You are my God." My times are in Your hands, deliver me from the hands of my foes and those who pursue me and persecute me.*

*Let Your face shine on Your servant, save me for Your mercy's sake and in Your loving-kindness. Let me not be put to shame, O Lord, or disappointed, for I am calling upon You, let the wicked be put to shame, let them be silent in Sheol. Let the lying lips be silenced, which speak insolently against the righteous with pride and contempt. Oh, how great is Your goodness, which You have laid up for those who fear, revere, and worship You; goodness, which You have wrought for those who trust and take refuge in You before the sons of men!*

*In the secret place of Your presence, You hide them from the plots of men; You keep them secretly in Your pavilion from the strife of tongues. Blessed be the Lord! For He had shown me His marvelous loving favor when I was beset as in a besieged city. As for me, I said in my haste and alarm, "I am cut off from before Your eyes." But You heard the voice of my supplications when I cried to You for aid. O love the Lord, all you, His saints! The Lord preserves the faithful and plentifully pays back him who deals haughtily. Be strong and let your heart take courage, all you who wait for and hope for and expect the Lord!*[19]

Daylight was upon them as David found his way to his bed; his thoughts were surrounding the Lord. He loved God so much. God was teaching him the importance of righteousness. God was showing him that every bit of his own righteousness was found in and through God. Righteousness, David said the word over and over in his mind, dwelling on the depth of its meaning. *Show me, Lord, all that You have for me to learn.* God had made one thing clear to him, "righteousness" meant his right standing with God. As David drifted off to sleep, he thought of the many inherited blessings that came to him because he was righteous in God. A peace flooded David's soul as he drifted off to sleep.

# Chapter 30

*"You make known to me the path of life; you fill me with joy
in our presence, with eternal pleasures of your right hand"*
*(Psalm 16:11, NIV).*

Depression settled upon David. Many of the men noticed that he wasn't his happy, jubilant self. Some of David's closest men went to Abiathar, the priest, the son of Ahimelech. They asked Abiathar to talk to David. It seemed that David became focused on King Saul's pursuit to destroy him. He became convinced that eventually, Saul would catch him off guard, and when he did, he'd kill him. David was certain that he was called to be king but was finding himself comparing his situation to that of Jonathan's or even King Saul's. The lineage of the king was originally supposed to be under King Saul and the Benjamin line. Jonathan was supposed to be the next king under King Saul. Perhaps, he, just as King Saul, had made some fatal error that had cost him his chance to be the next king of Israel.

The sky was dark as it ushered in the winter weather. It was not the beautiful sunny clouds that rays of sunshine could come through; no, not today. Today, the sky is gray and dark with a thick layer of cloud. Just as the sand of the desert seemed to go for miles and miles in every direction, so did the thick layer of gray clouds. It blocked every bit of sunshine that God must have out there. The path was wet with heavy dew, although it was almost noon. David slipped as he was walking. When he did, he was reminded of some words God had given him to write, "You make known to me the path of life; you fill me with joy in your presence, with eternal pleasures at your right hand."[20]

The sky seemed to hint at the darkness that draped over David's soul. Without giving any thought to his actions, David stepped high over vines of horsetail knotweed that grew across the path. The plant was named for the way it fans out like a horse's tail. Any other time, he might have taken time to appreciate its natural beauty. Its stem ascended in numerous directions, going even with the ground as well as straight up toward the sky. The leaves are oblong and wrinkled. It has clusters of pink and white flowers, with five partly fused outer petals. This plant is a big part of the area because they bloom the whole year. They are, however, done shedding now that summer is over. But not today; today, David didn't even see the plant. His focus was on the Lord. He was determined to break through this discouragement that oppressed his soul.

Having left camp and getting off away from everyone, David found a place to sit. He sat and wrote for a while, and then he'd get up and walk around. He'd seek God, praise God, and then talk to God. This went on for the entire day. David recalled many of the events over the past few years. He recalled the various times he'd run for his life or fought for his life. He meditated on putting his faith in God. He recalled various times in the past that he relied on God and trusted in Him. He experienced sadness but also hope and joy at the victories God brought.

Penning this song seemed easy as David recalled all the persecution he suffered from Saul. He recalled his narrow escape at Keilah, then in the wilderness of Maon, when Saul marched on one side of the hill and he on the other. Then, he recalled the cave in the wilderness of En Gedi. His heart was filled with a combination of prayers and praises. He confessed his confidence in God as he poured out his heart, being confident that God would deliver him out of his present trouble.

*In You, LORD, I have taken refuge; let me never be put to shame, deliver me in Your righteousness.*

In his thoughts, he said, God, *You are a just and fair judge. I thank You that You deliver me in Your righteousness...in Your righteousness.* David laid his quill down that he used to write on the parchment. He reached over to his harp and picked it up. A sweet melody flowed from his harp as his left hand strummed the strings, and his right hand picked the melody. He played a soft tune. He found comfort in his music. Then, he sang the lines he'd just written to the music, "In You, LORD, I have taken refuge; let me never be put to shame, deliver me in Your righteousness." Playing the strings, he reiterated the words, "In Your righteousness. In Your righteousness..."

After a few minutes of worshipping God, David laid the harp down and went back to writing the song that was in his heart.

*Turn Your ear to me, come quickly to my rescue, be my rock of refuge, a strong fortress to save me. Since You are my rock and my fortress, for the sake of Your name, lead and guide me. Keep me free from the trap that is set for me, for You are my refuge. Into Your hands I commit my spirit; deliver me, LORD, my faithful God.*

Praying, David said, "Please Lord, listen to me. I need You now to be my rock, my strong fortress, my refuge..."

He stopped writing for a few minutes to meditate on what these words meant to him. Rock... God is my cliff, my rocky wall to protect me from the enemy. David even imagined the heathen gods made of rock, but that was not his God. His God lives and walks with him just as He did with Abraham, Isaac, and Jacob. *God is my strong fortress. Not just my house and my shelter but my strong shelter. God is my strength, my fortified place, my defense. God is my castle, my strong place.*

David got up and walked around for a few minutes while he thought and prayed about what he was going to write next. His thoughts turned to the worthless communication that comes from some people. So many people lie and say what they want to say instead of being honest. King Saul would never stop pursuing him, and this bore heavy on his soul. Even though he trusted God, he was growing weary from the ridiculous chase he was dealing with.

*I hate those who regard lying vanities; as for me, I trust in the LORD. I will be glad and rejoice in Your love, for You saw my affliction and knew the anguish of my soul. You have not given me into the hands of the enemy but have set my feet in a spacious place.*

David thought about his home here in the wilderness and pinned the words, *You have set my feet in a spacious place, a large open area, the wilderness.*

*Be merciful to me, LORD, for I am in distress; my eyes grow weak with sorrow, my soul and body with grief. My life is consumed by anguish and my years by groaning; my strength fails because of my affliction, and my bones grow weak. Because of all my enemies, I am the utter contempt of my neighbors and an object of dread to my closest friends—those who see me on the street flee from me.*

Earlier, David had seen a pile of broken pottery lying off to the side of camp. He couldn't help but feel as discarded as that broken vessel. Rumors were also coming to him of gossip and people plotting against him. Most were people from around the area, but some from within his camp.

*I am forgotten as though I were dead; I have become like broken pottery. For I hear many whispering, "Terror on every side!" They conspire against me and plot to take my life. But I trust in You, LORD; I say, "You are my God."*

Reaching for his harp, David began to sing the words and play them to the melody. The music was taking on the words. They felt tense and almost devious when he sang of those plotting and conspiring against him. They sounded hopeful and light when he sang of his victory in God. He reiterated the words "You are my God" over and over again as he thought about all that these words mean to him.

*My times are in Your hands; deliver me from the hands of my enemies, from those who pursue me. Let Your face shine on Your servant, save me in Your unfailing love. Let me not be put to shame, LORD, for I have cried out to You, but let the wicked be put to shame and be silent in the realm of the dead. Let their lying lips be silenced, for, with pride and contempt, they speak arrogantly against the righteous.*

*Yes, Lord, let Your face shine on Your servant. Take away the clouds that are trying to take over my soul. Take away the despair and fill it with Your presence.*

*How abundant are the good things that You have stored up for those who fear You, that You bestow in the sight of all, on those who take refuge in You? In the shelter of Your presence, You hide them from all human intrigues; You keep them safe in Your dwelling from accusing tongues.*

*Thank You, God, that You protect me from human intrigues, the snares, plots, conspiracies of others.*

*Praise be to the LORD, for He showed me the wonders of His love when I was in a city under siege. In my alarm, I said, "I am cut off from Your sight!" Yet You heard my cry for mercy when I called to You for help. Love the LORD, all his faithful people! The LORD preserves those who are true to Him, but the proud, He pays back in full. Be strong and take heart, all you who hope in the LORD.*

How many hours had David been out here? He was not sure, but he knew the sun was growing long with shadows.

*****

Over the next couple of weeks, David spent much time dwelling on everything that had occurred up to this point. He became convinced of one thing above all else, "One of these days, I will be destroyed by the hand of Saul."

He thought over and over about what to do about this and determined the best answer was to escape to the land of the Philistines. *Then Saul will give up searching for me anywhere in Israel, and I will slip out of his hand.* With that in mind, he set up a meeting with his headmen and sat down to tell them his decision. They counted the cost, discussing the problems with that decision, as well as the solutions. Then, he sent out a small party of men to see if Achish, son of Maoch, king of Gath, was willing to sit down with him and discuss the possibilities. It saddened his heart to feel like he could turn to those who had naturally been his enemies from birth just because they serve other gods instead of those who said they served the same one true God of Israel.

# Chapter 31

*"All day long they twist my words; all their schemes are for my ruin. They conspire, they lurk, they watch my steps, hoping to take my life" (Psalm 56:5–6, NIV).*

Gath is one of five Philistine cities. It was established in northwestern Philistia. There were grape vineyards all around the area, as well as numerous vineyards surrounding the city. It was nice seeing the natural green growth of the land again. They had been so close to the desert that green trees and ground covering were sparse and not very attractive. Here, they were close enough to the river to have lots of green growth. The river flowed into the Great Sea. Gath bordered the Israelite territory to the south. David brought his two wives and sons. He also brought all six hundred of his men and their families. One by one, over the past few years, the men went home to get their families. Although they were concerned for their loved one's safety, they mostly missed them. As David's family grew, so did his camp. In some ways, they were creating their own city wherever they went.

David was still getting used to the idea of living in a Philistine city. He'd given some thought to this possibility since King

Saul first set out to kill him. However, he never really thought it would become reality, especially not his reality. David was walking through Gath early in the morning to go outside the city gates for a time of prayer. He told anyone who asked that he was going for his morning walk. They kept asking him why he didn't just walk in the city. He told them that he loved venturing down by the river. It offered a solitude that you can't get around people. Plus, he often saw deer and small animals wandering down to the river for a fresh drink of water.

David had learned much about the Philistines; in fact, he'd learn far more than he ever imagined. They don't pen their history like the Israelites do; they engrave their stories all over their walls. Almost every wall in Achish's castle was etched with a historical tale.

He'd seen the wall that depicted Samson marrying a Philistine woman from Gath and the riddle. David couldn't read the riddle because it was etched in their language, but he knew the riddle, and in his mind, he filled in the pieces. *Out of the eater, something to eat; out of the strong, something sweet.* They showed the wedding and the murder of his bride and her family. Sampson's adventures occupied a full, long wall. Next, they showed him catching three hundred foxes, tying their tails together, and them running in pairs. Their tails were on fire and spreading fire through the Philistines fields of grain, their vineyards, and some of their olive groves. These stories led up to Sampson and Delilah. As she sat stroking his forehead, a Philistine man with a razor was cutting his long hair off. His curls and long length showed falling to the floor. They etched the Philistines sticking hot rods of iron into his eye sockets and destroying his eyes. They showed him being bound in bronzed shackles and grinding meals in prison. Finally, they ended the story with Samson's hair growing back again. They drew him standing between the two pillars in Dagon's temple located right here in Gath. Leaning against the two pillars, they drew the walls tumbling down. Their drawings showed incredible details. They etched Philistines dead all over the temple mount. The huge sandstone blocks plummeting down on them. They showed bodies twisted and partially buried in and around the rubble.

*****

It seemed strange to David, but he and Achish actually enjoyed each other's presence. Of course, not in the same way as he and Jonathan, but they enjoyed talking about being on different sides of the battles.

One time while they were dining together, Achish shared with David how the men had come up to him and reminded him of David killing their war hero, Goliath. Laughing it off, he told how he humored them. He said, "David was a teenager with a slingshot. Any teen boy who could do that to our hero deserves my respect."

David heard good humor in his voice but felt as though he might be being tested to see his reaction. David didn't hide the fact that he worshipped the God of Abraham, Isaac, and Jacob, but he didn't promote it around the Philistines either. So he gave a light laugh and talked about how he couldn't believe that Goliath allowed his helmet to fall off. "By the way, speaking of armor, I'd love to see how you make your armor. Perhaps we can learn new details from each other." David knew they were years ahead of them in their iron smith work.

He decided to be honest and humble about their advanced technology, especially since it was obvious to both sides anyways. He complimented their achievements and asked if he'd mind sharing their process with him. They laughed, and Achish said he would, but perhaps he'd wait until he was certain of David's intentions. David smiled and said, "Fair enough."

Achish asked David if he'd like to see his wall. David was surprised to hear a wall called "his" wall. "Absolutely!" he responded.

David smiled as his curiosity peaked. He followed Achish through the castle until they reached a wall on the south side. There he was...up on the wall. This was amazing. He loved how their pictures told the stories. To emphasize he was a teenager, they drew him smaller than he remembered being. They had some sheep up on the hill the Israelites were on, emphasizing he was a shepherd. They drew frightened faces on many of the Israelites and bold, victorious faces on the Philistines. Then, they showed him slinging and a rock plummeting into Goliath's head. They drew him standing on top of their hero, lifting his head into the air by his hair with one hand. Blood was dripping down, and David was lifting Goliath's sword high in the air with his other hand. Next, the wall showed the Israelites chasing and killing many of the Philistines that day. The sun was setting on all the dead bodies as the story ended.

As David walked down to the river, he thought about Achish's plan of service for him as their new king. Bewilderment clouded David's mind as he thought, *How is it that Achish and I actually enjoy each other's presence?* David chose to view it as a divine blessing from God since he needed Achish's protection during this time of his life. So what if he had to fight with the Philistines against the Israelites. What had the Israelites ever done for him? Okay, he didn't really feel that way, but he didn't know how else to view the situation. Many of his men had misgivings about going down to Gath. David made sure that each man knew they had to make their own choice. He would not disown anyone for not coming with them, but he would not be able to provide protection for them or their families. One by one, they all agreed to stay with David, and since he entrusted his family to Achish, they would too. Word came to David just as he expected; King Saul had quit pursuing him when he learned where he was.

Gath was filled with much-advanced technology when compared to Israel or Judah. They had learned much about using iron in the development of weapons, but they'd taken this technology into their tools too. They were developing tools for gardening as well as tools for around the house. They'd also advanced in their pottery skills. Therefore, their pottery was more intricate in detail and versatility. Their painting skills also seemed more detailed and delicate.

The decor in Gath had many hints to their origin. They'd come across the Aegean Sea from ancient Greek, arriving approximately one hundred and thirty years earlier. It is said that they came around the same time the Israelites were entering the Promised Land.

Although there were enjoyable things about living here, there were also some problem areas. The Israelites followed

273

God's laws as completely as they knew to. The Philistines ate unclean animals. Their primary meats consisted of pigs and dogs, the wild wolf dogs, as well as other unclean animals. Any Israelite knew that wasn't acceptable. Most of the Israelites enjoyed the green grass pea lentils that were a huge part of the Philistine diet, but not the unclean animals.

Many of the men had commented to David about the evil they felt when they'd walked near the Philistine temples. Others expressed a small interest in checking them out. Their excuse was the more informed you are, the less likely you'd be pulled in. David prayed for each of his men and their families. He also sought God for answers.

After they'd been in Gath for a few weeks, David went to Achish and said, "If I have found favor in your eyes, let a place be assigned to me in one of the country towns, that I may live there. Why should your servant live in the royal city with you?"

Achish was very flattered by the honor that David showed him and assigned him the country town of Ziklag. It seemed a little funny to David since not all that long ago, he and his men protected the Israelites from the thievery of the men from Ziklag. Ziklag was located further inland. It was a few hours away on horseback and longer yet by foot. David also thought Achish's choice of cities was rather interesting. Years earlier, Ziklag had belonged to his ancestors. It had been given to Simeon's people. Achish told David he could have the nicest house there. Also, as long as he remained loyal to him, David could rule over Ziklag. David was very grateful and did just that. His wives loved having their own places again, and his men enjoyed being separated from such heathen people. David cautioned his men that such attitudes would show through in their behavior. For now, they must accept the Philistines as allies. Many times, throughout the years, the Israelites made allies with someone who was less than favorable for a specific purpose. This time was no different, and it was only for this season.

# Chapter 32

*"Be merciful to me, O God, for men hotly pursue me all the day long they press their attack" (Psalm 56:1, NIV).*

David enjoyed his newfound freedom living in Ziklag. He was excited to be walking through a town market again. He was enjoying buying foods and different items for himself. He didn't feel like he had to constantly watch over his shoulders for King Saul and his army anymore. He was enjoying simple pleasures he hadn't known in a while, such as buying the ripened fruits in season. He had given thought to bringing his parents here but knew how his father would feel about living in a Philistine community. No, he decided it was best to wait until he could secure their living amongst the Israelite community or back at their own home again.

The architectural design of Ziklag resembled the cities David had been raised in and around. This made Ziklag a whole lot more enjoyable than Gath. In some ways, David could almost forget it was a Philistine town. Ziklag had originally been given to Simeon's descendants when the Israelite children first came through to the Promised Land. Whereas the city of Gath had been designed and always owned by the Philistines, he had been told that many of their designs and culture came from the Egyptians. In fact, David learned that the Philistine people were originally brought over as slaves by Ramesses III. They were known as the Sea People who made seafaring raids upon the Egyptians. Ramesses tired of this and took them as prisoners. He then resettled them in the five different colonies they have as their coastal cities today. Ramesses was also known to have taxed them so severely in clothing and grain from their storehouses and granaries each year that he caused severe poverty to come upon them.

The Philistines were well advanced in creating metals. They'd learned much about this process. They made most of their tools and their armor out of metal. They'd learned extensively about it. Immediately upon pulling it out of the fire, it was soft. So they used hammers. By pounding the metal on an iron block, they could shape it into the various forms they were creating. They mostly used bronze and iron. They'd learn to dig rock out of the earth for this metal. Then they would cook it in a large outdoor furnace until it melted and separated into a pure iron liquid. They made shallow gutters carved out of rock and shaped in the sand with many channels. It flowed from the main trench to form a herringbone pattern. The iron was allowed to be set up hard in these sand channels. Once it was cooled, they'd break it into manageable pieces to rework. Many of the men compared the channels to a female pig suckling her litter. This was because of how it looked all laid out on the sand. They'd learned that remelting and recasting the molds made the metal harder and more durable. There were men who only did this job daily. Sometimes these same men created the new designs, and sometimes others did the designing. But they worked together as a team to create some very exquisite items, such as Goliath's armor.

* * * * *

After being in Ziklag for a few months, men started showing up to join David's army. Men had been doing that all along, but it was the first time since he'd come to live among the Philistines. These men were warriors who could help him in battle. They were armed with bows and excellent at archery. Most were able to sling stones with either their right hand or left hand. David was careful not to brag but did find it exhilarating that they were kinsmen of Saul. How exciting that they were from the tribe of Benjamin. The chiefs of these men were Ahiezer and Joash. A total of thirty men were in their small band. A few men in particular caught his attention; one of them was named Ishmaiah. One look told you he was a mighty man. He had huge shoulders with bulging muscles. This man looked incredibly strong and like he could lift a wagon alone when the wheels needed to be repaired. If he could shoot too, he'd make a great warrior.

* * * * *

The sun was setting as David looked around at the abundance of the day's plunder. Before coming to Achish, David and his men devised a plan. The Philistines raided villages and towns on a regular basis. David knew it would be necessary for them to either join in the raids or to go out on their own. This was the real reason David requested to live in another city. It would allow them to go out separate from the Philistines when doing raids. There were three groups of people David and his men could raid without going against God. These people were the Geshurites, the Girzites, and the Amalekites.

All three of these groups of people were supposed to have been eliminated by Joshua when the Israelite children entered the Promised Land, but the people were too anxious to get their families settled to fight and claim the land completely as God directed. All three groups had originally been native inhabitants of the northwestern portion of the desert between Egypt and South Palestine.

The Geshurites lived in the high land of the northwestern portion of the wilderness of Paran. The Girzites lived in Gezer, which lay far away in the west of Ephraim and in Mount Gerizim in central Palestine. Saul had been attacking the Amalekites and working on destroying them but had not yet succeeded. None of these people were allies to the Philistines, but they raided them as much as the Israelites. Therefore, David and his men knew they could raid them and present their plunder as an accomplishment of working against the Israelites. Since the Philistines knew no different, they were certain their plan would work. There was only one problem...they had to totally and completely destroy every living person when they went on these raids. David fully claimed the land. Killing every person on a raid was necessary and the only way to assure that no one went to Achish and told him what David and his men were doing. David knew it felt deceptive, but he also knew they needed to survive. He knew he and his men could never come against God's people. Since his men would fight against these three groups of people to protect Israel anyway, it seemed like a plan God could approve. Such violence still caused an aching in his heart, but again, that was the old law given down by God to keep the people from being led astray by sinful people who were determined to never serve the God of Abraham, Isaac, and Jacob.

There were all kinds of nice garments and robes among the plunder. David and his men were increasing their livestock, especially sheep, oxen, and asses. David always sent the agreed amount up to Achish, often taking the plunder to Achish himself. They were to give him half of the plunder, and then David was allowed to keep the rest. Achish gave him permission to keep the remainder or divide it as he chose. David split it up evenly, believing God would always provide for him.

Achish always asked him where they made a road. David knew he was asking where they had invaded or raided. He answered him, "Against the Negev of Judah," or "Against the Negev of Jerahmeel," or "Against the Negev of Kenites." Achish knew this meant they'd raided the south of Judah, the south of Jerahmeel, or the south of Kenites.

Achish was so excited over this news and held his cup to David in victory. He was overcome with smiles. Achish told his servant to fill his cup and to give David a cup of wine. They needed to celebrate. David gladly received his wine because it was some of the best in the land. He gave Achish his moment of pride. Achish thought about how David was totally cutting himself off from his people. The Jews must thoroughly and utterly abhor him. He found such pleasure in thinking about how David must stink to them. He had become completely offensive to his people. This excited him because he knew David would be his servant forever, creating great pleasure for Achish.

A few soldiers abducted David when he was leaving Gath. They beat him up and threatened him. They were chief men under Achish, and one of the king's generals suspected what David was doing. He accused him of lying to Achish about the raids and warned him that they'd be watching his every move. They would find out exactly what was happening, and they would definitely let Achish know what David and his men were doing. Then it would be his head upon the spear at the cities gates as a warning of what happens to people who lie to their king.

David couldn't get out of there fast enough, but he could hardly move. He was certain he had a broken rib. His face was bloody, and he felt like he'd kissed the dirt more than any other time in his life. He was slightly shaken from the severe beating. He always took a few men with him. They helped him up and back to Ziklag.

That night David took time to talk to God. Tonight, however, he stayed in the privacy of his house. He had the door open for fresh air to flow in. He was lying on his bed. He could hardly move because of how sore and stiff he felt. He called for the scripter so that he could write down the poem in his heart. Feeling discouraged and overwhelmed by the hatred of men, he started speaking. He had to pause at the end of each sentence so that the man could write it down. David told the scripter to name the poem "God Is With Me." He instructed the scripter to write a subtitle too, "This poem is to be for the director of music. I want it put to the tune of 'A Dove on Distant Oaks.'" This song had a sad sound as the bird sat high and safely above, watching the pain going on below.

Be merciful to me, O God, for men hotly pursue me; all day long they press their attack. My slanderers pursue me all day long; many are attacking me in their pride.

When I am afraid, I will trust in you. In God, whose word I praise, in God I will not be afraid. What can mortal man do to me?

All day long they twist my words; they are always plotting to harm me. They conspire, they lurk, they watch my steps, eager to take my life.

On no account let them escape; in your anger, O God, bring down the nations. Record my lament; list my tears on your scroll— are they not in your record?

Then my enemies will turn back when I call for help. By this I will know that God is for me.

In God, whose word I praise, in the Lord, whose word I praise—in the Lord, whose word I praise—in God I trust; I will not be afraid. What can man do to me?

I am under vows to you, O God; I will present my thank offerings to you. For you have delivered me from death and my feet from stumbling, that I may walk before God in the light of life.[21]

# Chapter 33

*"I was pushed back and about to fall, but the Lord helped me" (Psalm 118:13, NIV).*

The atmosphere of war had grown to the point that the Philistines were joining their armies together against Israel. Achish summoned David to come to him so that they could talk. Upon David's arrival, Achish invited him into his dining hall. He had his servants prepare a table of food, so they could leisurely discuss what might be a tense situation. After discussing the increasing tensions of war, Achish looked very seriously at David and said, "Understand that you and your men will go with me to battle."

Achish looked deep into David's eyes; he wanted to see where his loyalty lay.

When it came to King Saul, David had only the respect that one should have for his king. The love he'd felt not so many months ago was buried deep within him. He knew it was necessary to bury that part of him, or he'd end up dead at the hand of Saul or one of his men.

Being up to the challenge, David looked equally intent back into Achish's eyes. He said, "I find no pleasure in coming directly against King Saul, but it has always been my thought that God will strike him dead or that he will be killed in battle."

Continuing on, David said, "Perhaps it is his time."

A grin started to form on Ackish's face. It was accompanied by an "awe" that came from deep within his stomach, then spilled out into the words, "Perhaps it is…"

David paused and reached over to pick a small cluster of grapes from the wooden bowl. Plopping a grape in his mouth, he immediately formed a sour-looking face. Shaking his head at how bad it tasted, he thought, *Thank You, God, for sour grapes!* He had to eat another one quickly to replace the soured taste. This bought him a few more moments to form the correct words. Then he said, "We will go with you, and you shall know what your servant can do. My men and I came to you for protection; when we did, we swore our allegiance to you. We promised to serve you as you need us to. If it is war against the Israelites or raiding their cities, then so be it, King Achish."

Achish was so impressed with David that he instantly made David his bodyguard, for now and always.

Achish's bodyguard… David knew this was viewed as quite an honor. Unsure where that fit into God's plans, he responded with delight at the honor Achish had bestowed upon him. David thrust forth his arm and said, "Live forever, King Achish."

David knew his men feared things might come to this, and they always hoped it wouldn't.

Achish and David discussed different battle plans, the other armies that would join them, and David's position. Upon a comfortable amount of time and discussion, David excused himself from the presence of Achish. He needed time in prayer to know how to present this to his men. David knew his men were behind him, but how much would they take? How long? Would their patience run out? Yes, he needed time to pray and talk to God.

* * * * *

The Philistines were gathered into one large mass. With all four of the cities joining together, they must have numbered several thousand. They had all gathered outside the city of Aphek. Aphek was at the northern end of all of the Philistine territory and located the closest to the Israelite cities, and it was located halfway between Gath and Jerusalem. It was also a fortified city, although they never really went into the city.

The Philistines gathered in thousands. David and his men were in the rear with Achish. Upon stopping, the Philistine princes joined together and made their way to Achish. The prince of Ashdod made himself spokesman for all the princes. In a firm and disapproving voice, the prince of Ashdod demanded, "What are these Hebrews doing here?"

Achish was surprised by their attitude. He was quick to explain, "This is David, the servant of Saul, king of Israel, who has been with me these days and years. I have found no fault in him since he deserted Israel to serve me to this day."

The Philistine princes grew very angry with Achish. They started shouting disapproving hatred comments all at the same time. No one could really understand what was being said.

The prince of Ashdod raised his voice to make a statement. His thick dark eyebrows rose almost to an arched position.

His head was slightly tipped as if to gain more volume, and he shouted orders to Achish, "Make this fellow return that he may go again to his place where you have assigned him. Tell him that he is not to go down with us to battle, lest in the battle he becomes an adversary to us. It seems so simple to us, Achish, how easy would it be for David to reconcile himself to his master? Was it not be with the heads of the men here? Is not this David, of whom they sang to one another in dances, 'Saul slew his thousands, and David his ten thousands'? And let's not forget who they were slaying...our own men."

To emphasize his point, he raised the Philistine flag high in the air. Achish was disheartened and quite disappointed. He had looked forward to having David's notary victory to accompany him in battle. He knew with David on their side, their win was certain. But he chose not to argue any further with his countrymen.

*****

That evening Achish invited David to eat with him. Achish was just finishing a piece of meat when he brought up the conversation he'd had with the Philistine princes. He said, "As surely as the Lord lives, you have been honest and upright, and for you to go out and come in with me in the army is good in my sight, for I have found no evil in you from the day of your coming to me to this day. Yet the princes do not approve of you. So return now and go peaceably so as not to displease the Philistine princes."

Both men took a sip of wine. David did to gain the few seconds to think, and Achish to give him time to reply. David quickly guarded his emotions and was especially careful not to show his delight. As quickly as he thought of the joy of not fighting the Israelites and especially King Saul, he also thought of his position among the Philistines. He knew that without going out with them in battle, he'd never secure their place among them. He was uncertain how much longer he'd need their protection. The disappointment at the lack of trust rang strongly through David's words. Setting his cup down rather firmly, he set his jaw in a firm established way and said, "But what have I done? And what have you found in your servant as long as I have been with you to this day that I may not go and fight against the enemies of my lord, the king?"

Achish was careful to encourage David. He valued David's loyalty and didn't want to lose it. Sympathizing with him, he answered him, "I know that you are as blameless in my sight as an angel of God; nevertheless, the princes of the Philistines have said, 'He shall not go up with us to the battle.'" Continuing on, he added, "So now rise up early in the morning, with your master's servants who have come with you, and as soon as you are up and have light, depart."

As the sun was rising, David and his men finished packing their bedding and set out to return to their families in the land of the Philistines.

The Philistines were also packing up their belongings and continued on to Jezreel. They had one thought in mind, to destroy Israel. They gathered and encamped at Shunem, five miles south of Mount Tabor.

They encamped at Gilboa, a mountain-ridge at the southeastern end of the plain of Jezreel. They had tents surrounding the area. Of course, you could tell the prince's tents and camps; they were larger and more endowed. There were also more spears and guards surrounding the prince's camp. Every few feet, there seemed to be campfires safely set up for a few men surrounding that area.

# Chapter 34

*"For troubles without number surround me; my sin has overtaken me, and I cannot see. They are more than the hairs of my head, and my heart fails within me"*
*(Psalm 40:12, NIV).*

The Prophet Samuel had been gone for a while now, and much of Israel still mourned his death. Many people came to Ramah, Samuel's hometown, where he was buried. They came to leave flowers and ointments and to pay tribute to their prophet.

The people had turned to the wizards and mediums for their answers since their prophet was gone. Because of this, Saul had run the wizards and mediums out of the land, making it against the law to practice fortune-telling and séances. At least, that was the reason he'd given everyone. Saul was certain that he'd been bewitched when the Spirit of God left him. Because of this certainty, he was determined they must go in hopes that it would break the curse.

Riding to the top of a hill and looking over it, Saul and his closest men looked down on all the Philistines camped around Gilboa. Saul made a lame joke about how there weren't very many Philistines after all. Jonathan had seen the sheer look of terror in his father's eyes and encouraged him, although he, too, was losing hope. He knew that years before, he and his armor-bearer took on a small army, entirely and completely defeating them. He also knew that with God, they could do anything. There was story after story in Israel's history about how God sent in an army of angels to defeat armies, how God confused armies causing them to totally destroy themselves. There were countless stories and tales of what God had done. The question was, would God be with them?

Saul rushed back to his camp. He needed time to compose himself and devise a plan before fighting the Philistines. Saul knew God had not spoken to him in years but thought he'd try anyway. Crying out to God, he asked for help. Saul begged God to give him the same anointing he'd had years earlier. He pleaded with God to give him the fool-proof battle plan. He hollered... he cried...he begged...but all he got in return was silence. One might have thought God was being mean, but as usual, Saul was not reaching out to God with a heart of repentance. Saul was asking God to make sure he came out on top again. He was asking God to anoint him as the one true king ruling Israel. He was not crying from a repentant heart but from one of pride and fear.

Saul pleaded with God to give him a dream if he wouldn't speak to him directly. He tried lying upon his bed. He walked the floor of his tent. He made offerings; he called for the priest. He tried everything he knew to do, including sending for the Urim. The Urim was the high priest's breastplate. It was viewed as a holy oracle that allowed the priests to walk in

divine closeness to God. However, no direction...no answers...
nothing... No...nothing came from God. Saul called for the
prophets. But again...no answers. Two days had passed since
Saul started working on his battle plan. The men were pushing
for answers.

Saul needed help... He needed guidance...he needed Samuel.
Disgusted and overwhelmed in need, Saul whispered under
his breath, "Stupid old man... Why did he have to die anyway!
Samuel was never there for me! He was never there when I
really needed him, so why should now be any different?"

This was one time he really needed Samuel's advice. He
thought and thought until he came up with a plan.

He'd been fretting and complaining in the privacy of his
tent. Saul was determined that the answer was in speaking to
Samuel. Abner was there when all of a sudden, the idea came to
him. Walking back and forth across his rugs of animal skin, he
started talking to Abner. Looking down at the different printed
skins and the different colors, Saul supported his bearded chin
with his left hand. Covering his lips with his middle finger and
resting his thumb under his chin, he tapped his index finger
against the side of his cheek. His right arm was bent and across
his lower chest to support his left arm. His beard was smooth
due to all the years of growth. He liked the smoothness of it.
But his mind was on how he could talk to Samuel. There was
only one way.

Saul ordered his personal servants to find someone with a
familiar spirit. He wanted to go to them and inquire. Someone
who speaks to the dead could bring Samuel back. Saul knew he
probably shouldn't do this, but he was desperate for answers.

One of the servants knew of a woman who fit this description. "There is a woman who lives at Endor, just four miles north of Tabor."

*****

Wearing a disguise, King Saul dressed as an average man. He hoped to hide his true identity behind the regular pauper clothes he was wearing. He had two reasons for doing this. The first was so that no one knew what he was doing, and the second one was because he had banned all sorcerers from the area. He feared she would not help him if she knew who he was.

Saul took two other men with him. One of the men was the one who told him about the woman. Saul told them to dress in regular clothing so as to not draw attention. They came into Endor shortly after midnight; it was not all that far away. Endor was a small village that lay at the base of the Mountains of Naphtali. It was a small Arab village that boarded the Dead Sea. However, the Dead Sea was not visible due to the mountains in between. King Saul had always imagined going to the Dead Sea since he wasn't all that far from it, but tonight he was not thinking of the Dead Sea or any sea. He was thinking about the massive number of Philistines. If he lived through this war, he might make that one of his next adventures. Right now, he had a war to fight with overwhelming odds.

The moon was out and offering a natural light for the men. Saul was grateful for the moonlight. It was hard to travel by night when it was pitch dark. Saul wondered how the woman would receive him. He sent a messenger ahead of them so she'd be prepared for their arrival. Of course, the messenger did not know who was coming to her house. He only knew to tell her that it was someone who needed to talk to someone who was already dead.

Arriving at her house, Saul climbed down from his horse and gave the reigns to one of the men. Gently poking the man who knew of the woman, he told him to give his reigns to the other man. Then told him to lead the way.

The woman's house was small. There was an eerie feeling in the air as they approached her door. Saul recognized the feeling; it was one that accompanied soothsayers, magicians, and people who talked to spirits. The woman was middle-aged. She opened the door rather cautiously. She didn't really smile, but her expression wasn't one of hate or discontent either; it was more of an undecided look. Saul thanked her for seeing them. He explained that it was their journey as well as his need that caused them to be here at this hour.

He quickly glanced around the one-room house. She had a small humble home. There was a tiny table with only two chairs. She had a third chair sitting in one of the corners. In another corner stood a small bed covered in old worn-out quilts. Toward the kitchen area stood a small stand stacked with pots and pans. There were a couple of shelves showing all of her dishes above the cooking counter. She had a basin of water on the counter. There was also a small cooking oven in the house; it served for both cooking and heat. On the chair in the corner was a sleek black cat that appeared to be glaring at them. The cat was swishing its tail in a rather annoyed way. It might have been funny if it didn't create a feeling of anxiety. Saul almost expected the cat to pounce on him at any moment. There was a crow or a black bird up above the doorway. It seemed to have its own perch. He was chirping as if to offer his opinion. Both the cat and the bird added to the eerie feeling in the house. There was a candle in the center of the table. Normally, it might be viewed as extra lighting if not for the lanterns around the room. No, he was certain this candle was for the séance.

The woman was not into formalities, so she immediately gave Saul a look that told him to get to the point.

Clearing his throat, Saul looked at her and said, "I want you to consult a spirit for me and bring up for me the one I name."

The woman's suspicions showed all over her face. She didn't look worried but cautious that she was being set up. She replied, "Surely you know what Saul has done? He has cut off the mediums and spiritists from the land. Why have you set a trap for my life to bring about my death?"

Saul laid his hand across the heart area of his chest and said, "As surely as the Lord lives, you will not be punished for this."

The woman saw a pleading in the man's eyes. She thought, *Whoever it is, they must be very important to him.* She chose to believe him and asked, "Whom shall I bring up for you?"

"Bring up Samuel," he said.

As the woman sat down, she nodded toward the empty chair. A seriousness came over her as she stared into the candle. She started chanting. A few minutes passed, then she started humming in a low, rather unsettling tone. As she stared into the candle, with her low, gravelly voice, she spoke these words slowly, "Samuel... Samuel...we call you back from the dead... Samuel, there is someone here who wants to talk to you... Samuel...are you here?"

Each time she spoke the name Samuel, she said it as if to demand his attention. Fear came over the woman as she saw it was not any man named Samuel but the Prophet Samuel. She immediately cried out at the top of her voice, "Why have you deceived me? You are Saul!"

Her voice was so loud and shrill that it sent a wave of terror through everyone in the room. The cat jumped down and walked around his master as if to protect her. Its tail stood high in the air until the cat began to swish it back and forth again. Only this time, there was a heavy whip of its tail as if it intended to attack someone. The bird started flapping its wings and squawking. This in itself sent shivers up the men's spines. Even the candle flame was dancing.

King Saul looked at her, and in a calm, reassuring voice, he said, "Don't be afraid." Then he asked, "What do you see?"

With fear flowing from her voice, the woman answered, "I see a ghostly figure coming up out of the earth."

The woman looked terrified at the vision, which surprised the men. Since she did this regularly, they all determined that this time must be somehow different.

Saul asked, "What does he look like?"

"An old man wearing a robe is coming up..." her voice trailed off as if she was trying to gain more description of what or who she was seeing.

Relieved, Saul started to smile slightly. He knew it was Samuel. He looked around and started to see the same ghostly figure that the woman described appearing in the room.

Getting up from the chair, he kneeled down in front of the image on his knees. He bent his face to the ground to show the old prophet respect.

An unnatural voice came from the image that resembled Samuel. The two men with Saul backed away as far as they could. They looked at each other and wanted to run out the door. The whole situation sent spine-chilling fear through them.

Samuel asked, "Why have you disturbed me by bringing me up?" The voice sounded so far away, and yet the image was right in front of him.

Saul said, "I am in great distress; the Philistines are fighting against me, and God has departed from me. He no longer answers me, neither by prophets nor by dreams. So I have called on you to tell me what to do."

Samuel replied, "Why do you consult me, now that the Lord has departed from you and become your enemy? The Lord has done what He predicted through me. The Lord has torn the kingdom out of your hands and given it to one of your neighbors—to David. Because you did not obey the Lord or carry out his fierce wrath against the Amalekites, the Lord has done this to you today. The Lord will deliver both Israel and you into the hands of the Philistines, and tomorrow, you and your sons will be with me. The Lord will also give the army of Israel into the hands of the Philistines."

Immediately Saul fell to the ground. All of his strength was overcome with fear. Samuel's words had caused a fear he'd never known before. The odd thing was, he had a sense that somehow he'd known what was coming. Saul felt too weak to get up. He had not eaten anything for the last twenty-four hours.

The woman saw how greatly shaken Saul was and said, "Look...your servant has obeyed you. I took my life in my hands and did what you told me to do. Now, please listen to your servant and let me give you some food so you may eat and have the strength to go on your way."

Hopelessness flowed from every pore of Saul's body, but he still managed to answer her in a very sad voice, "I will not eat."

The men with Saul joined in with the woman. They didn't know what to do, but her suggestion sounded right. After a few minutes of what sounded like quiet sobs, Saul allowed the men to help him up. They lifted him up and placed him upon her bed.

The woman had a fat calf; she killed it and dressed it. Since she was working quickly, she only cooked up a portion for King Saul and his men to eat. She'd take care of the rest of it later in the day. She worked quickly around her kitchen and small area. She worked equally hard taking flour, kneading it, and baking some unleavened bread.

King Saul was grateful for an excuse not to leave immediately. He relived the entire conversation in his mind over and over. He never saw Samuel leave, but the words he spoke rang over and over in his head. Saul was getting pains in his head from the constant pounding the words left.

At first, Saul heard every word and the entire conversation replaying in his head.

"Why do you consult me, now that the Lord has departed from you and become your enemy? The Lord has done what He predicted through me. The Lord has torn the kingdom out of your hands and given it to one of your neighbors—to David. Because you did not obey the Lord or carry out his fierce wrath against the Amalekites, the Lord has done this to you today. The Lord will deliver both Israel and you into the hands of the

Philistines, and tomorrow, you and your sons will be with me. The Lord will also give the army of Israel into the hands of the Philistines."

After repeating the entire conversation over for what seemed like hours, the conversation dropped to a few key phrases...

*...the LORD has departed from you...*
*The LORD has done what He predicted...*
*The LORD has torn the kingdom out of your hands...*
*...and given it to one of your neighbors...to David...*
*...you did not obey the LORD...*
*...the LORD has done this to you today...*
*The LORD will deliver both Israel and you into the hands of the*
*Philistines...*
*...tomorrow, you and your sons will be with me...*
*The LORD will give the army of Israel into the hands of the*
*Philistines...*

Thought after thought ran through his mind, and he was overcome with grief. How could he tell his sons this news? He saw his sons' faces in his mind, Jonathan, his precious Jonathan... Hatred filled his heart for David. David... David... David. Saul still saw David as being the problem. He had been out to steal the throne from Jonathan from the very first time they met him.

Anger filled his heart as he thought of Jonathan being so blind and not seeing David's intentions. Next, his heart filled with sorrow as he envisioned him dead on the battlefield. Should he tell his sons to go home and not go with him? No, sitting there in silence, Saul shook his head, *No, our deaths are inevitable. David has won; God favors him.*

Abinadab was certainly not his favorite son, but he was still a good son. He was devoted and would follow him into battle even if he knew the outcome was death.

Malchishua was just spoiled. His mother had given him everything he ever wanted. He might turn and run if he knew the outcome, but Saul was certain that he'd die in battle tomorrow, and if his sons didn't, they'd be hunted down and tortured. No, it was more admirable to die in battle than to be hunted down and tortured. The Philistines would put each of them on display, just like they had done with their hero Goliath. He knew the drill. No, if they had to die, it was best to die in battle.

Each one of his sons had many of his traits. They were all close to his height. Malchishua was the shortest. He thought about his army and all of the men. As the woman worked on their food, he stayed lost in his thoughts. Every once in a while, one of the men would try to engage the king in conversation. But it never went anywhere. They'd recall the dooming words. What were they going to say?

One of the men did try to address the words by standing and making a loud proclamation, *"Long live the king!* My king...don't worry...it was only a dead spirit...it wasn't real..."

Surprised by the man's words, Saul glared at him. The man knew to shut up. His words faded out, and he dropped back into the corner.

The other man wanted to say something but didn't have the slightest idea what to say, so he kept offering his assistance to the woman. All he kept thinking was, *Am I going to die tomorrow? Am I part of the king's army? Will I become a Philistine prisoner? Should I run now? Do I tell the men what the dead prophet said?* Over and over, these questions and a thousand others ran through his mind. He was certain they were running through the other soldier's mind as well. Often, they would exchange looks that told the other they were thinking the same thing.

# Chapter 35

*"Keep me free me from the trap that is set for me, for you are my refuge" (Psalm 31:4, NIV).*

King Saul and the Israelites were camped along the Springs of Harod, near the foot of Mount Gilboa. The area was very beautiful, especially in the early summer months that they were now enjoying. The birds were chirping and singing their summer songs. Those watching closely saw squirrels scampering up the trees and jumping from limb to limb. Off in the distance at the base of the mountain, occasionally, they'd see an animal making its way to the stream. However, that was a rarity because the men were too noisy. The men were using the fresh water at the springs for drinking, and further downstream, they washed.

Some men told how this was the very stream that Gideon had brought his men to. Here at the spring, he was to sort them out on the basis of how they drank the water. They recalled the whole story, talking about Gideon as though they had personally witnessed the encounter. One man described how Gideon looked, about five foot eight and built muscular in the shoulders. They described him as having a short black beard and a very large nose, with ears to match. Another described him as walking with a cane, the way one would imagine Moses in his old age. They talked about Gideon's army and how the Midianites came against them. Some men had fun imitating the voice of God giving Gideon specific directions. When Gideon's army started out, he had twenty-two thousand men. Immediately, God spoke and told him this was too many men. The Israelites would believe they defeated the Midianites by their own hand. They'd glorify themselves and boast at their own success. No, God wanted them to know He caused their victory. God told Gideon to send anyone home who was afraid. His army instantly dropped to ten thousand. This brought many laughs and insults as they poked fun at the men who admitted openly to fear. Next, God led Gideon and his men to the springs. God told Gideon to tell the men to take a drink. Gideon was to set aside those who lapped the water with his tongue like a dog. The others were to go home. They'd not be fighting with him today. Some men took it personally, but God was separating the men, so Gideon and all Israel would see God's glory. His army was now down to three hundred men, and these would be divided into three sections. The army they were coming against was of overwhelming odds, even with the full twenty-two thousand men. The Midianites and the Amalekites and all their children lived in the east in the valley. The old text referred to them as "grasshoppers." It said their camels were without number as the sand of the seaside for multitudes.

Next, Gideon overheard a man telling of his dream. He understood this dream to be God telling him that they already had the victory. Then, God gave Gideon the battle plan, and it was a sealed deal. Gideon was now clear on how God was telling him to proceed. Before he knew it, the battle was won, and the men were victorious. They dramatized the lanterns that God had instructed them to carry. In good fun, the men imitated the sounds of the trumpet blasts. Saul's men were enjoying themselves, and it built them up to think of how their king must have gotten his instructions from God, just as Gideon had done. Why else would they even think of coming against so large a crowd of Philistines with so few men? Some of the men playing along even shouted, "For the Lord and for Gideon!" Those words became their theme as they prepared for battle. Throughout the camp, you could hear the men shouting, "For the Lord and for King Saul!" They'd raise their weapons in victory and shout together, "For the Lord and for King Saul!"

\*\*\*\*\*

Jonathan was sitting by the stream. His father had not been himself ever since he saw how big the Philistine army was. Rumor was that David was fighting with them. Jonathan couldn't believe David would really fight against them. He knew God would protect David's life, but to come against Israel... That just seemed out of the question. Jonathan was scripting a letter to his wife and the youngest children still at home. He had a bad feeling about this war. Maybe it came from his father's actions, or maybe it came from knowing God was with David. Either way, there was an unsettled feeling in the pit of his stomach. He'd tried to talk to his father about it but to no avail. Abner blocked him at every move as though he was protecting his father... From who? From him? Nothing seemed to make sense these days. He loved his wife, but in some ways, he felt as though his love and devotion ran deeper for David but not in any weird sinful way as some wanted to gossip. No...what he and David had was a deep love that is rarely shared between the best of friends. It was the deepest of friendships. Together they could rule the kingdom. It didn't matter to Jonathan if David was the king or him. At one time, he felt a tinge of jealousy. A smile crossed his face, and a sparkle appeared in his eyes as he thought of how hard it was to hang on to the jealousy when he so dearly loved David. He started to write a letter to David. "My dearest David..."שלי היקרה...

A tear formed in the corner of Jonathan's eye at the thought of possibly never seeing him again. If he should die today, would David remember the covenant he'd made with him? No words came to mind...or were there too many words to sort them all out? Jonathan tore the parchment paper up and tossed it aside. Time was short; he'd be going to battle soon. He needed to focus. He tucked his letter inside his things, hoping if anything happened, it would find its way back to his wife. Jonathan stood up, determined to join his brothers and father.

With God's help, today would be a good battle, and perhaps they'd not just win the war, but they'd once and for all defeat the Philistines and take home many spoils of war. Today would be the day the two armies would encounter each other. Today, fate would decide their outcome. *Today...* these thoughts were on everyone's minds as they knew it would be victory for one and defeat for the other. The odds were against the Israelites, but Jehovah God would be with them, wouldn't he?

King Saul gave orders to rally all the men together before going out. Feeling very defeated, he sent Abner to give the men some words of conquest. Everyone agreed to unite and fight to win. Some were even heard quoting David's words, "How dare these uncircumcised Philistines!" Of course, they never did this in front of the king or the king's guards.

Various conversations flowed from the men, including going back home as soon as this was over. They had the sparkle in their eyes telling the men closest to them that they were thinking of their wife or the way their little children were growing up so quickly.

Many of the men were glad that David was not fighting with them since their loyalty was with King Saul. However, David being among the Philistines seemed to spook a good number of the men. Some seemed to think of David as a good luck charm.

Seeing the kings' continence, Abner asked King Saul about the spiritist woman and what had happened. Saul only looked away. He didn't give him an answer. Upon Abner persisting, Saul looked at him and, in a very defeated voice, said, "David has won..."

The look in Saul's eyes sent a cold chill down his spine. Abner asked if they should turn around and go home immediately. In a very defeated whisper, he said, "It's too late—"

Abner pushed for more explanation but wouldn't get it...at least not today. Abner determined right then to keep a few of his favorite men with him. He'd keep his eyes peeled for a way out of this battle at all times. He was determined; *he* wasn't dying today! He wouldn't tell those close to him but would confide in them to stay close by to be prepared for his instructions should the battle turn on them. If he said to retreat, follow him as quickly as they could, for that might be all that saves their life. The question was, should he tell Jonathan his plans? No...Jonathan's devotion was to David and his father. He'd go directly to his father and tell him what he said. No...clearly, Jonathan was on his own.

# Chapter 36

*"When my spirit grows faint within me, it is you who watches over my way" (Psalm 142:3a, NIV).*

David and his men were a distance of almost three full days from Ziklag. The journey seemed long. The men had multiple conversations about how the battle would go. Many of them shared victory thoughts at not coming against King Saul and their Israelite friends. Some even had fun gambling and placing bets on the outcome of the war. However, they were careful not to bet in front of David's closest men. All in all, everyone was glad to not be fighting. Just a few more hours, and they would be holding their families in their arms. They'd be greeted by the hugs and kisses of their wives and their sons and daughters or their betroths. Not to mention the parents who worry about their sons, some of the men brought their parents with them for protection and to provide for them. Several of the men had young sons who begged their father to let them go and fight. These young lads were certain they were old enough, but the fathers, knowing the terrors of war, were thankful that they were not old enough. Especially this war, many were convinced that terrible consequences would come upon them for coming against King Saul and Israel. Many men questioned that David was going too far at this point. In their conversations, several recalled the story of Gideon, who came against the Israelites, or as many added, he tried to come against them. God did not allow him to because they were His chosen children.

***** 

Abner rode his horse up and down in front of the men giving the standard words of valor before war. It was critical to build the men up prior to any war, but especially when the odds were against them. He decided to address the fact that David was with the Philistines, but only by reminding the men that Israel and Judah had always had the hand of God with them. Today was no different. He talked of how they'd soon be back home with their families, enjoying themselves as they recalled the Philistines defeated in battle. He encouraged them with the spoils that they would receive when they went into these conquered cities. He spoke of the many times in their history when a few people defeated larger armies than they would encounter today. Since he'd heard the men's comments on Gideon, he referred to that victory to encourage them today. Together as one army, they lifted their swords and shouted, "For the Lord and for King Saul!" What a mighty sound it was indeed. Animals for miles must have run at their victory proclamation.

***** 

As they were approaching Ziklag, many of the men started commenting they were smelling smoke. At first, it was very faint. As they grew closer, it seemed to be getting stronger. David sent a couple of men on ahead to see what they could find out. The men had been gone for a couple of hours. David could now see them approaching. Suddenly, he got a sick feeling in the pit of his stomach. Maybe it was the downcast look on the men's faces. They weren't close yet, but they were close enough to see something was wrong; the way they were directing their mules, the way they were shaking their heads, the rush to their movement...all of it spoke danger. It was then that David noticed smoke in the sky. Now terror firmly gripped his heart. As the men approached, everyone stopped. All the soldiers strained to listen as the riders spoke. Their faces were filled with despair and hopelessness...and anger. One man was crying. The other was shouting curses. He was shouting so fast that you could barely catch what he was saying. But panic hit those closes to David as two words became quite clear, "Ziklag" and "destroyed." At that point, the man's words made sense, "The whole city of Ziklag is destroyed! They've taken our families. They've plundered our homes and taken everything we have. Our children...our wives...our livestock...our children... our gold...our children..."

David asked who they thought had done this. They said there were weapons around indicating it was the Amalekites. They also knew the Amalekites had been raiding the south, the Negeb. But they didn't feel like they had a choice in leaving any men behind. So they left some of the older teens, hoping that would be enough. The next hour was very emotional, with tempers flying as they finished their journey to Ziklag. The animals were tired, but upon hearing the news, the men rushed to get there. They had to see it for themselves. Some were already angry with David and threatening to stone him.

Most blamed him, saying he'd brought God's curse upon them by leading them out to come against Israel. Each man was angry and upset, whether he blamed David or not. David tried to calm the men and formulate a plan, but they were too upset. He was also upset. Didn't they understand his own family was taken too? No, each man thought only of his own loss. Tempers were flying as they talked of killing the Amalekites. Some men threatened to beat them severely before killing them if they so much as laid a finger on their wife or their children. Many men shouted threats and talked of what they'd do to the Amalekites. Darkness was approaching, and with it, deep despair settled over the men. There was no moon to give light, only total encompassing darkness. Their souls felt as dark as the night. They camped outside the city, but close enough that they barely slept from the smoke smell. The men were desperate to get their families back. David heard weeping until it seemed the men had no more strength to weep. "How has this happened, Lord? Is it my fault?" David's own heart was crying out to God for answers. They went through the motions of sleeping, but very little sleep happened during the dark night hours.

*****

Before tonight, David had never felt like he needed his own guards. Many of the men talked of stoning him. His soul ached for his family as well as his men. Many of the men were very bitter. Such hatefulness flowed from them. He'd never seen so much hatred in them before. David encouraged himself and strengthened himself in the Lord his God. He determined to grab hold of God and to hold on to Him until he had an answer. He needed God's direction, and every part of his being was determined to not let go of God until he had the direction needed for this moment.

Abiathar, the priest, was staying close to David. He was praying with him. David spoke to him and said, "I pray you, bring me the ephod."

David had a natural love for the ephod; this love stemmed from his Bible history knowledge. The ephod was sown together in the back and fastened together in the front. He used it to seek the heart of Yahweh. There was a special presence of God on the ephod, a presence that allowed David to personally hear from his Creator. Under the Aaronic Priesthood, the official clothing of the high priest was given by revelation from God. There was much symbolism, as well as practical significance to the many specific instructions.

Because David was seeking to come directly before God, he also knew he should not wear ordinary clothing. This garment was fastened at each shoulder and had an intricately woven band with which it could be fastened around the waist. In gold settings on each shoulder were onyx stones engraved with the names of the twelve sons of Israel. This was a memorial as the priest served before the Lord. Fastened to the ephod was a breastplate into which the Urim and Thummin could be placed, with four rows of three stones across the breastplate. The Urim were stones kept in a pouch on the high priest's breastplate used in determining God's decision in certain questions and issues. The Thummin were stones provided for the process of achieving a sacred lot. Wearing the ephod reminded David of God's concern for his people.

It also brought great comfort to David as he thought of the many generations of people before him. Wearing the ephod reminded him of the many covenants God has made with his people. This reminded him of Abraham and God's divine promises.

"I will make of you into a great nation, and I will bless you, and make your name great and you will be a blessing..."[22]

"All the land that you see, I will give to you and your offspring forever."[23]

In the same day, the Lord made a covenant with Abraham, saying, "To your seed have I given this land, from the river of Egypt unto the great river, the river Euphrates..."

*I will make you exceedingly fruitful, and I will make nations of you, and kings shall come out of you...*

As David heard those words echoing in his heart, he realized he'd be one of the kings to come from the seed of Abraham! Joy flooded his heart as he thought of the depth of those words.

As David put on the ephod, a new hope sprang up within him. He'd find God's will and walk it out. Then he'd have God's peace and direction. One way or the other, everything would work out.

＊＊＊＊＊

King Saul had just received word that the Philistines were approaching. It wouldn't be long now. His men lined up for the upcoming attack. Men with shields were placed in front; next, the archers, then chariots, and finally, men on horses and mules. King Saul was surrounded by his sons and his very best men...except for Abner and Abner's closest men. He'd told King Saul that he needed to be in another section to oversee the men there. It just so happened that it put them toward the back of the army. King Saul noticed his ploy and thought about ordering him to his side. But then his heart filled with despair, and he thought, *Why should we all die today?*

King Saul had given Abner specific instructions regarding his son at home, should anything happen to him and his sons today. Assuming that Abner made it out alive, he was to promote his son Ishbosheth. Do what he could to make certain that David didn't get his throne. The men were ready. The ground started to shake at the approaching of such a massive army. A few snorts came from the animals as they, too, felt the tension growing. Many of the horses lifted their feet, prancing and hoping to run free. Jonathan noticed that the birds he'd heard earlier were quiet or gone. The only sound now was the beating of their hearts and the approaching army.

*****

Nighttime was still upon them when Abiathar, the priest, brought David the ephod. David put the priestly mantle on with its magnificent breastplate. Aware of the priestly ordinance attached to it, he humbled himself before God. Because of this ordinance, David did not wear the entire priest outfit. He was not trying to operate in the office of the priest but to draw on the divine nature of the ephod so that he could find the necessary direction at this moment. Once David had the ephod on, he lay prostrate, and he praised God and rested in His presence. After some time, he inquired of the Lord and asked, "Shall I pursue this troop? Shall I overtake them?"

"Pursue them," the Lord answered, "for you shall certainly overtake them and succeed in the rescue."

God's voice was so loud that David was certain the men had heard Him. But as he'd learned earlier, only those God intends to hear Him audibly, hear Him.

David took a moment to cry in relief and to thank God for answering. He thanked God for giving him a clear direction. He knew his own families as well as those of his men would be safe and would soon be back with them. With God's words strong in his heart, David rallied the men together. He told Joab to spread the news that God was with them, and they'd certainly win this battle! The dawn was just breaking as they headed into the Amalekite territory.

# Chapter 37

*"In my distress I called to the Lord; I cried to my God for help. From his temple he heard my voice; my cry came before him, into his ears" (Psalm 18:6, NIV).*

The battle had begun; the soldiers were fighting, and men were already starting to fall on both sides. The crimson red of men's blood was starting to cover the ground now. Swords were clanking as men fought each other. Arrows were flying in every direction as the two sides met. Jonathan and his two brothers stayed as close to their father as they could. Jonathan was a mighty warrior and fought hard to defeat every uncircumcised Philistine. He couldn't help but think of his friend even during such terrible circumstances. Uttering a prayer in his mind, he said, "Dear God, please take care of both of us this day."

He'd heard rumors that the Philistines had not let David fight with them after all, but he didn't know if they were true or not. The thoughts of both of them coming face to face seemed more than he could handle. Then, filled with a new flood of energy, he laughed out loud and thought, *Funny, I am fighting for my life, and I'm wondering what I will do if David and I come face to face. I won't kill him, and I don't believe he'd kill me. Please Lord, let us join together and fight these uncircumcised Philistines...*

Shouts and cries were heard throughout the land, some of victory and others from the horrors of war. The Philistine princes violently drove their chariots through the soldiers. At the spokes of each wheel were wicked-looking blades. They were incredibly sharpened blades approximately eight inches long that were set vertical of the wheel to cut down all that came in their way. They were set in a slightly curved shape at the end to help them cut and gouge anyone or anything. The Philistine princes could be seen riding these chariots, pushing the horses hard, and cutting man after man and horses and mules as they went. The crazy thing was they didn't seem to mind that they were cutting down many of their own men along the way.

*\*\*\*\*\**

Besor Ravine was approximately fifty to sixty miles away from Ziklag. David and his men traveled the entire day. The men were slightly encouraged to be doing something. But the grumblings that made their way back to Joab was, "If the men didn't get everything back, especially their families, they would stone David." In fact, even that might not get him released from their wrath. The men had to be certain that David had not brought a curse upon them for going out at all against Israel. A few wanted to stop for lunch, but most didn't. David insisted that they all stopped for a short break. The animals needed it, and they also needed to keep up their strength. Once they reached Besor Ravine, some of the men were too tired to go on. David let those who were exhausted stay and wait for their return. Out of the six hundred men, two hundred stayed behind. Some of the men who went with David grumbled at the weakness of the men who stayed behind. The other four hundred took off with David.

\*\*\*\*\*

Out of the corner of his eye, Jonathan saw Malchishua fall. He was run through with a horrible-looking blade. As quickly as he could kill the Philistine he was fighting, he and Abinadab joined forces to kill the man who had just killed their brother. Feeling no time for tears, both men fought back to back, feeling a new surge of energy, as well as a new determination to win. Both men were doing their best to keep a watch on their father. Although he was older now, he still fought valiantly. His armor-bearer was fighting right alongside him. He was doing his best to protect his king as he fought next to him. Jonathan shouted to Abinadab that he was making his way back to their father. Swords continued to clank. Men were falling all over the valley. They were being pushed back up onto the mountain by the Philistines. Then, in a split second, Jonathan saw Abinadab fall. This time it was a flaming arrow that pierced him in the back. When he fell to the ground, he fell backward, making the arrow ascend through his chest. The flames were now catching his clothes on fire. Sickness almost overwhelmed Jonathan as he fought hard to concentrate on what he was doing. He wanted to run. He'd never felt more like running in his life. Although he was determined not to let tears come, there was a burning sensation in the corner of his eyes. Jonathan prayed for strength, *"Lord...we need You..."*

\* \* \* \* \*

It was early afternoon when David and his men were crossing a field, and some of his men noticed an Egyptian. He was lying in the sand, half dead. David sent men over to rouse the man and to see who he was. His skin was so dark it was almost black. The man was thin, very thin, and his high cheekbones were extremely profound under his eyes. He was especially tall. You could count his ribs on his bare chest. He had on only the loincloth of a slave, and he was barefoot. "Surely, they took his shoes," someone commented. He couldn't imagine that they'd expect their slaves to walk across the desert on the hot sand without shoes. The man's breathing was so shallow that some men thought he had already died.

Joab bent down, and raising his head, he held his drinking vessel to the man's mouth. Tipping his vessel back up, the small amount of water flowed over the man's lips. His lips were swollen and cracked. As the man started to stir, his mouth opened slightly. Although the man was still unconscious, he responded to the water.

After a few more sips of water, there was movement in the man's eyes as he tried to wake up. When he became conscious, David ordered his men to give him food and drink. He was weak, but as he started to eat and drink, his strength was quickly returning to him.

Upon eating part of a cake of pressed figs and two cakes of raisins, he started feeling strong enough to sit up. When they questioned him, he asked what day it was. When he knew, he said, "I have not eaten for three days."

David asked him, "To whom do you belong, and where do you come from?"

"I am an Egyptian, the slave of an Amalekite. My master abandoned me when I became ill three days ago." Still devouring his food and water, he paused to take another bite. Upon swallowing, he said, "We raided the Negev of the Kerethites and the territory belonging to Judah and the Negev of Caleb, and we burned Ziklag."

Tempers flared from those closest to the Egyptian slave, and one man drew his sword determined to run the man through. The man cowered as he put his hands up to protect himself and to block the blade. David held out his hand and shouted to his soldier to stop. Then, he gave Joab a look that told him to get this man out of here.

Speaking with compassion in his voice, David asked, "Can you lead me down to this raiding party?"

The man looked deeply into David's eyes and said, "Swear to me before God that you will not kill me or hand me over to my master, and I will take you down to them."

David looked just as sincerely back into the man's eyes and assured him of his request.

Joab was sent to spread the news that no one was to bring harm to the Egyptian slave. He'd agreed to lead them to the raiding party that has their families in return for sparing his life. It was approaching evening now. They were not far from their destination.

\*\*\*\*\*

It was hard to tell how long the battle had been going on. Jonathan's arms were feeling extremely heavy. But he knew he must keep going. If not for him and his father, then he must keep going for his two brothers and everyone else that had given their lives so far. How had it come to this...where was the one true Jehovah God? Had He deserted them? Questions flew through his mind, but there was no time for questions as he concentrated on fighting one more Philistine. He was covered in blood and dirt as the battle grew long. Then, as piercing as anything he'd ever felt, a Philistine's blade cut into his arm. At least it wasn't his main arm, but it was the arm that held up his shield. He wanted to look at how badly his arm was cut, but he knew better than to take his eyes off his target. As though his father was calling him, he looked over to find him. Suddenly, as if he'd been hit alongside his head, there was a ringing and a deafening sound. He felt himself collapsing to the ground. Something bad had happened, but Jonathan couldn't collect his thoughts enough to determine what had happened. As he breathed his last breath, prayers to Jehovah flowed from his lips, "Please Lord, protect those I leave behind... Yahweh, please take care of David... Yahweh, I love You..."

Jonathan lay among the many Israelites that fell that day. A sword had hit him in the neck, clipping his main artery. His death was almost instant as a pool of his blood surrounded him. His armor-bearer was the next to be killed. The hope that the men carried into battle was quickly fading. The men closest to Jonathan turned to run, but the battle was too thick. Their retreating cost some men their lives. Their open backs were easy targets for the archers.

*****

David and his men were almost to the location of the raiding party. They were very quiet as they led their animals. They hid behind trees and shrubs while assessing the situation. The Amalekite men were scattered over the countryside. They were intoxicated and dancing because of their great plunder. They were very pleased with their treasures, including the women and children.

At this point, most of the women and children seemed to be locked up. They, at least, were not being abused or tortured by the Amalekites. David made sure they were all ready to charge at the same time. As soon as everyone gave him a head nod, he gave them the charge signal. Giving shouts of victory and preparing their weapons, they rained down upon the drunken men. Although they were drunk, being evil men, they'd learned to keep their swords handy. Giving a shout of alert, the men jumped up, yelled for their women to bring them extra weapons, then to get to safety. They appeared to be shocked as though no one had ever stood up to them before. The battle was long, for the Amalekites fought hard. One by one, the Amalekite men fell to their swords. They fought for a total of one full day, from twilight that evening to the evening of the next day. As the next evening approached, David's men estimated that around four hundred men had escaped upon camels.

Upon securing the area and bringing final defeat to the Amalekites, David and his men found their women and their children. They retrieved all of their flocks and herds. They recovered their own spoils, as well as the spoils they took in the other raids. None of David's men were lost that day. David couldn't hug his wives quickly enough, but he watched his two sons as his wives smothered him with kisses and praises. Both were talking at the same time, exclaiming how they knew he'd come for them. They never lost hope, and they did all they could to encourage the other women. David knew this to be true of Abigail but wondered if it was as true about Ahinoam. She was much quieter and more likely to chime in on how desperate the situation felt. Freeing his arms for his two sons, he kneeled down to them and scooped them up into his arms. He couldn't describe how good this moment felt. With his two sons in his arms, he felt like a king. Perhaps he was not the king of Israel yet, but certainly, he was the king of his family and this small battalion of men. Twirling them around and around, everyone was smiling and laughing. Amnon was almost three years old now, and although he didn't totally understand, he'd felt the fear of knowing something was wrong.

Through a smile of relief, he looked at his daddy and said, "Bad guys...gone? Home...home now, Daddy?"

"The bad guys are all gone, and yes, son, we're on our way home." A lump formed in David's throat as he assured his little son.

The other men were as elated as David to hold their families in their arms. However, many of the men were anxious to collect all of the spoils they could find. Their spoils were extra great that day. They collected more than they had dreamed possible. The women prepared some food while the men packed the Amalekite carts and camels with all the spoils they could find.

Men were designated to guide the livestock. Those men headed out as soon as they were ready with the herds and flocks. As the men headed out, they were heard saying, "This is David's plunder."

Many of the women and children panicked when they looked for their own husbands and fathers and didn't see them. Sobs of horror filled the area as they supposed their men were cut down in the war. They cried so hard and so loud that David's commander, Joab, found it hard to get their attention. Eventually, he gained control and was able to tell everyone that no one had died here today or prior. Their journey had been long, and some men were not able to go the whole trip. Although all the wives were grateful, some were immediately filled with indignation at the thought of their husband not being among the others, causing them to quickly judge their husband's actions. Some of the men had insults for those who didn't come as well. As soon as everyone was set, clustered in families, they prepared to leave. Together, they headed out for Besor Ravine.

\* \* \* \* \*

King Saul was losing hope. He heard someone shouting, *"Retreat! Retreat!"* The voice was too distant to be certain, but it sounded like Abner. Would he really retreat and leave him and Jonathan alone out there to fight? King Saul determined, yes, he would!

Saul had lost sight of Malchishua and Abinadab. He had a sick feeling in his gut that they were not just separated. He caught sight of Jonathan. It was when Jonathan felt his eyes on him, and he looked in his father's direction. That was when a Philistine caught Jonathan in the arm, cutting him deeply. Too absorbed with what he had just seen, he kept his sword moving, but his eyes were on Jonathan. He saw the blade going toward his neck. He hollered at Jonathan, but it was too late. He knew Jonathan would never hear him over the noise of war, but he had to try. Saul was immediately distracted, allowing the archers to move in closer and closer, watching for their moment.

In the next second, intense pain shot through King Saul's body. It was so severe, and yet he couldn't be certain what happened. Then, he saw an arrow in his shoulder. Time suddenly seemed to stand still. Saul shouted to his armor-bearer to take his sword and kill him. Shaking his head no, the man refused. He was terrified at the king's words. Saul ordered him to run his sword through him as he described how they would capture him and torture him.

Pleading, he said he couldn't live through such torture. The armor-bearer still refused. The Philistines were moving in closer and closer. King Saul planted the hilt of his sword on the ground, and leaning into it, he fell to the ground. The armor-bearer was almost too shocked to move. He froze, but only for a split second. The king's words echoed in his ears. He knew he was responsible for protecting the king, and the Israelites would come after him. Taking up his own sword, he followed King Saul and planted the hilt of his sword into the ground and fell into it as well.

*****

Upon reaching the Besor Ravine, everyone rested and refreshed for the rest of their journey home. Home... David wasn't certain what to do, but if they needed to go back to the wilderness, they would. For now, he needed to be in the area when Achish returned. Achish... David hadn't thought of the war in hours. He had prayed over Jonathan but turned King Saul over to God. He'd asked God many times over the past few years to give him what he rightfully deserved. Then, he prayed for God to protect all those innocent of this fight. As they reached the men who had been exhausted and stayed behind, the men came out to meet David. There were many selfish men who had gone with David to fight the Amalekites. These men gathered together to stir trouble. A couple of the men made themselves spokesman for the others. In a rough intimidating voice, one man spoke up, "Because they did not go out with us, we will not share with them the plunder we recovered. However, each man may take his wife and children and go."

David was quick to reply, "No, my brothers, you must not do that with what the Lord has given us. He has protected us and handed over to us the forces that came against us. Who will listen to what you say? The share of the men who stayed with the supplies is to be the same as that of him who went down to the battle. All will share alike."

David didn't just make a statement; he declared this to be a statute and an ordinance for Israel from that day on. Those who had complained chose not to argue with David.

It was another happy reunion as these men were reunited with their families. David decided they'd camp there for the night and finish the trip home tomorrow.

# Chapter 38

*"How the mighty have fallen! The weapons of war have perished!" (2 Samuel 1:27, NIV)*

The battle was a horrifying defeat for the Israelites. The majority of men died, but some were able to escape by fleeing to Mount Gilboa. The mountain that had been so peaceful and beautiful that morning was now a place of refuge or a place of death. The local villages had been watching and waiting for word on how the battle was going. Word came that King Saul and his sons were killed and that the Israelite army was retreating. The people grabbed only their most treasured belongings and ran as fast as they could, leaving nearly everything. They completely abandoned their homes and their towns.

Sorrow filled the men who had made it up the mountain. Sorrow for their country, sorrow for their friends, and sorrow for their king. They were unsure what to do, other than they knew they had to get home to their families as quickly as possible. As the men came up the mountain, a few watched so they could regroup. The men knew they needed to get back home quickly, but they also knew they needed to join together as much as possible to ensure their safety. The plan was to circle around the mountain to the northern side and work their way back to their home area. Abner appointed himself commander over them. Darkness was coming quickly now. Since they could travel less noticed at night, there would be no sleep for them. Feeling the depression of the defeat, people were either very angry or very quiet. There didn't seem to be any in-between.

As they were walking, one of the men asked who would be Israel's king since the king and his sons were killed. A voice from behind him said, "Probably David."

Abner was quick to address that question. With anger in his voice, he said, "They were not the king's only sons; Ish-Bosheth will be the ruling king." Then he added, "Why do you think the king left him home instead of taking him to war? He left him home just in case anything should happen to him and his other sons."

Abner had answered him with such hostility that no other conversation followed. The only sound they heard was each man passing through the shrubs and brush and climbing over the rocks to form their own path. Occasionally, someone would wince as they hit their leg on a rock or got scratched by shrubbery. Though they spoke no more words, their hearts were heavy at the thought of Ish-Bosheth being their next king as they were over the brutal battle. Everyone knew that Ish-Bosheth was useless. He was lazy, fat, and very messy. Many of their thoughts went to what would happen to Israel under his leadership.

\*\*\*\*\*

The battle was over, and the field was littered with bloody and mangled men. There were men dead from both sides. It was an overwhelming sight. Philistine soldiers went around looking for those who were wounded and still alive. They'd run them through with their swords, finishing the task. The more violent the man, the more pleasure he had in finishing off the wounded. Some of the younger soldiers would be seen vomiting, as the bloodshed was too violent for them. A platoon of soldiers chased those that retreated up onto the mountain. They successfully killed many but estimated a few hundred still escaped.

Having finished killing the Israelites, the Philistines went into the towns closest to the battle to conquer them. Finding them empty, they decided to occupy them for the night. Tomorrow they'd decide whether to destroy these towns or start a new Philistine settlement. The princes would discuss it while dining tonight. They had other things to discuss, too, like the spoils, how to handle Israel now that they'd so completely defeated them, and much more. They set some soldiers to watch over the field of dead Israelites. Of course, the soldiers were warned what would happen if they took spoils for themselves. They even used a dead Israelite body as an example of the torture that would come to them as they dissected the body by cutting it open from the top of the stomach to the bottom. They would deal with all those issues tomorrow when they had fresh energy. It felt good to be the victors! Tomorrow they'd determine just how great their victory really was.

*****

The next morning, the refreshened Philistines went out to determine the full extent of their victory. The soldiers were to strip the dead of anything of value. They mostly wanted coins, weapons, and armor, but if they found anything else, they were given orders to collect it too.

A flock of ravens flew off as the soldiers approached the bloody battlefield. They'd been enjoying feasting on the bodies. Often, they had to fight off a persistent raven as they stripped the Israelites and the fallen Philistines of their possessions.

Suddenly, one of the soldiers shouted out very loudly, "I found King Saul!" It seemed like all the Philistines close by were gathering as bees swarming above clovers. One of the princes worked his way over and verified that the man was the Israelite king.

He ordered the man who found him to cut off Saul's head and strip him of everything. One by one, they clearly identified his three sons. Someone started to name the sons, Jonathan... Malchi...when he was cut off. A captain, snarling at him, shouted, "You fool! Do you think we care about their names! All we need to know is they are the king's sons, and now they're dead!"

The soldiers were ordered to prepare the king and his sons for travel. One of the soldiers thought he could pick up each body and place it on the back of the mule. Their bodies were already cold and very stiff. When the captain saw him floundering and trying to figure out how to move the stiff body, he ordered him to put the bodies in the back of one of the chariots. The captain shook his head at the ignorance of the man. When asked how they were to get the chariot in amongst all the bodies, he told him to carry the bodies to the chariot, with a few choice words to follow.

The princes ordered messengers to proclaim the news throughout the entire Philistine territory. The messengers were instructed to tell everyone, but specifically to have their victory proclaimed among the idols, especially in the temples. The people were to make offerings and sacrifices of thanksgiving to the gods. King Saul's armor was taken to the temple of Ashtaroth, their moon goddess. The Ashtaroth temples always had Ashtaroth pillars out front. She was known as the wife of Dagon.

Saul's head was instructed to hang in the temple of Dagon, their most sacred god. Although each city had temples and idols, the main temples were located in Ashdod. Both of these proclamations were made to announce that there was no god over their gods. Thinking of David, some of the men talked among themselves. They wanted David to get that message loud and clear. Other conversations talked of taking over Jerusalem. Still, others talked about their spoils, for they were consumed with them. Some men talked of the celebration they intended to have once they were home.

The king's body and his sons' bodies were instructed to be hung to the wall in Beth Shean. Beth Shean is located at the west end of the Jezreel and Jordan valleys and was a Canaanite city. They have a fortified city that is protected by mud-brick walls. The bodies were impaled to the walls. It was a gruesome sight that squeamish women were encouraged to avoid. Of course, the stiffer the bodies, the more unusual the bodies hung. The bodies were often displayed to make a statement of what would happen to others who fought them. Killing King Saul and his sons was an outstanding victory for the Philistines because of all the battles they'd had with him since he became king. As it is said, "He won the battle, but they won the war." The Philistines strutted with such pride for the next few weeks at their victory.

# Chapter 39

*"Saul and Jonathan—in life they were loved and admired,
and in death they were not parted. They were swifter than
eagles, they were stronger than lions"*
*(2 Samuel 1:23, NIV).*

David felt like they needed to share the plunder. There was such a vast amount that he divided it up, and as a token of appreciation, he sent a wealthy amount to the elders of Judah that had protected him and kept him and his men safe. Various towns were very helpful in giving food to David and his men. They also were helpful with keeping him informed of King Saul's whereabouts. The men who delivered the spoils were to deliver them in David's name and say, "Here is a gift for you from the spoil of the enemies of the Lord." The messengers were then instructed to explain their recent victory as they wanted to know. A few of the cities were Bethel, Ramoth of the Negeb, Jattir, Aroer, Siphmoth, Eshtemoa, Racal, the cities of the Jerahmeelites, and the cities of the Kenites.

The Kenites were from the south: Midian, Edom, and Arabah. They were mostly known for their craftsmanship and their tinsmith abilities. However, they are also known as the home of Moses' father-in-law.

These gifts were also taken to Hormah, Bor-ashan, Athach, and Hebron. All of these places were dwellings that David and his men had routinely sought refuge in. The gifts were received with joy and deep appreciation. Each group of men brought back a story to share with David about how much they appreciated the gifts. Each one also swore their allegiance to David as their new king.

With a teasing grin on his face, one of the men asked David if he'd be sharing the spoils with the Ziphites. Another man immediately asked David about the men of Keilah. David knew they were teasing by the looks on their faces, but he decided to goad the men back and ask them if they'd like to take the spoils to them. They quickly made excuses of how busy they were rebuilding. David had no intention of sharing anything with either group of men, for none of these men had shown him allegiance. They'd both dealt treacherously with him.

*****

Jabesh-Gilead is located east of Jordan and seventeen miles south of the Sea of Galilee. The land is very fertile, and the abundance of water caused it to often be called the garden of Eden in the land of Israel. It is one of the cities that King Saul ruled over. This city had been ruled by the Ammonites. Shortly after Saul became king, they conquered the city and claimed it for Israel. When the people of Jabesh Gilead heard all that the Philistines had done to Saul, their strongest and biggest men headed out to Beth Shean. They removed the bodies of Saul and his sons and brought them to Jabesh. Once there, they anointed their bodies with incense and perfumes to cleanse them. Next, they prepared them for a fire burial. After their bones were purged with fire, they buried their bones under a great tree in Jabesh. After they were buried, the whole town fasted seven long days to mourn their deaths.

Cremation was only part of their culture when a body needed to be cleansed and purified. The Philistines had paraded their bodies before Dagon and Ashtaroth. Also, King Saul's head had been displayed among the Philistine's god. Therefore, now they needed to be cleansed before burial.

*****

Israel fell into total disarray. Many were weeping and wailing and mourning for their king. Many people were unaware of all that had happened to cause their king to lose God's blessings. Most of those people presumed God had turned on them and blamed him for the current state of disarray. Sackcloth and ashes were everywhere. Wailers were hired to cry in the temple both day and night. There were no joyful sounds heard throughout Judea or Israel unless they were cities cheering for David.

David, his men, and their families returned to Ziklag. They were there two full days before news of the battle came to them. Each man and his family started to restore their home. The wives and daughters were busy cleaning and removing chard wood. They concentrated hard on making it a home again while the men worked on the building repairs that needed to be done. Each man was to take two hours a day to work on the walls. They needed to repair the mud-brick city walls.

On the third day, a man arrived from Saul's camp. His clothes were torn, and he had dust on his head. When he came to David, he fell to the ground to pay him honor.

As David asked him where he was from, he told the man to stand up.

With pride in his eyes and weary from the long journey, he said, "I have escaped from the Israelite camp."

David told him to continue and tell him everything that happened.

Skipping many of the details, the man jumped to the most important ones, "The men fled from the battle. Many of them fell and died. Saul and his son Jonathan are dead."

David asked, "How do you know that Saul and his son Jonathan are dead?"

Intent on pleasing David, he said, "I happened to be on Mount Gilboa, and there was Saul, leaning on his spear, with the chariots and riders almost upon him. When King Saul turned around and saw me, I asked, 'What can I do?'

"Saul asked me who I was, and I told him I am an Amalekite. He said, 'Stand over me and kill me! I am in the throes of death, but I'm still alive.'

"When I saw how badly he was injured, I felt I had no choice but to grant his request and kill him. He was so badly injured that I knew he would not survive. Upon seeing he was dead, I took the crown off his head and the band on his arm. I brought them to you, my lord."

David and all the men with him took hold of their clothes and tore them. There was mourning and weeping and fasting till evening for Saul and Jonathan and for the army of the Lord and the house of Israel. Their hearts were heavy because many had died by the sword.

David asked the young man, "Where are you from?"

"I am the son of a stranger, an Amalekite," he answered.

David then asked him, "Why weren't you afraid to lift your hand to destroy the Lord's anointed?"

Before the man could answer, David gave the order, "Go, strike him down!"

Then, he looked at the man and firmly said, "Your blood is upon your own head. With your own mouth, you testified against yourself when you said, 'I killed the Lord's anointed.'"

The man was shocked at David's response. He started to reply and argue his case, but before he could, the piercing of the sword stopped him. The Amalekite slumped to the ground as he breathed his last breath.

David sat there staring at the crown. One of his men offered to put it upon his head. David was quick to answer, "No! Not yet... Maybe not this crown at all..." David snapped at his loyal follower even though he never meant to. With each word, his voice softened. He knew the man never meant anything but loyalty and devotion.

That night, David wrote a lament concerning Saul and his son Jonathan. He ordered that it be taught to the men of Judah. At the funeral, David chanted these words over and over. They were pinned and written down so that everyone could learn them. They were also written in the book of the upright, also known as Jashar.

Your glory, O Israel, lies slain on your heights. How the mighty have fallen!

Tell it not in Gath, proclaim it not in the streets of Ashkelon, lest the daughters of the Philistines be glad, lest the daughters of the uncircumcised rejoice. O mountains of Gilboa, may you have neither dew nor rain, nor fields that yield offerings of grain. For there the shield of the mighty was defiled, the shield of Saul—no longer rubbed with oil. From the blood of the slain, from the flesh of the mighty, the bow of Jonathan did not turn back, the sword of Saul did not return unsatisfied.

Saul and Jonathan—in life they were loved and gracious, and in death they were not parted. They were swifter than eagles, they were stronger than lions.

O daughters of Israel, weep for Saul, who clothed you in scarlet and finery, who adorned your garments with ornaments of gold.

How the mighty have fallen in battle! Jonathan lies slain on your heights. I grieve for you, Jonathan my brother; you were very dear to me. Your love for me was wonderful, more wonderful than that of women. How the mighty have fallen! The weapons of war have perished![24]

\*\*\*\*\*

Over the next couple of weeks, most of Israel was in mourning for their losses. They mourned for their king and the many men that were killed in battle.

Abner, however, was busy with Ish-Bosheth, the last son of King Saul. Abner took pleasure in taking one of the king's crowns and placing it on Ish-Bosheth's head while making a proclamation that he was Israel's new king.

"Long live King Ish-Bosheth!" he proclaimed.

They would have a celebration feast, but not right away due to the grieving in the land. A few weeks from now, they could have the big celebration. Ish-Bosheth was in the height of his glory. He loved eating like the king. He was quickly gaining weight. He was the shortest of all of the king's sons and slightly on the chubby side. Currently, with his new fame, he was eating large celebration meals for every meal. Ish-Bosheth loved taking over his father's bedroom, his wives, and his father's concubines, excluding his mother, of course. As king of the land, nothing was withheld from him.

Abner found the second-best room in the palace. He and his family set themselves up there. He'd be heard saying he needed to be close to the new king for protection, of course. In reality, Abner didn't think Ish-Bosheth had the ability to be the king without someone telling him every little step. He decided he was the only one for the job. Abner was constantly whispering in his ear or giving him his next direction as a "suggestion."

Abner had a decree taken around to all the cities under King Saul, requiring them to show their loyalty to Ish-Bosheth. This was partly to declare the victory and partly to find out who was going to willingly follow him and who was going to follow David.

Abner fully expected David to rise up and announce himself as the new king of Israel. He was preparing the men for battle again. Not in a way they were aware of, but so that the new captains were put in place, and new recruits were being trained. This included young men who were only boys. He'd assigned men to build new chariots and to purchase new horses, mules, and camels for battle. If necessary, they were to take animals from the local people. After all, it was their duty to protect their king. Abner left no stone unturned as he prepared his new king for the battles to come with David. It was as though Abner completely forgot it was the Philistines who were responsible for King Saul's death. Abner had an inventory taken of all the current equipment, armor, and weapons. Then, he assigned men to work on replenishing them.

# Chapter 40

*"Oh, that the salvation for Israel were come out of Zion!*
*When God brings back the captivity of His people, let Jacob*
*rejoice, let Israel be glad!" (Psalm 53:6, NKJV)*

A few weeks passed since King Saul and his sons were killed. People were turning to David for direction. They'd begun to ask him about Judah, Israel, and his kingship. He decided it was time to seek God and ask for direction concerning the next step.

After singing songs and spending time worshipping his creator, David asked God, "Shall I go up to one of the towns in Judah?"

Answering short and precisely as God always did with David, he said, "Go up."

David asked, "Where shall I go, Lord?"

"To Hebron," the Lord answered.

Hebron was his home area. He'd be back closer to his childhood stomping ground. He was born and raised in Bethlehem, and Hebron was around twenty-one miles from Bethlehem, but David had covered many of those miles in between with shepherding and being a servant of King Saul.

A smile spread across David's face as he took pleasure in the thought, *In Hebron, I shall sit as the king of Judah.* David felt a giddiness of excitement, similar to that of a child.

He couldn't wait to tell both of his wives the news. He knew they'd both be excited. He shared things with Ahinoam first. He was most anxious to share things with Abigail but planned to stay the night with her to celebrate his news. Therefore, Ahinoam would be first. He also loved how they shared childhood memories. David loved the beauty of a younger wife and how she enticed him, but he also loved the maturity that Abigail had to offer.

Ahinoam was delighted for him, but it seemed that her main topic was not his throne but where her seat would be set and if her bedroom would be directly connected to his.

Slightly disappointed in her response and yet almost expecting it, he gave a slight nod of his head. Then, with a slight smile, he thought, *At least she's pleasant to look at and has given me my precious son, Amnon.*

Abigail was very excited for David, but in somewhat of a matter-of-fact way. She reassured him that this was clearly the next step and that someday he'd rule all of Israel, not just Judah. Together they celebrated a toast to the new king of Judah. They drank from the best wine he had. Tenderly and cherishing as his wife, she caressed his throat and his ear and whispered, "Long live King David." She had a long-awaited surprise that she was most anxious to share with him, but it could wait one more day. Tonight was a time to celebrate his kingship.

The next day, David set the move in motion with Joab. Over the years in the wilderness, his nephew Joab had become his right-hand man and a very valuable commander. Immediately under Joab were Abishai and Asahel, also his sister Zeruiah's sons, and Ahithophel, Amasa, Benaiah, and Hanun. Many other men were becoming part of his "mighty men" cabinet, but these men held a key position.

Joab told Benaiah and Asahel to get a group of men each to go up to Hebron early to clear the palace for his entry. They were to set up the stables and organize things. They'd be coming within the week. There was a palace in Hebron already from earlier years. However, Hebron itself had been ruled by King Saul. There was a small staff that maintained the grounds and the palace and others King Saul had allowed to live there. They were about to find a new home.

By the end of the week, the animals and carts were loaded, and everyone was ready to travel. David's family stayed close to him at the front of the line. Everyone else fell in behind, and they were off. Hebron was approximately twenty-five miles away. It would take longer than normal because they'd be walking over three large hills, and Hebron climbed in elevation. The most direct road was between Beersheba and Hebron. It ran along the mountain ranges. They followed the paths that led to the road going past Debir.

Therefore, it took two days to get to Hebron with six hundred men, their families, the animals, and their elderly. But once they arrived, they'd begin the next chapter in their lives, and David would become the king of Judah. It was a beautiful walk to Hebron. The mountain ranges were on the right side of them most of the way. On the left was a beautiful valley. They walked by fresh springs and enjoyed seeing the birds and animals that they passed along the way. The young men would take turns riding along the mountain ranges as a lookout. It was around lunchtime when they took their first break. They stopped nearby some fresh springs to eat, rest, and water the flocks. Again, at dinner time, they found another fresh spring and set up camp for the night. They would finish their journey after a good night's sleep. David had a messenger pass word to everyone that they were to be up and packing for the rest of the journey as soon as the day started to break. They'd be leaving early and waiting for no one.

Before they left Ziklag, Abigail had pulled out a beautiful robe for David. She had some very exquisite material she'd picked up when they were in Gath. She determined she wanted to make David a royal robe to wear when he came to his throne. It was a silk material said to have been spun from worms. They called them silkworms. It was hard to imagine, but the material was soft and sleek. It was brought by ship from across the sea. The material was such a royal deep red color that it hinted of purple. She sewed on jewels and added a shoulder cape of white fur. She used thread dipped in gold to sew on designs, jewels and to sew the cuffs and hems. Smiling at her achievement, she couldn't help but think it was very fitting for a king.

Abigail had worked together with Joab designing a new crown for him. Joab had assigned one of the men to make a most superb crown with stunning jewels. Of course, it was designed out of gold. It had very unique designs engraved in and around the jewels. They'd been very clever about how they attained his head size. They got it during a theatrical production. David never suspected a thing and was pleasantly surprised when they placed it on his head.

Among their men was an artist. They actually had several, but one man in particular. He'd been very busy designing a crest for David that could be used as a sign for the House of David forever. The man had already shown the symbol to David so that he could approve it and make appropriate changes. The artist came up with several designs, but the one David liked best was quite simple with theology behind it. It had two triangles intertwined. The top triangle points upward toward God, and a second triangle overlies and points downward toward earth, man, and His kingdom. At each point where the two triangles crossed, they alternated which one crossed over the top, giving an interwoven effect. When you counted all the sides, inside and out, there were a total of twelve sides, which represented the twelve tribes of Israel. The two intertwined triangles represented how Israel was inseparable, speaking volumes of the Jewish people. Two different metals were used to enhance the two different triangles.

One of David's mighty men saw it and jokingly asked if he'd just created the star of David. David smiled, rubbed his beard, and said, "I like that...the star of David."

# Chapter 41

*"The Lord of Host is with us; the God of Jacob is our refuge"*
*(Psalm 46:7, KJV).*

David sent word to everyone who had ever supported him that he was going up to Hebron; God instructed him to establish his throne there. Over the next two days, many men from Judah traveled to Hebron with the sole purpose of anointing David to be their king. Although they had not heard God speak to him, many of the men had seen God's anointing on David since the very first day most men remembered him, which often was the notable day he killed Goliath. Several of the men had also joined David in fighting the Philistines.

United together, the men of the area arrived to anoint David as their new king. A new prophet was becoming known throughout the land by the name of Nathan. David had sent one of his men to inform Abiathar, the high priest, that they requested his presence at the service, but, of course, the Prophet Nathan will be anointing him as king. Before anyone could leave in search of the prophet, Nathan arrived in Hebron, already prepared with his ram's horn and oil. He came seeking to speak to David alone.

It was such a glorious event. All of the discouraging moments he'd had these past few years now seemed swept away. He knew there would still be battles, but at least he was on his way to seeing the dreams God had put in his heart coming to pass.

The day started with pampering that a king would receive. His servants groomed his nails and massaged his hands and feet with special oils. People were busy preparing a feast not only fit for a king but made ready for the king and as many guests as they could fit in the palace. The palace area was rather small, but it was a start. They had time to build more rooms or a nicer palace. David's mind was spinning with new plans and ideas. Although he was excited about the possibilities, he determined to seek God on every step. He felt honored to wear the new robe that Abigail had designed for him. It was quite lovely. He enjoyed his new crown and his new sword and the well-designed new handheld staff. The women took the new design David approved and made flags to be flown in every town he was king over. The men made him a new throne chair with extra lumbar support and matching pillows. He enjoyed it very much. After the anointing, Abiathar prayed over David, and then, the men all together raised their swords upward and cried out in victory, "Long live King David!"

David knew he could handle the attention modestly, but it was hard not to succumb to the moment. To keep pride from entering, he took time to focus on God. He asked Asaph, his chief musician, to lead the men in a time of worship. David found himself calling on Asaph more and more to lead the men to worship God. He enjoyed the presence of God that Asaph ushered in. God was putting together a worship team, and Asaph was definitely a key part.

Sometimes David played his harp, and many of the men played various instruments. Still, more often, they'd sing a cappella. Occasionally, one of the men would sound just atrocious; if anyone was quick to point fingers, David would remind them that God loves us according to our hearts, not our voices. A few times, though, laughter took over as those around heard the screeches that came forth as a sound of worship. Today, however, his men had organized a small orchestra to play the music together. They had lyres, harps, trumpets, ram's horns, and many other stringed instruments. It was a very triumphant day, and David wanted God to get the glory. After all, if God hadn't protected him, he'd probably be dead. But that was another thought to be dismissed today. David went to sleep that night with his head full of ideas and excitement...and praises to God on his lips.

\*\*\*\*\*

The first line of business that David dealt with was to send a message to the men of Jabesh-Gilead. He thought much about Saul's burial and these men. He decided to send them a message as king over Judah. David's message read, "May you be blessed by Yahweh for doing this kindness to Saul, your lord, and for burying him. And now, may Yahweh show kindness and faithfulness to you! I, too, shall treat you well because you have done this. And now take courage and be men of valor. Saul, your lord, is dead, but the House of Judah has anointed me to be their king."

The messengers understood that in taking the message to Jabesh-Gilead, David was asking these men to acknowledge him as Saul's successor. The men were to bring their response. David was only slightly disappointed when no reply came, but perhaps they needed a little more time.

Ish-Bosheth, Saul's last living son, was making loud proclamations about being King Saul's successor. All Israel seemed to stand with him. Only Judah was supporting David. Although this was disappointing to David, he reminded himself of the past few years and how far they'd come since then. They had a palace now, not a cave. They had a full army to call on besides their own small army. They had food and supplies of a king with a kingdom. And to make things even more real, he had his own throne, crown, and armband. He also had the joy of seeing a flag representing his family's royalty flying in all the cities and towns that followed him. David went to God in prayer to see if he should just be happy with being king over Judah, and God reminded him that Samuel anointed him to be king over all Israel. As David allowed his thoughts to explore every aspect of the situation, he decided that this would most likely mean the death of Ish-Bosheth. David had never particularly cared for Ish-Bosheth, but he would not welcome his death either. One thing that he determined, though, was that neither he nor his men would be the ones responsible for his death. He'd have to make this clear to Joab and the rest of his men. Suddenly, David felt very weary as he realized Ish-Bosheth was probably around forty years old. How many more years could he live yet?

Displacing those thoughts, he found a good distraction in settling into the business of being king over those who wanted him. There was much to do, and God would take care of tomorrow. Today, he would be king over the people of Hebron.

# Section III

## *David Reigns as King in Hebron*

# Chapter 42

*"You make known to me the path of life; you will fill me with joy in your presence, with eternal pleasures at your right hand" (Psalm 16:11, NIV).*

The next few years were full of intrigue, challenges, and some regular life, or regular life for a king. For a while, it seemed David was taking a new wife every six months. He married Ahinoam the Jezreelitess. Next, he married Maachah, the daughter of Talmai, king of Geshur. After that, it was Haggith, then Abital. Then, he married Eglah. Each wife had her own beauty and brought something to the marriage. Most often, they brought either a bountiful dowry or a treaty from another nation. Most of his wives gave David at least one child. They all prayed for sons and that their son would someday be the next king. Of course, they all knew it was tradition for the first-born son to take the throne after his father, but history shows us anything can happen. They could only hope and pray that their son would be ready should he get his chance. History is filled with stories of princes who lost their chance to the throne because of plagues, wartime, sickness, and of course, evil men.

Each wife sought David's attention. His wives who could cook constantly sought to wine-and-dine him for a night together. The wives who could sew were always striving to outdo the other on apparel and royal clothing. In fact, one day, Haggith and Abital almost started fighting at the market over a fine piece of material. Their handmaidens intervened and stopped the women.

David cared about all of his children and tried to find time to know each one individually. He taught all of them the ways of Jehovah. The infant to toddler stage had some very overwhelming moments for David. He couldn't believe such beautiful little children could be such a handful. He often thought about how much easier it was to handle several hundred men than his small sons clamoring around his legs. Due to all of his responsibilities, David found it hard to spend a lot of time with the children before they were weaned from their mother. At that point, he encouraged them to go and spend time each week with Abiathar, the high priest. David wanted to ensure that his children were growing up under the Mosaic Law, especially since some of his wives were not Hebrew.

As soon as they were old enough to be taught, David assigned private tutors to each child, both for lessons and the rearing of being from royal blood. David loved watching Amnon and Daniel take riding lessons. Some days they seemed too little to be on horses. They started out being led around and getting comfortable with riding the large animals. Once they were old enough to have riding lessons, each son was given a horse of his own. They had much to learn, for someday, one of them would succeed him upon the throne. David had so many dreams about the tomorrows ahead. But for now, he determined to slow down and enjoy each day, each moment, and each child.

It was a wet fall day. Hebron receives a lot of rain during the fall months. The temperature was pleasant, though. It was neither too hot nor too cold but comfortable. The city was busy in preparation for the Feast of the Trumpets, which would begin tomorrow. The Feast of Trumpets was the first feast of the fall season. Many people referred to it as Rosh Hashanah. This feast signified the New Year. It was the anniversary of Adam and Eve, the beginning of mankind, and our part in God's creation. It was first spoken of in the old mosaic scrolls. Moses recorded them in the writings entitled "Relating to the Levites," also called the scroll of Leviticus. Just as David relived his father's teachings, he called all his sons to the courtyard. They had a nice covering that allowed them to stay out of the rain. All of his sons came, even the ones who were too young to understand. The mothers brought the babies. They would have the exposure to God's law just as the others and come to understand it and love it as they grew. David told of all the people sitting around as Moses explained the Levitical laws concerning the Sabbath and God's appointed festivals. Next, David told of each feast. As he named each one individually, he told the boys of God's specifications concerning them, the Festival of Unleavened Bread, the Offering of the Firstfruits, the Festival of Weeks, the Festival of Trumpets, the Day of Atonement, and the Festival of Tabernacles.

The Festival of Trumpets is in the seventh month and is to be a day of complete rest. That meant all the people were baking and cooking in advance. The fieldwork is being done, and all building is laid aside for the celebration. Each family was busy preparing themselves an offering made to the Lord by fire. David explained how they'd be sacrificing one young bullock, one ram, and seven lambs of the first year without blemish. As David explained how these sacrifices worked, Amnon said, "Ahhh, that's so cool!" And Daniel wrinkled his face as he said, "Uuuh, yuck! That sounds terrible." He smiled at his sons.

David explained the specific prayers they'd be praying tomorrow and some of the foods they'd be eating. He told them about how they'd have a piece of apple dipped in honey and how this symbolizes our desire for a sweet year. He had to stop often to answer various questions that came from little minds, but even though it was tedious, it was also fun. David had new insight to what it must have been like for his father with eight sons.

At David's request, one of the older men who blew the shofar came in to make the shofar sounds for his sons. The man explained some of the various sounds that they use so that the children could understand a feast blast from a battle cry blast. He gave an example of the different tones used to call everyone to a sacred assembly. David gave examples for each use so that his sons could understand them. Then, the man blew the shofar, creating the different blasts, so the older boys could identify which one it was. Amnon was the oldest and often had the answer first. Some of the boys followed him, while the others sought to beat him to the answer. David smiled when his young son, Absalom, joined in and very astutely gave his answer.

Absalom was David's third son. He came from Maachah. She was a princess and the daughter of Talmai, the king of Geshur. Years earlier, Joshua had been ordered to eliminate the Geshurites upon entering the Promised Land. God gave the land to the half-tribe of Manasseh. Instead of settling the entire land God gave them, they settled east of the Jordan River. The Geshurites were one of the groups of people who failed to obey God's command. Geshur was the territory east of the upper Jordan region.

Maachah's hair was dark brown and thick with long curly ringlets. She mostly wore it pulled back with ribbons, but small strands were always escaping and surrounding her face with tiny ringlets. The wind would catch these ringlets and cause her to often brush them out of her eyes. David thought she had incredibly beautiful dark long eyelashes. He admired her greatly, but his marriage to her was primarily an arranged marriage for a treaty between both groups of people. Geshur was located on the borders of Palestine and Syria. It was an Israeli settlement but of Arabic descent and independent of Israel. David was certain that Talmai had wanted peace and a covenant with him due to the raids while they were under Achish. Achish had the Philistines invading the Israelite communities. David and his men would never do that, but they would invade other communities outside the Israelite cities. Therefore, Talmai had sent a group of men to David asking for a treaty upon giving his beautiful daughter and a bountiful dowry to David. Upon praying about it, David felt like it was a good decision. Talmai was a large-built man. He stood almost a foot taller than David. He had broad shoulders and large hands. He reminded David of Goliath and how some of the Philistines were built. Fortunately, Maachah did not have her father's characteristics but her mother's smaller frame.

David looked down at his precious son Absalom. He had the same thick curly hair as his mother. Even though he was still so young, everyone who saw him admired his hair. They often had to run their fingers through it or touch it. It was so noticeable that it was the first thing that caught your eye when he came into the room or entered the courtyard. He was about to turn four years old. He had a smile that covered his whole face. He was a happy child, and when he smiled, his eyes smiled too. David saw something very special in Absalom. Even as a child, he had strong leadership skills. When he played with his older brothers, David observed that he tried to tell them how he wanted to play the game. The crazy thing was the older boys seemed to listen to him. What seemed like baby gibberish to others corralled all of his brothers and sisters together in a childlike order.

David enjoyed the time with his children and would enjoy the Feast of Trumpets. He wanted to be close to his sons so he could see their faces in the morning when the shofar was blown.

# Chapter 43

*"Turn to me and be gracious to me, for I am lonely and afflicted" (Psalm 25:16, NIV).*

The day promised to be a pleasant one. As David sat eating his breakfast of fresh fruit, eggs, and bread, he found himself contemplating, *Is it a new problem or a continuing problem?*

Judah recognized David as their king, but Israel aligned themselves with Ish-Bosheth, King Saul's last reigning son. Small wars were breaking out between Israel and Judah. Some days he found his faith faltering and just knew this situation would never end. *God could end all of this so easily; why must God wait to make me king over all Israel?* Why was it such a long, hard battle? If God anointed him to be king, then why didn't he make it happen in an easier manner? These questions plagued David, even though he gave the situation over to God as often as he needed to in order to obtain peace.

Ish-bosheth chose to reign from Mahanaim[25]. Mahanaim is east of the Jordan River. David was surprised when he learned Ish-bosheth hadn't stayed at his father Saul's palace in Gibeah. Word came to David that Ish-bosheth moved out of fear of David. Gibeah is about thirty-five miles northeast of Hebron, and Mahanaim is another thirty-five miles northeast of Gibeah. So now there was a distance of seventy miles and a river between them. It saddened David to realize how little Saul's family knew him. He'd never bring harm to any Israelite king, but especially not King Saul's family. "It's God's job to bring judgment. It is also God's job to place people in positions...and to remove them."

Although Ish-bosheth was Israel's king, David was certain that someone else was making most of the decisions. Someone... most certainly Abner. Ish-bosheth is not of strong character, and David was certain that he wouldn't be a good leader.

Mahanaim means "two camps." It also means "hill city." It is where Jacob had a vision of angels. Over the years, it became a haven for people. The land was designed in such a way that it offered protection from enemies.

Many small battles were breaking out, and report was coming to David of Abner and his men attacking while David's men were out patrolling. Sometimes, it would be David's men who did the attacking by catching a few of Saul's men alone and attacking them.

Then, one day, the battle intensified. Joab received a challenge from Abner to bring his soldiers and meet him at the Pool of Gibeon. The Pool of Gibeon was located east of Mahanaim. It sits outside Gibeon, an Arab village on top of the plateau. Gibeon was considered by Joshua as a great city, like one of the royal cities. Therefore, the people feared it greatly. The Pool of Gibeon is a huge pool or deep-water system. The pool was a large circle approximately forty feet in diameter. It went down around thirty-five feet deep to access the water table. They'd engineered a spiral staircase along the wall in the limestone. The staircase allowed a person to ascend and descend into the pool. The land surrounding the pool was very dry and barren. The plant life was more of shrubs and desert plants. Gibeon is a very ancient city that was given to the Benjamin tribe upon the Israelites entering the Promised Land. However, due to tricking Joshua into signing a treaty, the Hivites were never removed, and Israel never occupied this land.

Joab knew this was a challenge to fight. So he accepted the challenge. As the men arrived at the Pool of Gibeon, they sat down around the pool. Their feet hung over the side as they sat down, looking at each other and looking into this large architectural hole in the ground. Some of the men found pleasure in inspecting the hole. Others sat glaring with a hateful look at the other men. Some were just there to support their army, hoping nothing would come of this encounter. Many men seemed to have their hand on or near their dagger as if to make a statement. Neither army had brought a lot of men. They'd brought enough for a sporting match. This was to be more of a gladiator match, like the ones King Saul sat up from time to time with armies that were expendable.

As soon as Abner thought everyone had arrived, he spoke up and said, "Joab, let a few of our warriors get up and fight hand to hand in front of us."

Joab didn't trust Abner and already knew how things would end. So very astutely, he turned to a few of his men and nodded.

Joab chose twelve men from his army, and Abner chose twelve men from his. Joab was certain of the fate of these men before they ever stood up. He looked at each man as he stood.

They were all young, around their early twenties. He knew each man personally, but not full details of their lives. He knew they all had parents, and many had brothers or sisters. A lot of them had a wife by this age. But this was war, a war he was determined to help God and David win.

Each man stood up and walked to the side of the pool where they could face each other. Each man stood in a line, all twelve of Joab's men and all twelve of Abner's men. With a space between each set of men, they stood evenly facing each other. They stood for a few seconds. Each was waiting for the other to make the first move. Then, as quickly as everything began, it was over. Without hesitation, each man grabbed his challenger by the head, and with his other hand, he plunged his sword into his challenger's side. All twenty-four men died in just seconds. Twenty-four young men were never going to grow old with the love of their lives.

Instantly, the challenge turned into a fierce battle. The men fought intensely for a few hours. Abner and his men were strong, but David's men were stronger. They backed them toward the side of the hill. The ground was rocky, with mounds of rocks protruding from the ground. This made it extra challenging, and every once in a while, a man would trip on a rock. Sometimes they'd recover very quickly, and sometimes, it meant their death. Joab's two brothers were with him, Abishai and Asahel. They are both excellent fighters. Abishai and Asahel both listened to Joab as the commander; therefore, they were also leaders under Joab.

Asahel was known for his fast-running ability. He is slightly taller than both of his brothers, giving him long, agile legs. His nickname was "Asahel the Gazelle" or just "Gazelle." He was very swift and fast. Having been in Joab's counsel for so long, he understood the need to take Abner out. His eyes immediately found Abner, and his fast legs seemed to have a mind of their own. They seemed to take flight after Abner. Unlike Abishai, Asahel had very dark brown hair. At his young age, he already showed signs of a receding hairline. His eyes are dark brown and alert, watching the ground and keeping his eyes steadfast upon Abner.

Immediately, Abner realized that he was being chased, and he took off running to the side of the hill. He darted around rocks and scraggly desert trees and other soldiers. He was certain Asahel was the one pursuing him. So glancing back over his shoulder as he ran, he called out, "Is that you, Asahel?"

With determination in his voice, Asahel answered him, "Yes, it is!"

Abner paused and turned to him and said, "Turn aside to the right or to the left, take on one of the young men and strip him of his weapons."

Asahel huffed at that and ran all the faster after him. "You'd like that old man, wouldn't you! You're going down today!"

This time Abner turned to face the approaching Asahel. He called out a stern warning. As Asahel drew closer and closer, Abner shouted out a command, "Stop chasing me! Why should I strike you down? How could I look your brother Joab in the face?"

Asahel was close now, and without further hesitation, with quick action, Abner thrust the butt of his spear directly into Asahel's stomach. He caught him just below the fifth rib. Abner hit him with so much force that the spear came out through Asahel's back. Asahel died immediately where he fell. As Joab's men chased Abner's men down the mountainside, each man stopped when he came to Asahel. All except Joab and Abishai. Seeing Joab's determination, all of his men that were not injured pursued Abner with them. They were more determined than ever to catch Abner, so they pursued him until that evening when the sun was setting. Abner and his men had made their way to the hill of Ammah, near Giah, on the way to the wasteland of Gibeon. A group of Benjamin men rallied behind Abner and formed a troop. As Abner and his men took their stand on top of the hill, there were no further options for the two brothers and their small band of men at that time.

From his safe distance, Abner called out to Joab, "Must the sword devour forever? Don't you realize that this will end in bitterness? How long before you order your men to stop pursuing their fellow Israelites?"

Joab shouted back, "As surely as God lives, if you had not spoken, the men would have continued pursuing them until morning."

Upon that, Joab blew the trumpet, and their troop came to a halt. They no longer pursued Israel, so there was no more fighting that day.

\*\*\*\*\*

Abner shook his head whenever he thought of killing Asahel. He knew from that moment on, Joab would make it his personal goal to kill him. He'd have to be extra careful now. Joab did not look like a person to forgive something like that easily. As the night progressed, Abner and his men marched through the Arabah and crossed the Jordan. They continued on through the morning hours and came to Mahanaim. He knew they were hit hard by Joab and his men but was surprised when the count came in and they'd had three hundred and sixty men die.

\* \* \* \* \*

Joab vowed Abner would pay for killing his brother. It might not be today, but it would happen. The two very tired and weary brothers and their army worked their way back to find Asahel and to carry his body back to Hebron. Sadness always surrounded them when a soldier died, but today, too many soldiers had died, the twelve men who challenged his brother Asahel and seven other men, totaling twenty-one men. Joab listened as they walked home. No laughing and joking, which so often accompanied their group. Occasionally, a soft cry would escape the lips of someone, often followed by a cough to chase away the embarrassment of showing emotions. Although it was war, the loss brought much emptiness and sadness to their hearts. Every man who died was buried right there in the field where they died, every man except for Asahel. From that day on, the area became known as Helkathhazzurim or the Field of Blades.

With heavy hearts, Joab, Abishai, and his men took their brother's body home. Both Joab and Abishai had feelings of heaviness. They not only grieved for Asahel but the memories of the loss of their father flooded them once again. They buried him in Bethlehem in their father's tomb beside him. Pausing only for a few moments of silence, they continued on until they reached Hebron the next morning.

# Chapter 44

*"Blessed be the Lord, who daily loads us with benefits, even
the God of our salvation" (Psalm 68:19, NKJV).*

Over the next few years, war continued between the house of David and the house of Saul. David found favor with God and man, and his army grew and increased daily. On the other hand, Saul's army, or Abner's army for the house of Saul, grew weaker and weaker. It seemed as though daily, David would get a report of spies watching everything they were doing. The spies were primarily from King Saul's house, but there were also spies from the Philistines. Or rather who were hired by the Philistines, for a Philistine was obvious, and his appearance would stand out in the midst of the Israelites. All of them were watching for opportunities to come against him. They also watched to make sure David's kingdom didn't become too powerful. David's heart grew heavy, and he found his greatest comfort in taking time alone with God and laying his burdens on Jehovah.

During this time, David's family also grew. His first son Amnon, born to him from Ahinoam, was now six years old.

Daniel, his second son, given to him by Abigail, was now five years old.

His third son, Adonijah, came from his fourth wife, Haggith. She was a Gadite dancer. David thought she danced so gracefully, and he loved to watch her dance. He met her through the Gadite men who joined his army while they were in the wilderness. Every time the praise music began, she danced and honored Jehovah. She draped long scarves around her neck and arms that flowed in the air as she worshipped in God's presence. Her thin, long fingers would flow over her skin and her arms with praises. With every movement, she ushered in God's holy presence. Other women joined her in dance, but she had an anointing that intrigued David and drew him. She was the sister to one of his mighty men, Benaiah. Her hair was long and flowed down her back, thick and light brown with strands of blond flowing through it. She was a sweet lady. David got the impression that she could have a "bad side," and it might be best to never get on it. Over time, she gave David his son Adonijah. He had the same dark Jewish features that made David proud. He thought Adonijah resembled his brother Eliab. Just as Absalom, everyone who saw him remarked at how beautiful of a baby he was. David's heart beamed at his sons. Even as an infant, Adonijah was built slightly larger than most babies his age. David was certain this meant that he'd be a big boy as he grew.

Some months after he married Haggith, David took another wife, Abital. His sixth wife was a Hebrew lady. Just like David, she was raised with all the Jewish customs. She is not as strong in her dedication to God as David, but she loves Jehovah and worships Him. Her name means "my father is as fresh as the dew." She grew up very close to her father, but she found joy when she thought of her Father God in heaven and applied this meaning to Him. She caught David's attention when he heard her saying how each day is new and fresh as the dew on the ground when we serve Jehovah. She said it with such meaning in her voice.

Abital takes her role in the Mitzvot or commandments of the Jewish tradition very seriously. She loves lighting the candles to mark the beginning of Shabbat or a holiday. Sometimes David teased her because she might vary thirty minutes here or there on when Shabbat begins. Shabbat begins at sundown, but if she didn't have everything in order, she might delay the lighting of the candles for a few minutes to get the last few things finished so that she could enjoy Shabbat. He found humor in it and loved to tease her about it, "Shabbat begins when Abital decides so." It was all in good humor, though.

Abital also prided herself on making the best Challah. She spent much time perfecting it as her offering to God. She was honored to prepare the Challah and to have it ready for the breaking of bread. Although these customs were regularly expected of Jewish women, she found pleasure and honor in these two traditions especially. She loved taking time to braid the sweet golden eggy bread for the Rosh Hashanah festival. She made sure its texture was so pleasing. The bread was shaped differently for different festivals and events. Another feature David enjoyed was her long black wavy hair. Her hair was thin and easily tangled in the wind.

David's fifth son, Shephatiah, came from Abital. Shephatiah is a small boy and not as alert as Adonijah. David was surprised to see how he favored some traits in his sons more than others. He was determined never to have favorites like his father had, but it was hard. Certain children outshine others with their attitudes and behaviors. Perhaps that is why his father favored his oldest three brothers. Was this how his father saw him compared to his older brothers? Did his father compare him to his brother's physical build?

This was a good reminder for David. Had God not looked more at the heart than the stature or beautiful appearance, then I might not be where I am today. Perhaps he'd never been anointed as the next king of Israel. He decided to work on developing Shephatiah's heart and directing him toward the one true God. *Perhaps he will enjoy playing the harp like I do and creating an atmosphere of praise.*

Another year later, David took Eglah as his next wife. David met Eglah when he was buying heifers for their own herd. A host of men traveled to Bashan with David. Bashan is located east of Jordan. They knew that the best heifers in the land were from this region. While there, the men of Bashan prepared a feast for David as their new king. The owner of the herd brought his finest daughter out before David. Although she was fully covered, she was a very voluptuous female indeed. Her robe was beautifully designed. She caught his attention, for she had a shapely curvaceous top. The father sought David's favor to marrying his daughter. He insisted she'd make him a good wife and bring him many sons. He said this based on how many sons his wife, her mother, had given him. Then he offered the herd David was prepared to purchase as a dowry. David decided it would be good to marry her. It would cement his relations with this region of Judah.

Ten months after their union, her handmaiden placed their beautiful little son into his arms. They chose to name him Ithream, which means "profit of the people." They plan to raise him to be the "excellence of the people." Ithream would grow up tending the cattle as his mother requested. She desired for him to know her family and to learn the benefits of herding cattle just like her family.

David often gave specific instructions to Abiathar for different sons. For Ithream, he instructed Abiathar to make certain he was taught the necessity of a *pure* heifer sacrifice. He also thought he should learn the importance of a spotless offering. The baby was truly of Jewish descent, with the desired, however, lighter Jewish features. He had fairer skin. He had lots of rolls for a baby. Maybe it was his diet of breast milk, but he sure was a healthy little guy.

*****

David took time to reflect upon all God was doing for him and how his family was growing. He now had six sons to watch grow. They seemed to grow as fast as the weeds outside. The older two were starting to do more activities with their father when David was not out to war.

# Chapter 45

*"Restore unto me the joy of thy salvation; and uphold me with thy free spirit" (Psalm 51:12, KJV).*

Life went on for David as had become the norm, and then in one day, everything changed. Messengers brought word to David that Abner and Ish-Bosheth had a falling out. They told David the argument regarded a concubine of Saul's named Rizpah, the daughter of Aiah. David knew who Rizpah was, but he only knew her by name. Jonathan did not particularly care for her and had pointed her out to him. He had commented how her sons were jealous because they were not in line for the throne, and yet, they had the same father.

It was a known fact that Abner had an eye for her. He flirted with her whenever he thought no one was looking. Now that King Saul was gone, he couldn't stay away. But Ish-Bosheth knew that sleeping with a king's wife or concubine was often a declaration to take over another's kingdom. Ish-Bosheth had seen how Abner was growing stronger before the people. He already feared that Abner might be planning to take over. Then, last night he'd been seen coming out of Rizpah's chambers when he thought no one saw him. When Ish-Bosheth confronted him,

Abner became very angry. He nearly spit out his words mixed with deep resentment at the accusing words, "Am I a dog's head on Judah's side?" Hostile and belligerent, he continued, "This very day, I am loyal to the house of your father, Saul, and to his family and friends. I haven't handed you over to David. Yet now you accuse me of an offense involving a woman! May God deal with me, be it ever so severely, if I do not do for David what the Lord promised him on oath and transfer the kingdom from the house of Saul and establish David's throne over Israel and Judah from Dan to Beersheba."

The messengers told David that Ish-Bosheth dared not say another word to Abner because he was very afraid of him.

*****

Later that day, David was visited by messengers sent from Abner. They carried a message from him, saying, "Whose land is it? Make an agreement with me, and I will help you bring all Israel over to you."

David knew that Abner was the one creating the alliances and that it was he who brought about their loyalty to Ish-Bosheth. He'd been thinking a lot lately and mostly about how his wife Michal had been taken away from him. He forgave King Saul, but David was determined to get her back. She was his wife, and it was wrong for her to have been given to anyone! He knew he didn't love her the way he once had. He'd known love in many different ways by this time. Then, there was the fact that she never conceived a son for him after all their times together. It was rather certain by this time that she would never give birth to her own child. But again, she was still *his* wife. She shouldn't be with anyone else. She was only King Saul's daughter to give the first time. It was because of King Saul's attitude that they were not together these past ten years. David knew this was his opportunity to negotiate for her return.

He would make his alliance with Abner and get Michal back. Abner's promise to gain him the kingdom didn't mean much to David. David recalled the words written by Moses when he was leading the children of Israel through the wilderness. Moses said to the people, "Remember the Lord your God, for it is He who gives you the ability to produce wealth, and so confirms His covenant, which He swore to your ancestors, as it is today."

Right before Moses spoke these words, he said, "You say in your heart, 'My power and the strength of my hand have produced this wealth for me.'" Abner believed it was he who controlled Israel's destiny. David gave a slight head nod as he thought about Abner's stand on things and where he must stand with God.

Because it is God who gives the power to get wealth, God will give him the kingdom in His time, and no one, not Abner, nor Ish-Bosheth, nor anyone else, will keep it from him.

David sent the messengers on their way with his reply, "Good! I will make an agreement with you. But I demand one thing of you. Do not come into my presence unless you bring Michal, the daughter of Saul, with you when you come to see me."

Then David sent for his own messengers and sent this message to Ish-Bosheth. David demanded, "Give me my wife Michal, whom I betrothed to myself for the price of a hundred Philistine foreskins!"

David knew Abner would bring about his own death if he tried to get Michal without Ish-Bosheth's approval. Just for fun, David added the reminder of how he earned Michal and what God could do through him. Perhaps it would wake Ish-Bosheth up and put a little bit of healthy fear in his heart.

*****

Michal's heart skipped a beat when she heard that David wanted her back. In the same breath, she'd built a life with Paltiel and knew this would break his heart. Twelve years ago, this past spring, David and Michal had been married. Their love had been so young and tender. She had loved David with her whole heart. She believed she might have loved David more than he loved her because he shared his love for her with Jehovah. She loved Jehovah too, but David had made Him more important than she. That was the only problem, that is, until her father decided David was out to steal his kingdom. Over and over, her father told Jonathan that David would kill both of them, maybe in their sleep or poison or by the sword. The paranoia her father dealt with was so sad. She'd deceived her father in helping David escape, and they both knew it. Instead of charging her with treason, he gave her to another man. It was her father's way of keeping her alive and still punishing her.

Paltiel was a very tender man, and he devoted all his time and attention to her. Sometimes, it made her sick the way he doted over her. But she smiled as she thought again, *He really is a good man.* Paltiel came from Gallim Springs, which is located north of Jerusalem. For over five years now, she'd been a mother to her nephews. She and Paltiel had taken them in and were raising them. Adriel had asked this of them when Merab died giving birth to their fifth son. Michal had been concerned about her having the children so close. She seemed so weak the last pregnancy. Michal had requested an extra handmaiden from her father for Merab. It helped but was not enough. The boys were still young when they moved in with them. The oldest was seven years old, down to the newborn. Paltiel never hesitated for even one minute to take on the responsibility of five growing boys.

Michal had stayed close to Merab even after they both married. She was there for Michal during those first days when her husband was being pursued by their father. Merab let her cry and listened to her worries. Then she was there to guide her through the "forced upon her" union with Paltiel. It was never in Michal's heart to be with anyone but David, and it saddened her deeply. To fill Michal's time, Merab encouraged her to become a midwife and assist with her pregnancies and births. Losing her sister was incredibly hard for her, but becoming a mother of five young boys overnight was even harder. She'd spent enough time with the boys that they had a good relationship. But still, the daily tasks of laundry, cooking, and sewing were very overwhelming at times. She'd learned to treasure the good and stable man that Paltiel had become to her.

That morning, Abner and some soldiers showed up with an enclosed carriage. From inside the house, the carriage appeared empty. This filled Michal with questions and worries. The man of the house was the one who went out to greet the riders. To her surprise, she heard loud howls and protesting cries come from Paltiel. Michal's heart filled with fear at what else could be wrong. The last time several riders came was when her brothers and her father were killed in battle. She waited anxiously for Paltiel to come and tell her what terrible news they'd just received. Soon, Abner came inside the house and found her. He told her to gather her things; she was being returned to David, the king of Hebron.

Her heart skipped a beat at the thought that David, her David, might still love her; then, her heart filled with anger and jealousy at all his other wives. Next, it filled with sorrow for Paltiel, as well as questions about her sons. The boys were now six years older than when they came to her. Almost six years ago, David became king over Hebron. She'd waited and wondered if David would come for her then. When he didn't, she settled back into the daily joys and tasks of being a mother and a wife. Why the sudden change? She could only wonder. Why now, now that she'd settled into the idea of completing her life here in this simple house with Paltiel and raising her nephews as her own sons?

She had a hard time reasoning with Paltiel. He was certain he could change the king's decree. He was determined to go see Ish-Bosheth immediately. Michal grew up under the laws or decrees of a king, and she knew it was useless. Besides, David had never divorced her; she was still legally his wife.

Slowly, to drag out the process, she started packing her things. She needed time to think. Michal chose to take only her personal items. Everything else could stay here for Paltiel and the boys. Paltiel was so lost in his grief that she had to make all the decisions and tell Paltiel what she was doing. She looked around at the small bedroom she'd shared with him. Silently, a few tears swelled in the corner of her eyes and rolled down her cheek.

Michal chose to leave the boys at this time. She wasn't certain how things would go with David. Over and over, she'd been told it was good that she was not with David. They said he'd kill everyone from the house of Saul. Although in actuality, David had never done this. However, in case there was any truth to this, she wanted the boys as far from David as she could get them. Plus, they were not David's sons and would be treated as such. Here, with Paltiel, they were the most important sons a man could have. Paltiel taught them everything he knew. Although Adriel stayed away often with work, he came by frequently enough for the boys to know him. However, it was interesting how the two men had changed roles. Now, Adriel seemed more like the uncle and Paltiel, their father. Adriel never recovered from the loss of his wife. He barely took time to know his youngest son. Michal was certain that he held resentment toward the child for the loss of Merab. How sad it seemed to Michal. The boy had no bearing on what happened to his mother. Why should he pay such a high price when he was growing up, never knowing the arms that would have held him and feel the brush of her fingers against his face? *No, the boys need to stay here with Paltiel.*

Michal tried to explain it to the boys, but it was too much for them to understand. They'd lost their mother, then their father, and now the only mother the younger ones had ever known. She told the boys she'd be back as soon as she could. She knew Paltiel would take care of them well. The younger boys were crying and shouting at the soldiers. The youngest one even went and kicked one of the soldiers in the shins as he hollered, "Don't take my momma away!"

The whole scene was filled with sorrow. Michal packed her clothes, and the soldiers loaded them on the carriage. Michal's heart was breaking as she looked from one face to the next. She touched each boy's face and spoke encouraging words. She gave them very tight hugs; then, she kissed her boys goodbye. Finally, there was only Paltiel left to say goodbye to. He begged her to stay and give him time to talk to Ish-Bosheth. She looked at him with sad, sorrowful eyes and pleaded for him to understand. There was nothing she could do but obey. David had never divorced her, and technically, she was still his wife. In fact, should they decide to, she could be killed for being married to more than one man, even though this was not of her doing.

After one last round of hugs and kisses, she climbed into the carriage. The next few miles broke her heart as she realized just how much Paltiel loved and needed her. He ran behind the carriage crying for Michal and begging them to leave her. He pleaded; he bargained; he tried everything he knew. He followed them all the way to Bahurim. He followed her until they were between Jerusalem and Jericho, just beyond the Mount of Olives on the way to Jericho. Finally, Abner turned to him and ordered him, "Go back home!"

Upon Abner's command, with a sorrowful heavy heart, Paltiel stopped in his tracks. He stood there weeping and watching the carriage disappear out of sight. Then he returned home to pick up the pieces of their broken lives.

\* \* \* \* \*

As Michal looked out the window, she saw his lips form the words "I love you." He put his hand on his heart, and she heard the words his lips spoke in her heart, "I will always love you."

She loved Paltiel, but not with the same deep love he had for her. That love went to her first husband. But Paltiel felt her love as he saw the tears running down her face as the carriage put a distance between them both.

\* \* \* \* \*

The next day, Abner sent soldiers to Hebron with Michal. She was immediately taken to the palace. David had the servants prepare the nicest room separated off from his wives for Michal. She would have her own room. It would not be closer than the other wives; however, as his first wife and as King Saul's daughter, it would be the nicest one. She looked around at this small room. She knew then her life was not going to include the romantic young love they'd once known. Her heart grew heavy when she was not greeted by David but his servants. She was encouraged when she was told to rest; David would dine with her tomorrow evening. He wanted her to have the necessary time to prepare and to rest from her long trip.

\* \* \* \* \*

David was surprised when he found himself excited with butterflies in his stomach at seeing Michal again. Little questions formed in his mind. Would she be excited to see him? Would she feel rescued and honored to be back with him? What about Merab's sons? Why didn't she bring them with her? Would they pick up the love story they'd had years ago? Would she conceive a son for him now that they were back together? Had she learned who Jehovah was, and was He everything to her? How had she dealt with the loss of her brothers and father? Had she gotten word that he had nothing to do with their deaths? Did she blame him as her father did? Was she still the beauty she'd been when they married twelve years ago? Did she take Merab's death hard?

David determined to wait on all these questions. He decided to plan a romantic dinner and see where things went. That would answer a lot of questions.

*****

Both David and Michal were disappointed in the evening. They both wanted the other to run to them with open arms. They wanted the other to say how happy they were to be with them again, but that is not how the evening went at all. It seemed as though every topic they tried to talk about led to the distance that had grown between them over the years.

*****

As Michal returned to her own room for the night, David thought about their evening together. Maybe they just need time to get to know each other again. Could she still be his Michal? She flinched when he reached out and brushed her cheek like he had so many times before. Was she in love with Paltiel? Had she stopped loving him? Was it he or his other wives? Did she think she should be the only wife he had, even if she couldn't bear children? Maybe she just needed time to adjust and to remember how much she had loved him.

*****

Michal was on the brink of tears as she returned to her room. Why hadn't he proclaimed how much he loved her? Why hadn't he captured her in his arms and swept her off her feet? Why did they find it so difficult to talk? Had so much changed over the years? Did he love all those other women more than her? Then her heart wept as she thought of Paltiel. She thought of her boys and the family they had made together. She knew beyond a doubt he was struggling with their separation. She also knew that she'd never see him again. That didn't bother her so much as she felt like she was in for a long lonely life with David. She was not his only wife but one of many... She'd seen how her father's wives would compete to get an evening to sleep with their husband, the king. Did he think she would join such competitions? No, she'd rather be alone than scheme or plot for an evening with him!

She cried herself to sleep in her pillow once her handmaiden left the room. The evening had been full of disappointments. She asked him why he didn't return for her sooner. His answer seemed so disappointing; in fact, he didn't really have an answer other than her father... Everything came back to her father...was it truth or an excuse? Maybe they just needed time to get reacquainted with each other... Maybe...

# Chapter 46

*"But thou, Lord, art most high forever" (Psalm 92:8, KJV).*

Word came to David that Ish-Bosheth was greatly depressed. Abner was going out just as he promised, and one by one, he was turning the alliances from Ish-Bosheth to David.

Abner called the elders of Israel together and said, "For some time, you have wanted to make David your king."

With a smile on his face and encouragement ringing through his voice, he clapped his hands together and continued, "Now is the time to do it! For the Lord promised David, 'By my servant David I will rescue my people Israel from the hand of the Philistines and from the hand of all their enemies.'"

Abner had also talked to the whole house of Benjamin. The house of Benjamin was a special project because they were the relatives of Saul. These men were there when Saul became Israel's first king. Bound in tradition, they would never understand the kingdom being given to someone outside of Saul's family. In fact, the uncles and cousins were lining up, looking for their chance to claim the throne. Therefore, Abner had spent time personally talking them into following Ish-Bosheth and turning them against David. He knew it would take a little time and effort, but the men always listened to him, and they would this time too.

Abner was very proud of all he was accomplishing and was anxious to tell David. He began to envision himself working for David as a leader in his army. In fact, he saw himself as David's right-hand man, taking over Joab's position. Of course, David would quickly realize his value. He'd come to see how much he'd built relationships with the elders of Israel over the years. His age would prove to offer knowledge that Joab wouldn't have.

Abner recalled the triumphant entry into Jerusalem many years ago. He'd been slightly irritated about following behind David in the king's parade as they rode into town. King Saul had expected the people to praise him. Actually, they did praise him, but they praised David more. He heard their words, "Saul has slain his thousands, and David his tens of thousands." Abner wanted to kick himself for not seeing God's hand upon him back then. Maybe things would have gone much differently. This time he envisioned himself following behind David again. Only this time, he held no resentment, only admiration for Israel's new king. The king he'd help to gain his place over all Israel *and* Judah.

He'd helped the house of Saul to go as far as he could. David had God's help and His blessing. His kingdom was prospering. Abner remembered how fun it had been to be in such a kingdom years ago. At one time, it was Saul who had the Lord's favor. His kingdom was advancing, and it seemed that little went wrong. Then instantly, everything changed. With one sin, Saul lost God's favor, and from that time on, everything became a challenge and usually ended in defeat. Now was the time for

Abner to get back on the winning side, the "God-blessed" side. He almost wanted to kick himself for not having seen this revelation sooner. But no matter, he did see the truth now and would align himself with the winning side. He was still young enough to make a difference for the kingdom of David and play a part in reuniting all of Israel and Judah.

Abner sent word to David that he was coming to give him an update. Later that day, Abner showed up with a small army of twenty men. The first thing David and Abner did was seal their agreement with a covenant. They both cut into the palm of their hand and shook hands, mixing their blood to seal the covenant. Next, David had a feast prepared for them so that they could sit and discuss Abner's accomplishments. Abner said to David, "Let me go at once and assemble all Israel for my lord, the king, so that they may make a covenant with you and that you may rule over all that your heart desires."

Abner knew that David intended to rule over all Israel and all Judah. David intended to be king from Dan in the north to Beersheba in the south. What Abner failed to notice was how this was God's plan, not David's. Abner, as with most men, saw his successes coming mostly from his own accomplishments.

David sent Abner on his way in peace. Aware that Abner was coming, David sent Joab and his men out to pursue a troop of Amalekites. They'd done this so many times that Joab didn't think anything of it. David was getting Joab away from Abner to assure his safety.

On the way back with a great wealth of plunder, Joab and David's men passed a small company of men. Joab had been excited about the gold and treasures they'd gained in the spoils.

He'd been anxious to present them to David, but now Joab was quite curious about what was happening. Upon arriving back in Hebron, Joab was brought up to speed on what had occurred in their absence.

It was customary for Joab and his leaders to come before David and report all that happened on each raid. He was determined to come before David now, and instead of reporting, he intended to confront David. Joab was very angry. Voicing his anger rather loudly, he demanded David give him an answer, "What have you done? Abner came to see you. Why did you dismiss him and let him get away?"

Joab went on accusing Abner, "You know perfectly well that Abner, the son of Ner, came to deceive you and observe your movements and find out everything you are doing."

David knew to let this kind of insubordination go on was wrong. He also knew Joab was still hurting over the loss of his brother. David didn't argue back, and he didn't justify his actions to Joab. He let Joab have his say. David determined to remind him later that he would not be allowed to talk to him that way. He was the king, and Joab would be held to the same level of accountability as everyone else.

David's response was to tell Joab that he knew what he was doing and that Joab should trust him. Everything would work out in time.

Joab disagreed and was certain that David was betraying him and his family by not killing Abner. In his eyes, it was justice to kill him. He deserved to die for murdering his brother Asahel. Joab completely overlooked the fact that they had been fighting in war. Joab was certain that Abner was deceiving

David; he didn't trust Abner. He had been a captain under King Saul and should never be trusted. He never had trusted Abner and couldn't understand how David could or why he would.

*****

Upon leaving David's chambers, Joab sent messengers to catch Abner. They were to tell him that David had more to say to him and would like him to return to Hebron. Joab knew David would not approve of his actions, but he was determined that Abner had to be stopped! Abner had to be taken out. He deserved to be punished for killing Asahel. As commander of David's army, Joab made the decision that it was his responsibility to do the job. He did, however, consult Abishai about his plans.

*****

Abner was no longer in Hebron, where David could protect him. He'd left in peace. David had blessed him, and he was excited about the next adventure in uniting the kingdom of Israel and turning it over to David. He was surprised when messengers came to him asking him to come back. The messengers said David had more to say to him. Abner had traveled all the way to the Cistern at Sirah, approximately two and a half miles northwest of Hebron. They were enjoying a fresh drink of water when the messengers caught up with them. Abner was so excited that he turned around immediately. His imagination got the best of him as he imagined all kinds of good promoting conversations with David. He imagined David exalting him in his military position immediately.

\*\*\*\*\*

Upon arriving back at Hebron, Joab came out to greet Abner. Abner had left his men outside the city. He trusted David so completely that he never suspected harm would come upon him. Joab laid his hand upon Abner's shoulder and spoke good supportive words concerning him and David's covenant. He thanked him for all his efforts and then led him to the inside gate. They walked into the inner area, between the outside city gate and the actual entrance into the city. It was a private place. Abner's anticipation grew within him. He was most anxious to hear what he'd been called back for, and because of this, he didn't suspect what was coming.

Joab pulled his right arm out from under his battle coat. He had a dagger in his hand, and with as much force as he had, he jammed it into Abner's abdomen. He purposely aimed for underneath the fifth rib, right where Abner had shoved his spear into Asahel. Abner looked at Joab with shock and fell down, dying instantly. The sound of a dagger being forced into a man's abdomen was a very sick sound. Abner's blood splattered on Joab's hand and on his battle coat. The blood of many enemies had splattered on his coat before; this time was no different.

Joab spit on him as he fell to the ground. Abishai stepped out from the shadows and spit on Abner as well. Together, they both kicked him in the ribs and then left his body where it fell. Together they walked back to their army and declared the victory of another defeated foe. They lifted their weapons in the air and shouted shouts of victory.

David inquired what the excitement was all about. It was then that his heart sunk at Joab's actions. He realized that moment; he should have dealt harsher with Joab for his insubordination. David knew he should have gone to God instead of moving forward in what felt like God's favor and direction.

Taking immediate actions, David made sure he was not associated with the murder of Abner. He would deal with Joab later. Right now, he needed to order a time of mourning for Abner.

David stood before the people and said, "I and my kingdom are forever innocent before the Lord concerning the blood of Abner, son of Ner. May his blood fall on the head of Joab and on his whole family! May Joab's family never be without someone who has a running sore or leprosy or who leans on a crutch or who falls by the sword or who lacks food."

The curse David had just pronounced upon Joab and his family was a harsh one. David intended for everyone to know that he had absolutely nothing to do with this murder and this deception.

Then David turned and looked directly at Joab and then to the rest of the people, giving specific orders, "Tear your clothes and put on sackcloth and walk in mourning in front of Abner."

King David wore his best royal robe in order to give his greatest dignity to Abner. He walked behind the bier, the bed they made for Abner to be buried on.

Joab hated pretending to mourn for Abner, but he knew he'd pushed the king far enough. He was certain that this curse was David's way of punishing him before the people. He'd talk to David and make certain he hadn't really meant it later. They buried Abner in Hebron, in the cave of Machpelah. David cried and wept for Abner. All the people followed the king. If he wept, they knew they were supposed to feel his sorrow, and they wept too. Most of them didn't have a clue why they should cry for Abner, nor his part in their lives, but they did it anyway to honor their king.

As David stood at the grave weeping, he raised his hands toward the tomb where Abner lay, and with a loud voice, he said, "Should Abner die as a fool or as a wicked man? Your hands were not bound, or your feet put into fetters. There were no metal chains or copper fastened around your ankles. As a man falls before wicked men, so you fell."

And all the people wishing to comfort David came and urged him to eat. David had not eaten since he'd had the feast with Abner. That was hours ago.

David replied to his people, "May God do so to me, and more also if I taste bread or anything else before the sun is set."

Again, not understanding all that it meant, the people declared that they would not eat before the sun set along with their king. A few people who felt weak did not quote David's words because they did not want what had happened to Abner to come upon them, nor the "more also." They would try to fast, but, feeling weak, they were not sure they could follow through. Of course, they would not let the king know that.

However, there was one thing the people did understand. It was important to their king for them to know that he was not the one who had killed Abner. No! That deceptive task fell to Joab and Abishai. Maybe now they would feel their vindication for the murder of Asahel. This message was carried throughout all of Judah and Israel so that all people would know that David had nothing to do with his death.

Later, when David was alone with his six hundred mighty men, he asked them, "Do you know that a prince, a chief ruler, a noble captain, and a mighty man has fallen this day in Israel?"

He went on to say, "I am this day weak, though I am anointed with oil to be king. These sons of Zeruiah are too difficult. They are too stiff-necked for me. May the Lord repay the evildoer according to his wickedness."

David's heart was heavy. He'd explained so many times why he did not take vengeance upon people. He'd let Saul live when he clearly had reason to kill him, and after all this time, his nephews had failed to learn anything from him.

# Chapter 47

*"Your word, Lord, is eternal; it stands firm in the heavens.*
*Your faithfulness continues through all generations"*
*(Psalm 119:89–90a, NIV).*

Word came quickly to Ish-bosheth that Abner had been killed. The exact details were unclear to Ish-bosheth, but he felt certain that Abner received what he deserved. However, Abner's death brought deep fear and depression upon the Israelite king. The king was trembling with fear. He knew he was not strong enough to be the king without Abner, his right-hand man. All of Israel was alarmed. The people formed in clusters throughout the city, talking and worrying about what was next. They were certain that David and his raiding parties would fall upon them, and they would all die or be taken prisoners. Saul's words of warning against David echoed fear in many of their heads.

Ish-bosheth was unsure who he could trust now. His two closest men had more alliance with Abner than himself. They were brothers and captains of two of the main raiding bands. Their names were Baanah and the other Rechab. They were sons of Rimmon the Beerothite. Beeroth is considered part of

Benjamin because the people of Beeroth fled to Gittaim and have lived there ever since.

These two brothers were both rough in character. They were dirty from seldom bathing. Both men had a tooth or two missing or broken off from fighting. Yet they both thought they would be doing Israel, or at least David, a favor by plotting to kill their king.

Ish-Bosheth was correct to question these two men's alliances. They were not to be trusted. It had been an incredibly difficult morning for Ish-Bosheth as he worried and dreaded the days ahead. He fell into a massive state of depression. Ish-Bosheth had taken to his bed with sleep as his mechanism of dealing with the issues. He slept far more than an active king should. He knew he must make some active changes quickly but was uncertain as to how to begin. His deep fear seemed to paralyze him. He justified his thought for sleep by comforting himself, *Besides, it is noon, and a noon nap is permissible, isn't it?*

Only a few days after Abner's death, Baanah and Rechab gained access to King Ish-Bosheth's bed-chamber by pretending to come for wheat. The guard at the door had become complacent and wasn't watching and had wandered toward the kitchen for lunch. The men snuck into the king's bed chambers. Ish-Bosheth's breathing was labored by his weight and his depression. Quietly, the men climbed the step up to the king's bed. The men could not help but notice how nice the bedding was. It was much nicer and plusher than anything they had.

Next to the bed was a table with a tray of food that had clearly been picked over. A remnant of cheese, crackers, figs, dates, walnuts, and lamb meat was still on the tray. Next to it was a goblet of wine and a pottery bottle filled with more wine. There was still a little bit of fresh herbs smoldering to offer a relaxing smell into the air. Also, on his stand was a vase with hyacinth flowers, probably brought to cheer him up. Ish-Bosheth's bed had solid oak carved pedestals with a wooden cover above the bed. There was a thin draped curtain tied to the corners of the bed. They knew it was oak because of the light wood color. The top and the bottom of the pedestals were covered in engraved leaves and grapes. Wooden trim went around the entire room. There were oil sconces all over the place and a couple of pottery bowls for cleaning and bathing. Seats were placed near the window for viewing out over the city.

Rechab pulled his sword out from under his robe. Feeling the presence of someone in his room, Ish-Bosheth stirred. His eyes fluttered slightly as if he was waking up. Baanah reached down and clamped his hands tightly over the king's mouth. To this, the king's eyes opened instantly. He tried to sit up, but Rechab stabbed him in the stomach, mortally wounding him. The king's eyes rolled back in his head as he collapsed back into the bed. The men started to leave the room when Ish-Bosheth let out a soft, painful groan. Immediately they feared they had not killed him. Baanah rethought their plan. He whispered to Rechab his next intentions. Baanah decided that murder was not enough. He sold his idea to Rechab. If they presented Ish-Bosheth's head to David, they would be rewarded quite handsomely. After all, everyone knew David intended to take over the kingdom of Israel. With Ish-Bosheth out of the way, David could take over. He was the last of Saul's true sons.

The two men turned around and went back to Ish-Bosheth. Rechab stabbed him in the abdomen a second time. It was a little more gruesome than Baanah had thought it would be to cut through the bone, sinew, and the tissue in the neck. Blood squirted everywhere, especially when they cut into the blood veins that run up the neck. It turned his stomach slightly, even though it was his idea. Rechab looked around for a sack to hide the head in. They settled upon wrapping it in bed linen to contain the blood. Next, they put it in the sack they'd brought with them for wheat. They snuck out of the palace, pleased with their task. Although misguided, the men were certain they were doing what was best for Israel. Baanah's words had been, "Besides, if we don't kill Ish-Bosheth, someone else will."

As soon as they were away from everyone, they talked about the rewards they were certain to get from David. They left immediately and traveled all night by way of Arabah, which was along the road to the plains.

The two men traveled fast and directly to Huron for two key reasons. The first reason was so that they were out of Mahanaim before anyone knew Ish-Bosheth was dead. There were those loyal to the king that would search for his murderers, and they would most certainly be tortured and killed, they and possibly their whole family. The second key reason was their excitement over the treasures they were sure to get from David.

Arriving at Hebron, the men were very excited and immediately requested a meeting with King David. When asked what their meeting concerned, they smiled at each other. Rechab spoke for them, "We have important news concerning Ish-Bosheth that should make the king very happy and..." Both men were grinning with broken teeth, as well as missing teeth. They looked at each other, and he continued, "and gain us a handsome reward..." They laughed together at the joy of this thought. "We have also brought him a gift that will most certainly give him the kingdom of Israel."

Guards ushered the two brothers into the presence of King David. He was sitting on his throne chair at the head of the large gathering room. They bowed low, showing full respect to the king. David told them to rise and get to their business. He asked what this meeting was all about and what news they had concerning Ish-Bosheth.

Baanah reached into the wheat sack and pulled out a bloody sheet and started to unwrap it as he smiled. Seeing the blood, David's soldiers had their hands on their weapons, ready for whatever came next. Looking very pleased with himself, Baanah said, "Here is the head of Ish-Bosheth, the son of Saul, your enemy who tried to kill you. This day the Lord has avenged my lord, the king, against Saul and his offspring."

They continued on explaining the plot. Each man was quick to break into the conversation, sharing his steps to their achievement. They had not yet noticed the expression on the king's face due to their excitement.

David was appalled at the sight before him. He pointed to the guards and then to the men. The guards were instantly standing behind them.

David rose up out of his chair with a most displeased look, almost glaring at the men as he spoke, "As surely as the Lord lives, who has delivered me out of every trouble, when someone told me, 'Saul is dead,' and thought he was bringing good news, I seized him and put him to death in Ziklag. That was the reward I gave him for his news! How much more—when wicked men have killed an innocent man in his own house in his own bed—should I not now demand his blood from your hand and rid the earth of you!"

Both brothers' continence changed instantly. Their jaws dropped in surprise. David ordered his men to remove these worthless men from his presence and to kill them. He repeated his words with a firmness that gripped everyone's heart, "Rid the earth of them!"

He also commanded their hands and feet to be cut off and their bodies hung by the pool in Hebron as a sign to everyone. The men couldn't talk quickly enough, pleading and asking what they did wrong. They begged for their lives and even told David to forget about a reward, just please let them live! David turned away as the men were removed from his presence.

One of the young servants later asked David why he ordered their hands and feet to be cut off. He was very humbled upon asking the king. He did not wish to get in trouble but clearly didn't understand. David smiled slightly at the young man. He asked, "Do you know why they were killed?"

The servant's words came with a question, "You said they took innocent blood?"

David told him that was correct. "Ish-Bosheth was considered innocent because he was not fighting in battle, but rather he was sleeping in what should have been a safe place for him." Pausing, David looked down at his hands and rubbed them together. "They had to pay with their blood because of the Levitical law spoken of by Moses, 'Anyone who takes the life of a human being is to be put to death.'" David continued, "Their hands and feet were cut off as a sign to everyone that they were traitors to their king. The hands were specifically cut off for stealing from Israel."

The young man looked slightly puzzled by David's last comment. David continued, "They stole their king's life and his head. Their feet were specifically cut off because they used them to quickly flee and come to Hebron. They intended to bring their news and to collect a reward. Of course, their bodies were displayed near a public place so that everyone would see these two men's shame and know that I had nothing to do with King Ish-Bosheth's death or any plot to come against him. It is very important that all of Israel and Judah know that I had absolutely nothing to do with his death."

The young man gave David an affirmative look of approval. Then, he thanked him for explaining the particulars of their punishment to him.

David couldn't help but smile and recall some of his conversations with God as a young shepherd boy. He was simply one day attending sheep, and almost in the next moment, he was asking questions concerning the actions of a king over him and of himself as a future king. God had him studying the Levitical law and any other texts he could get his hand on. He took the Shabbat so much more to heart than he had before, and he'd always loved his time with God. Now, suddenly he was talking to God, and God was talking directly to him.

David instructed messengers to send word to Israel of these men's actions. Also, to let them know that they'd given Ish-Bosheth's head a proper king's burial and placed his head in the tomb with Abner. David was also very clear about these men's punishment and that he had nothing to do with these men's actions.

David knew they'd need to make quick decisions about the next king but felt like he needed to give them a couple of days to grieve for their king. Again, David felt like he should let God direct him and place him in position.

# Chapter 48

*"I will proclaim the decree: the Lord hath said unto me,*
*'Thou art my Son; this day have I begotten thee. Ask of*
*me, and I shall give the heathen for thine inheritance..."'*
*(Psalm 2:7–8a, KJV)*

David went into prayer over the next few days. He was most anxious to become the king of Israel. Although he had nothing to do with Ish-Bosheth, nor Abner's death, their deaths paved the way for David to step in as king. But then, he thought that when the Philistines killed Saul and his sons. He didn't make any move to become king, though. Instead, he prayed and trusted God. He was determined to seek God's direction.

Within just a few days of Ish-Bosheth's death, all the elders of the tribes of Israel came to Hebron. It was quite an assembly of men that requested to see King David. It was such a large assembly that some people's hearts sunk. They were certain all of Judah had come to stomp them out. Rumor was, they blamed them for the death of Ish-Bosheth and were coming to destroy them. Although the townspeople didn't know it, word had already come to David that the men of Israel were coming to see him to request that he be their king. The camels and donkeys stirred up an incredible amount of dust. David's soldiers were still on alert, although their messengers came early and said the elders came on friendly terms. Even David wondered at first if he should lock the gate as fear threatened to grip his heart. In his heart, David heard God telling him to trust and wait. He did, however, send a servant to get one of his nicer kingly robes. It was actually the one Abigail made for him when he was crowned king over Hebron. The men brought their weapons for war, which was also quite alarming. However, God put peace in David's heart, which he shared with all his leaders.

David's stood upon an overlook that allowed him to see out over the valley outside the city gates. He could not believe the astronomical amount of people who came before him. It appeared all of Israel came to see him. Although all the elders came, one from each tribe stepped forward to speak to David.

The men approached the city and asked if David, the king over Judah, would come out before them. David quickly climbed down and went out to meet them.

The men fell before David when they saw him. He allowed them a few seconds to pay homage and then motioned upward with his right hand and told them to rise.

Once they were standing, David took in the sight of each man. A few men who knew him personally smiled a smile full of satisfaction and joy. A couple of men had a slight tear in the corner of their eyes. One of the elders stepped forward and introduced himself. Then, he proceeded to speak for everyone, "We are your own flesh and blood. In the past, while Saul was king over us, you were the one who led Israel on our military campaigns. And the Lord said to you, 'You will shepherd My people Israel, and you will be their ruler.'"

David wanted to fall prostrate right then and there, but he didn't. He determined to save that for his personal time with Jehovah.

Memories of leading these men into successful battles started flooding David's mind. He recalled leaving excited and coming back even more excited as he personally saw the power of God. The praises from the townspeople as he entered their cities had been very invigorating.

Many of these men were there when the Prophet Samuel spoke God's words of rejection to Saul, Israel's first king. The prophet's words still rang in some of their minds, "The Lord has torn the kingdom out of your hands and given it to one of your neighbors." Those words alone are why many of the men knew the next king was not to be from the house of Benjamin.

Upon the death of Ish-Bosheth, these leaders met together and discussed their options. Many of the men never thought there was another option besides David. Others wanted to make the next king another member of Saul's family. Still, others suggested a contest among Israel to find their next king. As the elders prayed, those that knew God was preparing David for such a time as this led the conversation. It didn't take a lot of persuasion because David as king was God's will for Israel. Those who lacked God's vision saw it strong in those who did. Once they all agreed on David, they assembled together to come before David.

Each leader from a tribe of Israel gave account of how many men he brought with him. Two of David's scribes were busy writing everything down and tallying the numbers. Later, the number of men who came was totaled, and the number was outstanding! The total ended up being three hundred thirty-six thousand one hundred men. They all came to honor him as their king. He was truly astounded. After waiting all these years for God's promise, God surely was making his kingship an incredible event. As the men stepped forward one by one, they told David of the various skills his men had and how many he brought. David raised his arms in praise to God. He did not allow himself to get lost in worship, but he still praised God in his heart as he listened to the leaders give account.

Each leader stepped forward to give an account of the men he brought. Upon speaking, he bowed slightly and took a full step backward.

"From the tribe of Judah come six thousand eight hundred men. We come before you carrying our shield and spear. We are ready for battle, my king."

"Simeon brings warriors ready for battle, seven thousand one hundred, my king." This man remembered fighting alongside David. Therefore, he gave him a smile and a slight wink as he stepped back.

"Levi brings four thousand six hundred men, King David." Proud of their achievements, he continued, "This includes Jehoiada, leader of the family of Aaron, and Jehoiada has three thousand seven hundred men, and Zadok, our brave young warrior, plus twenty-two officers from his family."

The next man to speak gave an account, "The Tribe of Benjamin sends you three-thousand men."

David breathed deeply, feeling a huge sigh of relief slip through his lips. These were the men most dedicated to King Saul, his own family. Suddenly aware of his actions, David hoped the men either didn't see him or took no offense to his response.

With his chest puffed out, the next man spoke, "From Ephraim comes twenty-two thousand eight hundred brave warriors; these are all famous in our clan. We come to you, King David." He proudly stepped back in formation.

"From the half-tribe of Manasseh, eighteen thousand men elected to come and make you our king."

"Issachar sends two hundred chiefs, men who understand the times and know what Israel should do. This includes all their relatives under their command. Fifty thousand experienced soldiers who are prepared for battle with every type of weapon come from Zebulun. We come prepared to help King David with undivided loyalties."

The next man stood there until David's eyes had finished looking over the crowd and the men Zebulun had sent. Then he said, "Naphtali sends one thousand officers along with thirty-seven thousand men carrying shields and spears."

Stepping back, the next man spoke out, "Twenty-eight thousand six hundred men come from Dan ready for battle, King David." This man had incredible eyes filled with integrity. David couldn't help but notice.

Just two men remained to give account. The elder man looked at David and said, "Asher brings forty thousand experienced soldiers prepared for battle."

Finally, the last man looked up at David and said, "From east of Jordan, from the tribe of Reuben, Gad, and the half-tribe of Manasseh, I bring one hundred twenty thousand men, all armed with every type of weapon."

David's heart rejoiced at the large way in which God was making him king over Israel. As the last man stepped back by the other men, they all bowed forward to give respect to David.

Then they asked if they could anoint him to be their king. He set the crowning for that evening as the magnitude of all that was taking place flooded his mind. He'd make a covenant with them, and they'd have a royal feast for the next few days.

David sent messengers throughout Hebron to invite all the elders. He called for both Nathan, who had anointed him as king over Hebron, and Abiathar, his high priest. They came prepared, both having a horn full of oil. Nathan loved the thought of anointing David again. Later that day, David received a double anointing.

David smiled when he thought about how this was his third time being anointed as king. Then he smiled and thought, *If you want to get technical, it's the fourth time I've been anointed to be king...*

A command was sent to the kitchen staff to prepare as large of a feast as they could for all his men and many more. When David asked, "How do we prepare a feast for everyone?" the men told David that they'd come prepared with food to feast for three days. Each tribe would prepare its own meals.

Messengers were sent out to the surrounding cities of Judah. They invited the leaders of the cities and their men in for the festivities and for the covenant relationship that would be happening that evening. They were also invited to bring their tents and men and come prepared to celebrate with them for the next three days.

\* \* \* \* \*

The night was a night to remember. David made a covenant agreement with the leaders who had come. He read his covenant agreement with Israel out loud. Although not everyone could hear him, the leaders were surrounding him enough to catch what was said. The ceremony was very intense and yet very exciting.

Hours earlier, while in prayer, God put a new song in David's heart. He now knew why. God planned on it being a part of this ceremony. The new psalm was written in honor of the united Israel.

Why do the nations conspire, and the peoples plot in vain?

The Kings of the earth rise up and the rulers' band together

against the Lord and against his anointed, saying,

"Let us break their chains and throw off their shackles."

The one enthroned in heaven laughs; the Lord scoffs at them.

He rebukes them in his anger and terrifies them in his wrath, saying,

"I have installed my king on Zion, my holy mountain."

I will proclaim the Lord's decree:

He said to me, "You are my son; today I have become your father. Ask me, and I will make the nations your inheritance and the ends of the earth your possession.

You will break them with a rod of iron; you will dash them to pieces like pottery."
Therefore, you kings, be wise; be warned, you rulers of the earth. Serve the Lord with fear and celebrate his rule with trembling. Kiss his son, or he will be angry and your way will lead to your destruction, for his wrath can flare up in a moment.
Blessed are all who take refuge in him.[26]

This song came in four parts. The first part talked about how the nations see Jehovah upon His throne and the Messiah coming in victory. He found himself angry and upset at the nations. They denied God and His anointed one. The witness upon David's heart was that the anointed one had a dual meaning. Today, it was him, but in the future, it would be the Messiah and how people would view the Messiah. David found himself shaking his head at stubborn-hearted people.

Next, David heard God laughing at their futile efforts with contemptuous laughter. This part was extra awesome because this was when God spoke to David about establishing his kingdom in Zion or Jerusalem. With a smile on his face and joy in his heart, David marveled at how God spoke to him and directed him. He also marveled at being called a son of God. The thought took his breath away for a few seconds as he thought of the intensity of His Father's love for him. The song ended with David giving his counsel to the leaders of the nation, *"Serve the Lord...celebrate His rule...kiss His Son..."*

He sat in the presence of God, meditating over the song after finishing it. The words God spoke to him had been incredible. He allowed them to ring through his thoughts again. What an unbelievable promise he'd just received from God, "You are My son; today, I have become your Father. Ask of Me, and I will make the nations your inheritance, the ends of the earth your possession. You will break them with a rod of iron; you will dash them to pieces like pottery."

The whole celebration had been incredible. God had given Asaph a Maschil as well. This one was filled with instructions. Asaph started by recapping Israel's history in the wilderness. He gave instruction to the fathers. He talked about the stubbornness of their hearts, even in the midst of God's divine provision. He talked about how the people would flatter God with their mouths but lied to Him with their tongues. Asaph recapped all that God did in Egypt so that they'd know His power and dominion. God had so righteously lifted up Joseph to lead the Israelites through a difficult time, and yet it was not his line that God chose to rise up, but David's, the tribe of Judah. He concluded by telling how God, in His own sovereign power, chose David, a shepherd. The last few lines brought humility to David, "And David shepherded the people with integrity of heart; with skillful hands, he led them."

Before climbing in bed that night, David heard one more miktam rising inside of him. This one was a prayer concerning his reign as king. It also was a prophetic psalm, as God gave him words concerning the future Messiah, the Son of God. This time, the words from God spoke of the Messiah's death and resurrection, *"Therefore my heart is glad, and my tongue rejoices; my body also will rest secure because you will not abandon me to the realm of the dead, nor will you let your faithful one see decay."* Then, he heard these words as His Father would have said them:

...my heart is glad, and my glory rejoices: my flesh also shall rest in hope. For thou wilt not leave my soul in hell; neither wilt thou suffer your Holy one to see corruption. Thou wilt show me the path of life: in thy presence is fullness of joy; at thy right hand there are pleasures for evermore.[27]

David's heart was so full from the events of the day that he had no idea if he'd sleep at all. Well, at least he was the king and could declare when the festivities began in the morning. With a smile and an exceptionally warm heart, he stared off into the darkness as he once again praised God.

**The End**

Join me in a sneak preview of the second part of King David, a Man after God's Own Heart. *There are so many events yet that will unfold in our young king's life. It is full of adventure, disappointments, lessons, and love. The love he learns and shares with his wives and with his children is from the Father Jehovah. Learn of David's regrets and the various hardships that come his way. Learn what makes him stand out more than any other king, except our Lord Jesus.*

# Book 2

## Section I

## *David, King Over a United Jerusalem*

עִיר דָּוִד

(The City of David)

# Chapter 1

*"I will establish your seed forever and build up your throne to all generations" (Psalm 89:4, AMP).*

The morning air was refreshing, and everything was still quiet from the peaceful night. David found comfort sitting alone in his beautiful garden. He had a gardener that loved to tend the plants. The man took time to find good soil for nurturing the ground. He'd learned that animal dung enriched the soil. He'd take the time to nurture the dirt away from the palace first. Once the strong, potent smells dissipated, he'd bring the rich soil in and mix it into the gardens. David knew this because any guest who saw his garden asked what his gardener did to bring about such results. Therefore, he'd inquired himself. David always found it humorous when he answered they use animal dung. Sometimes the ladies would be admiring a particular flower, and suddenly they'd wrinkle their nose while pulling away as though the dung was right there or they could suddenly smell it.

Excitement rang through the palace at the growing kingship. David was talking about moving to Jerusalem. Even though things were not finalized, everyone started to prepare for the move. David liked his current staff and had informed everyone that he would like them to come to Jerusalem. He gave them the option and asked if anyone wanted to stay at their home in Hebron. Only a few chose to stay. Those who chose to stay were given orders to assist in the move. They would then be expected to stay until their position could be filled.

David was in awe as he thought about the time that had passed since he was crowned king over Judah. It had already been seven and a half years. Now, finally, it was time for the next chapter to begin... Excitement filled his thoughts as he dared to dream of all that was ahead. His imagination traveled to Saul's palace and all that he would do with it. To his knowledge, there was not a palace in Jerusalem but a fortress. He could easily remedy that. The Jebusites had governed themselves as their own tribe of people. A smile crossed David's lips as he imagined the Jebusites when he and his army showed up. After all, it was God who told him, "Zion" and "Ask of Me and I will give you the nations..." What a loving Father, what incredible promises, and how awesome to be His son.

David's thoughts traveled to his loyal men... They would take up residency closest to him in Zion, and he'd leave the dispersing of housing to Joab. He imagined leading his men victoriously into more battles. He saw them defeating the Philistines and possibly destroying the Amalakites. He pictured himself gaining a lot of new land for Israel. He saw himself taking back all the land God gave to Joshua when they first came into the Promised Land. He saw himself bringing the people into worship with a full orchestra. This would then usher in the presence of the Holy. He imagined bringing the

Ark of the Covenant into Jerusalem. He saw himself building the most exquisite tabernacle for God and all the people worshipping Him there. He saw his sons riding with him in battle. He envisioned his sons growing up and reigning with him. He tried to imagine Amnon on the throne succeeding him, but that seemed too far away. He wasn't done dreaming about his own succession as king. Besides, he couldn't really see himself as an old man with a grey beard and being too old to enjoy life...or his wives. Then, he thought about taking more wives and bringing up an even stronger legacy of sons and daughters. A smile turned the corner of his lips and caused a rush of excitement to pass over him.

David reflected over his life. He had recently turned thirty years old. He had been almost thirteen when Samuel first anointed him to be king. Wow! Many years had passed since then. David marveled that he spent more years getting to this point than years he'd lived before being anointed by the prophet.

Later, he walked through his wives' house and thanked God for his sons. He couldn't help but admire his little daughter Tamar. She looked a lot like her brother Absalom. She had the same thick beautiful black hair with ringlets falling around her shoulder. It seemed as though her curls bounced with every step she took. She had her mother's slender build, even for a child. She had the same incredible eyes as Absalom. His eyes shined with love for life to everyone who saw them. Tamar had her father's attention. David knew the honor in having sons, but he loved his little girl. Besides, a king needs some daughters. A daughter was a man's property to be bargained with, or as with he and Michal, to be given as a reward. He might need lots of daughters to advance the kingdom a lot less violently. He thought about his wives and smiled at each one he saw. David had spent some time with Michal recently, but not as much as he had hoped. She still was not with child. He'd hoped she'd give him a son. She was his first wife, and he'd had a special love for her at one time. But it appeared a child from her womb might never happen.

*****

David and his men were preparing to go up to Jerusalem. God was directing him to establish his kingship from there; the "Throne of David" was to be established in Jerusalem. He smiled when he heard his kingship referred to in those words. They needed to check out the land before moving. The Jebusites lived in Jerusalem currently, and they had not asked David to be their king. Therefore, David took enough men to defeat them should they need to. This clan dwelled in Canaan during the time that Joshua brought the Children of Israel into the Promised Land. God had ordered them to totally destroy the Jebusites. However, Judah and Benjamin chose to dwell together with them instead. They were a people of war, and the Israelites were not able to defeat them. The Jebusites built on a mountain top, establishing Jerusalem from its very beginning. It was said that they were direct descendants of Noah's son, Ham.

Abraham was the first to approach the Jebusites. He wanted the cave of Machpelah to bury Sarah and his descendants. They agreed to sell it to him but said, "We know that God will give this country to your descendants. Now, if you will make a covenant with us that Israel will not take the city of Jebus against our own will, we will agree to you the cave and a bill of sale for it." Jebus was the ancient name for Jerusalem.

Abraham eagerly made the covenant and engraved their covenant upon a bronzed statue. When the Israelites came to destroy them, they couldn't because of Abraham's covenant with them. The Jebusites stood the statue with Abraham's engraving on it in the middle of the city for all to see.

David knew the history of Jerusalem and knew that the covenant they had with Abraham would be a problem. He believed the covenant could be broken if the bronzed figure were destroyed, so he made an announcement, "Anyone who conquers the Jebusites will have to use the water shaft to reach those lame and blind who are David's enemies."

The Jebusites had heard David was coming and were so confident of their ability to stand against him and his army that they taunted David saying, "Even the lame and the blind can defend our city."

Feeling angered by their mockery, he set a challenge before his men. In the midst of his anger, he thought back to when he was challenged and offered the king's daughter. So he called a meeting with his top military generals and gave this challenge, "The warrior who successfully captures the fortified stronghold of Jerusalem will get to be the commander of my army."

Joab immediately jumped to the challenge. He was not about to let another warrior take over his position, even though he knew he'd have to earn it. He was slightly irritated to think that he had to earn it for any reason. But he also knew the military strategy in such a challenge. They'd already been given the way in. He told them to go through the tsinnor, also called "the water conduit." David organized a small group of men to go in and take the city while instructing the others to be ready to come in once they broke through and opened the city gates. The water tunnel was only wide enough for one person to pass through at a time. It ran north to south and measured fifty meters in length or fifty yards long. The walls were of bedrock and ran along the upper part of the eastern slope of Jerusalem.

The victory came easy and swift. Joab had secured his position once more. The enemies of David had been killed and the city secured. In a short time, his men had the city cleaned up from the Jebusites, and David and his army were free to move in.

There was a small fortress in the middle of Jerusalem, a citadel. David moved his family into the fortress he built around the Millo, the fortification for Jerusalem. The new king had fun roaming through the fortress, looking at it, dreaming, and planning. Immediately, he set people to extend the walls on the right and the left. He had a small group of men walk through with him. One was his sketch artists noting all of David's changes and plans. It was truly a highlight for him as he saw God's plans coming together in his life. Next, they walked through the city as David talked out loud about his plans and purposes to carry out God's directions in his life. Truly, it was an extremely victorious moment.

# Characters

**Abiathar:** He was the High Priest under David. He was the son of Ahimelech, who was the son of Ahitub. He was also the only one who escaped King Saul when he murdered Ahimelech and his whole family of priests. I Sam. 22:20.

**Abigail$_1$:** David's sister and mother of Abishai, Joab and Asahel. I Chron 2:16

**Abigail$_2$:** She was David's second wife. She had been Nabal's wife prior to his death. I Sam. 25:3

**Abinadab$_1$:** Keeper of the Ark. I Sam. 7:1

**Abinadab$_2$:** He is the second son in David's family. I Sam. 16:8

**Abinadab$_3$:** One of King Saul's sons who died with him in battle. I Sam. 31:2

**Abishag:** David's nurse. She was a young girl brought in to nurse King David in his old age. I Kings 1:3

**Abishai:** David's nephew and his sister Zeruiah's son. He was the oldest of three brothers; Joab, Asahel. I Sam. 26:6. *In this story, he is almost 5 years older than David.*

**Abital** or **Avital:** She was the fifth wife of King David. Abital was the mother of David's fifth son Shephatiah. Her name means my father is [the] dew. 2 Samuel 3:4

**Abner:** King Saul's top advisors and cousin. He was also the commander of Saul's army and later he was the top advisor to Ish-bosheth. I Sam. 14:50

**Abner₂:** Father of an officer for David. I Chr. 27:21

**Absalom:** Son of David. Absalom, the son of Maachah. He tried to take over his father's kingdom. 2 Samuel 15:11

**Achish:** King of Gath and an ally of David. I Sam. 21:10

**Adonijah:** David's fourth son while reigning in Judah. II Sam. 3:4.

**Adriel, the Meholathite:** He married Merab and was from a city in the territory of Manasseh. I Sam. 18:19

**Ahinoam of Jezreel:** Wife of David. She is of the tribe of Issachar, the fourth son of Jacob and Leah. She comes from the fertile valley of the Jezreel River, a western tributary of the Jordan, and in the low hills southeast of Mount Tabor. I Sam. 25:43

**Ahithopel:** Adviser to David and also to Absalom during his rebellion. II Sam. 15:12

**Amasa:** Nephew of David, army commander for Absalom. II Sam. 17:25

**Amnon:** David's oldest son, who also violated Tamar. II Sam. 3:2

**Aram:** The sixth brother in David's family. I Sam. 17:13

**Asahel:** David's nephew and brother of Joab. He ran as fast as a deer. II Sam. 2:18

**Asaph:** Is a Levite and chief musician for David. I Chr. 6:39

**Baal:** A Canaanite god. Judges 2:13

**Bathsheba:** Wife of Uriah and later David. She is the mother of Solomon. II Sam. 11:3

**Benaiah:** Father of Jehoiada, David's counselor, I Chr. 27:34

**Beniah$_2$:** Captain of David's bodyguard and later, Solomon's commander. II Sam. 8:18

**Benaiah$_3$:** One of David's 30 warriors. Note: he is named here in the list of the 30 warriors. II Sam. 23:30

**Boaz:** Ruth's husband and great-grandfather of David. Ruth 2:1

**Dagon:** Philistine god of grain. Judges 16:23

**Daniel also called Chileab:** second son to King David. 2 Samuel 3:3

**David:** He was a man after God's own heart and main character in this story. He was the second king of Israel. His blood line carried on to the birth of Jesus and beyond. 1 Sam. 13:14

**Eliab:** David's oldest brother. The firstborn son in David's family. I Sam. 16:6

**Gad:** He was the Prophet who advised David. I Sam. 22:5

**Hadad:** He was an Edomitee who escaped the slaughter of Edomites. 1 Kings 11:14. As a child he witnessed the takeover of his homeland by King David. Although many of his countrymen were killed, Hadad managed to escape and make his way to Egypt. I Kings 11:19. When he was older, he came against Solomon.

**Hanun:** He was one of David's 30 warriors. I chr. 11:43

**Hadadezer:** He was the Armamean King of Zobah and defeated by David. II Sam. 8:3

**Haggith:** She was David's fifth wife. She was a Gadite dancer. She was also the sister to one of his mighty men, Benaiah. Over time, she gave David his fourth son, Adonijah. 2 Samuel 3:4

**Hiram:** King of Tyre, an ally of David and Solomon. II Sam. 5:11

**Hushai:** A very dedicated counselor of David. II Sam. 15:32

**Ish-bosheth:** Son of King Saul who succeeded King Saul in death. II Sam. 2:8

**Ittai:** He was one of David's 30 warriors. II Sam. 23:29

**Ittai$_2$:** He was from Gath and a supporter of David. II Sam. 15:19

**Jesse, the Bethlehemite:** David's father and the son of Obed; who was son of Ruth & Boaz. 1 Sam. 16:1

**Joab:** He was David's nephew, and his sister Zeruiah's son. His name is pronounced YOAB. Joab means, "Yahweh is father." He became David's commander in Chief. I Chron 2:16

**Jonadab:** Son of Shimeah and David's nephew. II Sam. 13:3

**Jonathan:** King Saul's oldest son and a best friend to David. I Sam. 13:2

**Jonathan$_2$:** Uncle and counselor of David. I Chronicles 27:32

**Jonathan$_3$:** One of David's 30 warriors. II Sam. 23:32

**King Saul:** He was the first king of Israel and anointed by the prophet Samuel. After turning his back on God, he lost his anointing. God raised up David to take his place as the King of Israel. I Sam. 15:1

**Mephibosheth:** Son of Jonathan, and he was crippled early in life. II Sam. 4:4

**Merab:** She was King Saul's oldest daughter. I Sam. 14:49

**Michal:** She was King Saul's youngest daughter and David's first wife. I Sam. 14:49

**Micah:** He was a Levite under David. I Chr. 23:20

**Nathan:** He was a Prophet and advisor of David. II Sam. 7:2

**Nathaneel:** He was the fourth brother in David's family. I Chron 2:14

**Nitzevet bat Adel:** She was David's mother. Her name Nitzevet means 'to stand'. **NOTE:** The name of David's mother is not written in the Torah, but rather is recorded in the Talmud, Tractate Bava Batra 91a.

**Obadiah$_2$:** Father of an officer of David. I Chr. 27:19

**Obadiah₃:** A Gadite who joined David. I Chr. 12:8-9

**Obed:** The son of Ruth and grandfather of David. Ruth 4:17

**Obed₂:** One of David's 30 warriors. 1 Chr. 11:47

**Ozem:** David's brother closest to him in age. I Chr. 2:15

**Palti:** King Saul gave Michal to him to be married, although she was still married to David. I Sam. 25:44

**Rahab:** Ancestor to Boaz. She was also a prostitute of Jericho, Josh. 2:1

**Raddai:** The fifth brother in David's family. I Chr. 2:14

**Rizpah:** She was a concubine of King Saul. II Sam. 3:7

**Ruth:** She was a Moabite and the wife of Boaz. Ruth 1:4

**Samuel:** He was Judge, Priest and Prophet. He anointed David to be Israel's second king. I Sam. 1:20; I Sam. 8:1-5

**Shammah:** He was the 3rd brother in David's family. I Sam. 16:9. He was one of David's 3 chief warriors and one of David's 30 warriors in II Sam. 23:11.

**King Saul:** He was Israel's first king. He lost God's anointing when disobeying God's command. I Samuel 9:2

**Sheba$_4$:** He was a rebel against David. II Sam. 20:1

**Sheba$_5$:** He was a clan leader in Gad. I Chr. 5:13

**Shimei** or **Shimeah:** David's brother who slew a giant. II Sam. 21:21

**Shimei$_2$:** He was an overseer of David's vineyards. I Chr. 27:27

**Shimei$_9$:** Benjaminite who cursed David. II Sam. 16:5

**Solomon:** Son of David and Bathsheba and successor to the throne after King David. II Sam. 5:14

**Tamar$_2$:** Daughter of David. II Sam. 13:1

**Tamar$_3$:** Daughter of Absalom. II Sam. 14:27

**Uriah the Hittite:** One of David's 37 mighty men. Husband of Bathsheba. He was intentionally murdered in war at the orders of King David. 2 Samuel 23:29

**Uzzah:** Son of Abinadad. He touched ark and died instantly. II Sam. 6:3

**Uzzah$_2$:** Levite clan leader in the time of David. I Chr. 6:29

**Zadok:** A High priest for David and Solomon. II Sam. 8:17

**Ziba:** He was a servant of Saul's family and later Mephibosheth, the son of Jonathan. II Sam. 9:2

# DAVID'S BROTHERS

They are listed in order of birth: Eliab, Abinadab, Shimmah, Nathaneel, Raddai, Aram and Ozem and David. I Samuel 16:13, I Chron. 2:16-17. NOTE: *1 Chron. 2:16-17. This passage only lists seven brother's total. It does not name Aram, which suggests that he might have died early in life.*

# DAVID'S CABINET

**David's Cabinet or chosen men:** Abishai, Joab, Asahel, Ahithophel, Amasa, Benaiah, Benaiah2, Hanun, Hushai, Ittai, Jonathan2, Jonathan3, Obed2, Shammah.

# DAVID'S SONS

*According to I Chronicles 3*

Born in Hebron: 6 sons were born to David in Hebron, where he reigned seven and a half years. This list is according to I Chro. 3:4 and II Sam. 3:2.

1. Amnon, of Ahinoam the Jezreelitess, the firstborn
2. Daniel, of Abigail the Carmelitess, also called Chileab (2 Sam. 3:3)
3. Absalom, the son of Maachah the daughter of Talmai King of Geshur
4. Adonijah, the son of Haggith

5.  Shephatiah of Abital
6.  Ithream by Eglah his wife

**Born in Jerusalem:** Of Bath-shua [Bathsheba] the daughter of Ammiel: Shimea; Shobab; Nathan; and Solomon. *NOTE: Solomon was the youngest son from Bathsheba. The story indicates he was the second son to Bathsheba.*

**David's Concubines:** Ibhar; Elishama; Eliphelet; Nogah; Nepheg; Japhia; Elishama (again); Eliada; and Eliphelet (again).

# PLACES

**Cistern at Secu:** The great cistern at Secu laid approximately half way between Gibeah and Ramah.

**Gath, Gat,** or **Geth:** (Hebrew: גַּת, Winepress; Latin: *Geth*), referred to as Gath of the Philistines. It was one of the five Philistine city-states, established in northwestern Philistia. The king of the city was Achish during the times of Saul, David, and Solomon.

**Gilgal:** was about sixteen miles away from Shochon. Gilgal was seven miles north of Bethel and was where the united tribes of Israel formally received King Saul was as their King. It is also where King Saul's palace was located.

**Geshur:** was a territory in the northern part of Bashan. It was given to the half-tribe of Manasseh. In the time of David, Geshur was an independent kingdom, and David married

Maachah, a daughter of Talmai, king of Geshur. Her son Absalom fled to his mother's native country, after the murder of his half-brother and David's eldest son, Amnon. According to Israeli archaeologists, Geshur laid east of the Sea of Galilee, in what is now the southern Golan Heights.

**Naioth:** It was Samuel's home town. It became known as a prophetical college town. Samuel was the one who started the school. The men who came were often referred to as "sons of the prophet."

**Ramah:** Ramah was up on top of a hill. Ramah was where Samuel's parents had lived and as an adult, he returned to his home area.

**Shochoh in Judah:** Where the battle with Goliath happened in the valley of Elah.

**Desert of Maon:** Is a town in the mountain of Judah named along with Carmel and Ziph. Joshua 15:55. It is the home of Nabal. 1 Samuel 25:2 In the genealogical list of 1 Chronicles 2, it is located about a mile South of el-Karmil, the ancient Carmel.

**Madiam$_2$:** Maon is named along with the Zidonians and Amalek as having at some time, oppressed Israel. Judges 10:12

**Hakilah:** A darksome hill, one of the peaks of the long ridge of el-Kolah, running out of the Ziph plateau, "on the south of Jeshimon" I Sam. 26:1-5

**Jabash-gilead:** Jabash means "dry". It is a town in the territory of Gilead. It is beyond the Jordan, 6 miles or 10 kilometers from Pella. It is on the mountain road to Gerasa.

**David's Wives:** He had eight wives. They are listed in order: Michal, a daughter of King Saul; Ahinoam of Jezreel; Abigail, previous wife of Nabal; Maachah; Haggith; Avital; Eglah and Bathsheba.

## EXTRA'S

**Bedouin:** In the story this name was given to David's horse. King Saul gave him the horse upon killing Goliath. 'Bedouin' is an Egyptian bred of horses that was brought in from Egypt. The name comes from desert dwellers.

**Dyes:** The deep red dye was taken from the plant, papaver rhoeas found between Jerash and Anjana, Jordan. The papaver rhoeas was quickly being nicknamed as the 'poppy plant'.

# Endnotes

1 The name of David's mother is not written in the Torah but rather is recorded in the Talmud, Tractate Bava Batra 91a. Chapter 1.

2 1 Samuel 17:46 (KJV).

3 It was here in 1 Samuel 17:54 that Golgotha became known as the "Skull." Golgotha was the hill where Jesus was crucified, and the place where David took the skull too in Jerusalem. Chapter 4.

4 1 Samuel 15:28 (KJV).

5 Psalm 5 (NASB, 2020). King David writes this psalm at a discouraging time of his life. Chapter 18.

6 Psalm 59:1, 9–10, 13b (ESV).

7 Psalm 34:17–18, 22 (NIV).

8 Psalm 34:1–22 (NIV).

9 Psalm 52:1–10 (NIV). David wrote this Psalm after learning about the evil in Doeg's heart and King Saul's order to kill the priests. Chapter 21.

10 Psalm 109:1–12 (NIV). David wrote this psalm asking God to punish his enemies. He calls down a curse on one enemy in particular. Although it is not certain who, it is presumed that this is referring to Doeg for killing the priests. Chapter 22.

11 Psalm 109:30–31 (NIV).

12 Psalm 13:1–6 (NIV). This psalm was written by David. It was entitled "Rejoice in His Salvation." In this story, David wrote while learning to find his alone time while surrounded

by the men who came to support him. Chapter 23.

13  Psalm 22:1–18 (NIV). According to the Chronological Bible, this was written shortly after David saw Jonathan again in 1 Samuel 23. This was a prophetic psalm about the death of Jesus. Chapter 23.

14  Psalm 22:19–31 (NIV). According to the Chronological Bible, this was written shortly after David saw Jonathan again in 1 Samuel 23. This was a prophetic psalm about the death of Jesus. Chapter 23.

15  Psalm 54:1–3 (NIV). "God Is My Help." It was written by David around the time Saul chased him in the Desert of Ziph. Chapter 23.

16  Psalm 54:4–7 (NIV). "God Is My Help." It was written by David around the time Saul chased him in the Desert of Ziph. Chapter 23.

17  Psalm 14 (ESV). Written by David and believed to have been written after Nabal insulted him. 1 Samuel 25. Chapter 28.

18  Psalm 53 (ESV).

19  Psalm 31 (NIV) paraphrased. David has just allowed King Saul to live a second time. Chapter 29.

20  Psalm 16 (NIV). Chapter 30. David takes confidence in God's ability to take care of him.

21  Psalm 56 (NIV). David was taken and beat by Achish's top men while in Gath. Chapter 32.

22  Genesis 12:2 (NIV).

23  Genesis 13:15 (NIV).

24  2 Samuel 1:19–27 (NIV). This is a lament that David wrote for all the men to be taught. It is written in the book of Jashar. Chapter 39.

25  Today, Manahaim is called Tell edh Dhahab el Gharbi and is located in Jordan, about thirty-three miles NE of the Dead Sea and north of Jabbok River. Gibeah is called Tall al-Fūl.

26  Psalm 2 (NIV). This psalm was written for David's coronation over a united Israel. Chapter 48.

27  Psalm 16:9–11 (KJV).

CPSIA information can be obtained
at www.ICGtesting.com
Printed in the USA
BVHW052336060723
666783BV00013B/1252

9 781637 699621